Sacrifice in the Post-Kantian Tradition

SUNY series in Contemporary Continental Philosophy

Dennis J. Schmidt, editor

Sacrifice in the Post-Kantian Tradition

Perspectivism, Intersubjectivity, and Recognition

Paolo Diego Bubbio

Published by State University of New York Press, Albany

© 2014 State University of New York

All rights reserved

Printed in the United States of America

No part of this book may be used or reproduced in any manner whatsoever without written permission. No part of this book may be stored in a retrieval system or transmitted in any form or by any means including electronic, electrostatic, magnetic tape, mechanical, photocopying, recording, or otherwise without the prior permission in writing of the publisher.

For information, contact State University of New York Press, Albany, NY
www.sunypress.edu

Production by Eileen Nizer
Marketing by Kate Seburyamo

Library of Congress Cataloging-in-Publication Data

Bubbio, Paolo Diego, 1974–
    Sacrifice in the post-Kantian tradition : perspectivism, intersubjectivity, and recognition / Paolo Diego Bubbio.
        pages cm. — (SUNY series in contemporary continental philosophy)
    Includes bibliographical references and index.
    ISBN 978-1-4384-5252-4 (paperback : alk. paper)
    ISBN 978-1-4384-5251-7 (hardcover : alk. paper)
    1. Sacrifice. 2. Philosophy, Modern—19th century. I. Title.

BL570.B828 2014
203'.4—dc23   2013032629

10 9 8 7 6 5 4 3 2 1

To Sofia and Alessandro

*May they always be willing to make room
for other points of view.*

Contents

Acknowledgments — xi

Abbreviations — xiii

Introduction: The Notion of Sacrifice — 1

1 Kant: Sacrifice and the Transcendental Turn — 19
    Kant's Kenotic Turn in Epistemology — 20
    Kant's Practical Philosophy: "A Sacrifice Before
      the Moloch of Abstraction"? — 25
    Symbolic and Regulative Value of Sacrifice — 31

2 Solger's Sacrificial Dialectic — 39
    Sacrifice as Double Negation — 39
    Negation and Privation — 49

3 Hegel: Sacrifice and Recognition — 61
    Sacrifice in the *Phenomenology of Spirit* — 61
    Sacrifice and Incarnation in Hegel's Philosophy
      of Religion — 75

4 Kierkegaard: Sacrifice and the Regulativity of Love — 87
    Sacrifice in *Fear and Trembling* — 87
    Kierkegaard's Kenotic Sacrifice — 104

5 Nietzsche: The Sacrifice of the Overman — 117
    Three Meanings of Sacrifice — 117
    Political Implications of Sacrifice — 126

6	Conclusion: The Long Way of Sacrifice	141
	Sacrifice from Kant to Nietzsche . . .	141
	. . . And Beyond	146
	What Theory of Sacrifice?	160
Notes		167
Bibliography		197
Index		209

Acknowledgments

A book is always, to some extent, an intersubjective effort. I therefore thank a number of people for help and encouragement along the way.

I was encouraged to pursue postgraduate research on the notion of sacrifice in contemporary philosophy by my teacher Marco Ravera in 1998 at the University of Turin. In 2004, when my PhD dissertation was published (in Italian), I was already convinced of the need to consider the Kantian and post-Kantian tradition of the nineteenth century to really understand the notion of sacrifice and its implications. I am grateful to Marco who, since then, has shown all his hermeneutic generosity in discussing various philosophical issues concerning my research, even when my approach was somehow diverging from his own. I would also like to thank Maurizio Pagano for introducing me to the work of Hegel and for several years of conversation about different interpretations of Hegel's philosophy.

Proper research for this book commenced by way of a Postdoctoral Fellowship from the University of Sydney (2006–2009). Originally the research was limited to the notion of sacrifice in Hegel and Nietzsche, and was extended to Kant, Solger, and Kierkegaard in the following years up to 2012. Across all these years, Paul Redding has been a great scholarly mentor. His intellectual openness, philosophical rigor, and patience have been key factors in pursuing this research. Without him, this book would not have been possible. I am also grateful to the School of Philosophical and Historical Inquiry at the University of Sydney for its financial support for conference travel during those years.

Thanks are also due to the Department of Philosophy at the University of Warwick for accepting me as a visiting research fellow into that stimulating environment in the first half of 2008. During that short visit, I enjoyed profitable discussions on Solger and Hegel with Stephen Houlgate.

In May 2009, Douglas Hedley kindly invited me to present my work on sacrifice in Hegel's philosophy at Clare College, University of

Cambridge. It was great to discuss my preliminary outcomes with him and his postgraduate students. I regret that, due to geographical reasons, I did not have many opportunities to discuss with Douglas our respective views on sacrifice.

During this book's long gestation, I have been helped by a number of other individuals who offered valuable suggestions about sections of the manuscript or my general interpretation of sacrifice. Although I cannot thank them all individually, let me mention Damion Buterin, Ingo Farin, Christopher Fynsk, Sebastian Gardner, Wayne Hudson, Heikki Ikaheimo, Jeff Malpas, Justine McGill, Dalia Nassar, Annette Pierdziwol, Philip Quadrio, and Herman Siemens. A special word of thanks is due to Talia Morag, who graciously provided invaluable insights and shared her critical eye in checking my arguments in the chapter on Nietzsche. More recently, I have also gained much from conversations with my colleagues in the Philosophy Research Initiative at the University of Western Sydney, where the final work on this book was made. In their capacity as readers for the press, David Kolb and Douglas Moggach were helpful in pointing out problems, opacities, and hazards in the original manuscript. I am grateful for all of this help. For the book's shortcomings, I claim credit myself. I am also very grateful to Dennis Schmidt, Book Series Editor, and Andrew Kenyon, Editor of Philosophy at SUNY. Thanks are also due to Charles Barbour for his insights on a variety of particular style matters; to Rory Dufficy for his meticulous preparation of the index, and to the Dean of the School of Humanities and Communication Arts at UWS, Professor Peter Hutchings, for the financial support of the same.

During my long engagement with this project, a number of friends in both the Northern and the Southern hemispheres of the globe have been sympathetically and emotionally supportive: Stephen Buckle, Damian Byers, Luigi Dentis, Fabrizio Gallino, Andrea Lasagna, Daniele Limerutti, Emanuele Miroglio, Luca Moretti, Sebastiana Nervegna, Alessandro Rodani, and Dimitris Vardoulakis. Their humor, encouragement, and friendship continue to be a genuine blessing.

To my family, I owe more than I can acknowledge. My children, Sofia and Alex, gave me lots of pleasure and taught me the importance of a fresh point of view. And, first of all, I thank my wife, Silvia, for her help, support, and understanding throughout the long period of this book's composition.

Most of the chapters that follow recast material that has appeared earlier, often in altered form, in other settings. I thank the following journals and publishers for allowing me to draw on that material:

Chapter 1 is an extended version of "Kant's Sacrificial Turns," in *International Journal for Philosophy of Religion* 73:2 (2013): 97–115 (with kind permission from Springer Science+Business Media).

Chapter 2 draws from "Solger's Notion of Sacrifice as Double Negation." in *Heythrop Journal* 50:2 (2009): 206–214, and "Solger and Hegel: Negation and Privation," in *International Journal of Philosophical Studies* 17:2 (2009): 173–187.

A version of section 1 of Chapter 3 appeared as "Sacrifice in Hegel's *Phenomenology of Spirit*," in *British Journal for the History of Philosophy* 20:4 (2012): 797–815.

Section 2 of Chapter 3 draws from the first half of "God, Incarnation, and Metaphysics in Hegel's Philosophy of Religion," in *Sophia. International Journal of Philosophy and Traditions* DOI: 10.1007/s11841-013-0391-z (with kind permission from Springer Science+Business Media).

Chapter 4, section 1 draws from "Kierkegaard's Regulative Sacrifice: A Post-Kantian Reading of *Fear and Trembling*," in *International Journal of Philosophical Studies* 20:4 (2012): 691–723.

A version of Chapter 4, section 2 appeared as "Kierkegaard is Standing by Himself—Through Hegel's Help," in P. D. Bubbio and P. Redding (eds.), *Religion After Kant. God and Culture in the Idealist Era* (Cambridge: Cambridge Scholars Publishers, 2012), 173–196.

A shorter version of Chapter 5 appeared as "The Sacrifice of the Overman as an Expression of the Will to Power. Anti-Political Consequences and Contributions to Democracy," in H. W. Siemens and V. Roodt (eds.), *Nietzsche, Power and Politics: Rethinking Nietzsche's Legacy for Political Thought* (Berlin and New York: de Gruyter, 2008), 269–296.

Sydney, 2013

Abbreviations

KpV Immanuel Kant, *Kritik der praktischen Vernunft* (1788). *Critique of Practical Reason*, translated by Werner S. Pluhar (Indianapolis, IN: Hackett Publishing, 2002).

MS Immanuel Kant, *Metaphysik der Sitten* (1797). *The Metaphysics of Morals*, translated by Mary J. Gregor (Cambridge: Cambridge University Press, 1991).

RGV Immanuel Kant, *Die Religion innerhalb der Grenzen der blossen Vernunft* (1793). *Religion Within the Boundaries of Mere Reason*, in *Religion and Natural Theology*, translated and edited by A. W. Wood and G. Di Giovanni (Cambridge: Cambridge University Press, 1996).

NS Karl Wilhelm Ferdinand Solger, *Nachgelassene Schriften und Briefwechsel* (1826), Herausgegeben von Ludwig Tieck und Friedrich von Raumer (Heidelberg: Verlag Lambert Scheider, Reprint 1973).

PG G.W.F. Hegel, *Phänomenologie des Geistes* (1807). *Phenomenology of Spirit*, translated by A. V. Miller (Oxford: Clarendon Press, 1977).

Rel G.W.F. Hegel, *Vorlesungen über die Philosophie der Religion* (1827). *Lectures on the Philosophy of Religion. The Lectures of 1827*, edited by P. C. Hodgson, translated by R. F. Brown et al. (Berkeley: University of California Press, 1988).

FT Søren Kierkegaard, *Frygt og Bæven. Dialektisk lyrik af Johannes De Silentio* (1843). *Fear and Trembling*, translated by Sylvia Walsh (Cambridge: Cambridge University Press, 2006).

WL Søren Kierkegaard, *Kjerlighedens Gjerninger* (1847). *Works of Love*, translated by Howard V. Hong and Edna H. Hong (Princeton, NJ: Princeton University Press, 1995).

JGB Friedrich Nietzsche, *Jenseits von Gut und Böse: Vorspiel einer Philosophie der Zukunft* (1886). *Beyond Good and Evil. Prelude to a Philosophy of the Future*, translated by J. Hollingdale (Harmondsworth: Penguin Books, 1973). References are to the section/aphorism number.

GM Friedrich Nietzsche, *Zur Genealogie der Moral* (1887). *On the Genealogy of Morality*, edited by Keith Ansell-Pearson, translated by Carol Diethe (Cambridge: Cambridge University Press, 1994).

WM Friedrich Nietzsche, *Der Wille zur Macht* (1901). *The Will to Power*, translated by W. Kaufmann and R. J. Hollingdale (New York: Vintage Books, 1968). References are to the section/aphorism number.

Introduction

The Notion of Sacrifice

What is sacrifice?

If we look at twentieth-century philosophy, we find the notion of sacrifice employed in the philosophical analysis of religion, culture, faith, and violence. In twenty-first-century thought, sacrifice remains at the heart of discussions on religious and political issues, and even ethical debate. In the field of philosophy, sacrifice has become the object of intensive research activities, especially in the so-called "Continental philosophy." Several philosophers, such as Bataille, Derrida, Nancy, Girard, and Žižek (just to mention a few) have engaged in discussions aiming to clarify the status and implications of the notion of sacrifice. Nevertheless, after a few decades of discussions and philosophical debates, it would seem that a significant degree of clarity has not been reached. Sacrifice has been considered from the point of view of each specific philosophical approach, so that we have studies on the notion of sacrifice in Bataille's philosophy, Derrida's philosophy, and so on. However, these studies provide very little assistance in clarifying sacrifice *in itself*.[1]

Another element that adds to the lack of clarity on sacrifice is the fundamental ambiguity of the notion. Oddly, very few accounts of sacrifice are concerned with the provision of a preliminary definition of the object of investigation. In other words, what do we mean by "sacrifice"? This is probably the case because it is generally assumed that the notion of sacrifice to which one refers is the standard one, so common and well known that even to mention it is considered a waste of time. In fact, "sacrifice" is usually regarded as meaning the suppression or the destruction of something for the sake of something else. For example, an animal can be sacrificed as a means of appeasing gods or of changing the course of nature. Even self-sacrifice can be considered in this way; I can kill or mutilate myself to appease gods or (in more secularized forms) to save my country. There is, however, *another* meaning of sacrifice, which is very different from the standard one mentioned above, and which is rarely identified because of its peculiarity. It is *kenotic* sacrifice, or sacrifice as *withdrawal*.

The term "kenotic" derives from the Greek word *kenosis*, meaning "emptiness."[2] The use of the term in connection with a "sacrificial" dynamic (but different from the traditional meaning of sacrifice mentioned above) dates back to the Christian New Testament, in particular Philippians 2:7, where, to describe the incarnation of Christ, it is said that he "withdrew" or "emptied himself." In the previous verse (Philippians 2:6), it is written that Christ did not consider his divine form (*morphe*) something "to be grasped" or "to be kept," but was willing to "empty" or "annul" himself to assume a different "form." What is implied is that God gave up those divine privileges that are incompatible with the finite nature of a human being (omnipotence, omnipresence, omniscience, etc.) to become fully human. Retrospectively, and through a connection with the Jewish Kabbalistic notion of *tsimtsum*,[3] the term kenosis has also been used by some theologians to describe God's original act of creating the universe: God created the universe by voluntarily limiting his divine infinity, *withdrawing*, and allowing room for the universe and finite beings that are free to be themselves.[4]

The kenotic conception of sacrifice represents a minor and often hidden, but nonetheless significant, theological interpretation in medieval and early-modern philosophy and theology. It is beyond the scope of this book to provide a detailed history of the kenotic conception before the nineteenth century; however, it is worthwhile to mention at least two names. The first is that of the German philosopher, theologian, and mystic Meister Eckhart, whose life spanned the thirteen and the fourteenth centuries. One of Eckhart's most peculiar doctrines concerns the notion of *Abgeschiedenheit*. This term, usually translated as "disinterestedness" or "detachment" in English, effectively refers to the kenotic emptying of the self as a result of the imitation of Christ.[5] Eckhart was a seminal figure, and through the work of his disciples (among them John Tauler and Henry Suso) his doctrines had a significant impact, particularly on Martin Luther and the Reformation. The second name that should be mentioned is that of Jacob Böhme. Eckhart's conception of kenosis resurfaces in this German Christian mystic, defined by Hegel as "the first German philosopher."[6] However, while the process of kenosis for Eckhart was leaving God "intact," without substantially affecting his divine prerogatives (Eckhart remained consistent, in this respect, with Thomas Aquinas's conception of a perfect and immutable God—which basically replicated the Aristotelian conception of God as "unmoved mover"), Böhme conceived of the kenotic process as an emptying that "involves a change in the underlying substance."[7] In short, Böhme's God can change and, most importantly, can suffer—and in fact, he *does* suffer.

In German, the distinction between "suppressive" and "kenotic" sacrifice is often marked by the use of two different terms, *Opfer* and *Aufopferung*, respectively. *Opfer* is commonly used to refer to a specifically religious concept, originally meaning the act or practice of destroying or renouncing something (first fruits; best lamb or animal of the herd; slaves; sexuality; etc.) in order to receive something more valuable in exchange (divine support, help, benevolence; a place in heaven; redemption from evil; etc.). *Aufopferung* indicates the process of *giving something up*, with an emphasis on reflexivity—sacrifice as *self-sacrifice*. This is not always a neat distinction, and sometimes *Aufopferung* and its derivatives are still used to refer to the suppressive sacrifice. Other terms that are sometimes used to refer to the kenotic sacrifice are *Verlassen*, which is often used in kenotic literature to describe Christ's act of relinquishing his own divinity in the incarnation, and—more rarely—in philosophy as well,[8] and *Freilassen*—literally "to release" or "to set free,"—introduced by Fichte in the context of his theory of recognition to refer to the concept of mutual liberation,[9] and used by Hegel in the *Encyclopaedia of the Philosophical Sciences* to describe the final stage of the process of recognition, but with a meaning closer to the kenotic dynamic: *Freilassen* is liberation from one's own self and, at the same time, a "leaving space" to the other.[10]

"Standard" or "suppressive" sacrifice (the destruction of something for the sake of something else) on one hand, and kenotic sacrifice on the other, have different ethical implications. In the suppressive sacrifice, the goal is represented by the purported achievement (the satisfaction of needs, gods' benevolence, or even a simple manifestation of power). In this case, the ethical value of sacrifice is dependent on the ethical value of the purported achievement. Conversely, the kenotic sacrifice has an *intrinsic* ethical value, which can be immediately grasped from the passage in Philippians. In fact, with his description of the incarnation of Christ as a "withdrawal," the author of the letter to the Philippians clearly intended to call for an imitation of Christ: Christians are required to follow Christ's example by sacrificing themselves. However, the sacrifice to which Christians are called is different from traditional sacrifice (the destruction of something for the sake of something else); here, the sacrifice of Christ is assumed to be a paradigm for a sacrifice conceived as a withdrawal or a "making room" for others.

Once the conceptual opposition between suppressive sacrifice and kenotic sacrifice has been set, the notion of kenosis should be analyzed further—and here it is important to note that the notion of kenosis is far from uncontentious. As one of the main contemporary theorists of kenosis,

Sarah Coakley, puts it, various exponents of kenosis "can disagree even on such basic matters as: whether kenosis implies pre-existence (or not); whether it implies a temporary loss of all or some divine characteristics (or neither); whether the 'emptying' applies to the divine nature or the human [. . .] and whether the effects of kenosis pass to the eternal nature of the Godhead [revealing divine power to be intrinsically humble] (or not)."[11] In other words, how radical is this sacrifice supposed to be? Should it be the sacrifice of one's life? Or an everlasting sacrifice of one's identity, in the form of self-denial? What does kenotic sacrifice mean, *in concreto*?

In order to answer this question, it is useful to refer to the accurate taxonomy of kenotic sacrifice provided by Coakley,[12] and amended and improved by Groenhout.[13] In fact, Coakley and Groenhout have elaborated a "scale of gradations" of kenotic sacrifice (that is, the second type of sacrifice in the above-mentioned opposition, and indeed the focus of this book). Coakley had originally introduced a "sliding-scale of meanings" of kenosis, constructed on the prototypical kenosis of God. From the lowest to the highest they are: risk (the risk taken by the creator in submitting Godself to "the free process" of creation[14]), self-limitation, sacrifice (exemplified by Christ's forswearing of any triumphalist interpretation of Messiahship[15]), self-giving, self-emptying, and annihilation (Moltmann's idea that God chooses to "wait" for created beings to repent and turn back to God[16]). Groenhout simplifies the scale by removing "risk" and "annihilation," which are respectively judged too weak and too strong to describe Christ's incarnation and death, and "sacrifice," which is judged too broad. Thus we are left with self-limitation, self-giving, and self-emptying. Groenhout distinguishes these three levels of kenosis in relation to the notion of selfhood. While in self-limitation "the self retains some sense of robust identity,"[17] in self-giving, some "*prerogatives* that are due one on the basis of one's nature"[18] are given up. Finally, we have self-emptying (also defined, more simply, as self-sacrifice) when "in some significant way the self is actually lost."[19]

In this book, I accept Groenhout's taxonomy and I consider kenosis as self-limitation, self-giving, and self-emptying (depending on the context). Thus, for example, I can renounce my position of privilege so that someone else can benefit from it; or more fundamentally (and we will see that this is indeed a central point), I can put my point of view in perspective to take into consideration the perspectives of others. Kenotic sacrifice is not suppressive. It does not suppress or destroy anything; rather, it requires a withdrawal of my identity for the benefit of others.

The main thesis of this book is a simple one: I submit that there is a strict interrelation between the kenotic conception of sacrifice and the tradition of Kantian and post-Kantian idealism that developed in Germany and continental Europe in the nineteenth century. By "interrelation" I mean that, on one hand, the kenotic conception of sacrifice exerted a cultural influence on the conceptual development of the idealist tradition from Kant onwards and that, on the other hand, most of the thinkers of the post-Kantian tradition employed, more or less explicitly, this particular notion of sacrifice as a component of their philosophies.

Here I want to emphasize that the methodology I use in this analysis is informed neither by analytic nor by contextual history of philosophy, but rather by a combination of the two. Thus, for instance, I will not enter into further analysis of Böhme's rendition of kenosis because, while I believe that the topic of the historical influence that Böhme has exerted on Kant and Hegel certainly deserves to be pursued, I am more interested in acknowledging the presence of an array of common features and problems dealing with a notion of kenosis broadly conceived as self-limitation, self-giving, and self-emptying, and connecting some philosophers in the post-Kantian tradition.[20]

More specifically, the book has two specific aims regarding the notion of sacrifice. First, it aims to show that the origins of the modern philosophical treatment of sacrifice have to be traced back to the Kantian transcendental turn and to its development in the nineteenth century from German Idealism to Nietzsche; and furthermore, that the notion of sacrifice can be adequately understood only against this background. Second, it shows that the different, and sometimes opposing, positions of these thinkers compose a philosophical strategy that allows the notion of sacrifice to be dealt with in a way that avoids the problems implied in other approaches. It follows that the approach suggested in the Kantian and post-Kantian tradition is the most appropriate strategy to deal with sacrifice.

Essentially, this book reconstructs the history of the notion of sacrifice and its employment in nineteenth-century philosophy in a way that emphasizes how all these thinkers are indebted to Kant and that also brings out a group of recurring features. As the idea of a Kantian legacy conceived as the "least common denominator" of nineteenth-century Continental idealism suggests, my investigation into the notion of sacrifice is situated against the background of a distinct approach to this tradition. For a very long time, the stereotype of Continental idealism as "dark" and "obscure" (not to say "irrational" or "lunatic") has dominated the reception of this tradition in the Anglophone world. From the point of view of this stereotype, the specific subject of this investigation might only make things worse. After all, what might be "darker," more "irrational" and more exposed to allusive and metaphorical forms of expression than the notion of sacrifice? In this respect, I would like to reassure the reader that I personally regard the approach of post-Kantian philosophers to the notion of sacrifice as *anything but abstract*, and that I have tried my best to show the meaning of this notion, and the transformations it went through, in their clarity. To a significant degree, this was possible thanks to several studies published in the last few decades, and to their achievements. Three of these achievements are particularly relevant for the development of my argument and it is therefore worthwhile to briefly mention them here. The reader will have no difficulty in recognizing their presence and their influence throughout the entire book.

The first achievement concerns Kant's ambiguous use of the term "metaphysics." Traditionally, the *Critique of Pure Reason* has been interpreted as representing a radical skepticism about metaphysics. Sometimes, however, Kant seems to suggest that metaphysics is somehow *possible*—not the traditional (pre-Kantian) metaphysics that treated metaphysical objects as if they were empirical objects, but a new (idealist) metaphysics, conceived as that discipline in which reason is concerned *with its own products*. This possibility of reading Kant's account of metaphysics in two different ways has been suggested by Sebastian Gardner (who distinguishes between an "analytic" and an "idealist" way of interpreting the *Critique of Pure Reason*)[21] and articulated more fully by Paul Redding (who calls these two viewpoints "weak transcendental idealism" and "strong transcendental idealism," respectively).[22] This is important because it allows us to read post-Kantian idealism as a development of Kant's critical philosophy and in continuity with his project (or at least with one of the possible interpretations of his project, one that Kant himself advanced). With regard to our investigation, this provides the framework within which the development of the notion of sacrifice can be situated; moreover, it suggests that sacrifice itself has to be regarded as *a product of reason*, hence endowed with a normative feature (I examine this aspect in more detail in Chapter 1).

The second achievement I rely upon is still primarily concerned with Kant studies, but has major consequences for the entire post-Kantian tradition: It is Terry Pinkard's diagnosis of the "Kantian paradox." According to Pinkard, the Kantian idea of self-legislation (the idea that one has to be bound by laws of which one is also the author) implies a paradox.[23] Pinkard reads the entire history of German Idealism as a history of attempts at responding to this paradox and finding a solution to it. Influenced by Klaus Hartmann[24] and Robert Pippin,[25] Pinkard came to identify the most appropriate solution to the Kantian paradox in Hegel's philosophy. A pivotal role in the Hegelian solution to the Kantian paradox is played by the notion of recognition (*Anerkennung*), an issue that was already identified as central by other "non-traditional" interpreters of Hegel, such as Robert Williams[26] (who in turn drew upon the work of Ludwig Siep[27] and Andreas Wildt[28]). Therefore, from the point of view of an interpretation that follows Pinkard's account of the Hegelian solution to the Kantian paradox, recognition becomes the "organizing principle" of that "metaphysical realm" in which reason is concerned only with its own products. This new, post-Kantian metaphysics becomes the realm of objects of reason that exist insofar as we recognize them as existing (we can think here of human rights, for example). The fundamental act of recognition, however, is the recognition of the other:[29] that is, human beings themselves exist *qua* human beings (and not merely qua empirical biomechanical agglomerates naturalistically conceived) only insofar as they reciprocally *recognize* themselves as existing. If I do not recognize "the other" as another human being (equally capable, as such, to recognize me as a human being), the very possibility of a "realm of reason" made up by values and norms, disappears. My interpretation of the importance of the notion of sacrifice in the post-Kantian tradition, and particularly in Hegel's thought, is indebted to, and to some extent depends on, this reading. Hegel's recognition-theoretic approach and his emphasis on kenotic sacrifice are reciprocally connected, and they are both evidence of his belonging to perspectivism, which I take as a fundamental feature of the post-Kantian tradition. This leads me to the third major achievement of recent scholarship that represents the background of my interpretation of sacrifice.

The third achievement that has oriented my research, partially derived from the previous two, is Paul Redding's interpretation of the history of the post-Kantian tradition of the nineteenth century from Kant to Nietzsche (the type of thought Redding calls "Continental idealism") as the history of perspectivism, conceived as the philosophical viewpoint derived from Kant's transcendental turn.

In pre-Kantian metaphysics, from Aristotle onward, the image of God as "thought thinking itself" was an image of the knowledge aspired to in philosophy connected with a conception of metaphysics as expressed by the phrase "God's-eye view." Kant's transcendental turn determined a change in perspective. This change in perspective implied the renunciation of the idea that the world can be examined by the subject objectively, that is, from a God's-eye point of view. The Kantian turn has an intrinsic kenotic structure: the subject *withdraws* from its pretension of absolute objectivity.

However, Kant's perspectivism does not extend to his practical philosophy. Evidence of this is Kant's repeated insistence that moral commands generated by practical reason "be regarded as commands of the supreme

Being."[30] Kant's view of God as "the source of norms" is an attempt to solve the paradox diagnosed by Pinkard. Consequently, while the coincidence between human reason and the God's-eye view is rejected in the theoretical domain, the same coincidence resurfaces in the practical domain. This problem was noted by Nietzsche, who saw in Kant's practical philosophy a regression to the idea of "a real world," that is, the metaphysical idea of a world conceived as what is there "anyway," independently of us,[31] and hence a world that is possible to grasp objectively. Kant's ethics, Nietzsche also remarks, is a formal or "pale" version of Platonic-Christian ethics, implying a *sacrifice* of one's own instincts and natural dispositions. Insofar as Kant's morality effectively implies the negation, or suppression, of instincts and desires for the sake of duty, Nietzsche is certainly right.

Given the formal nature of Kant's practical philosophy, one of its main concerns becomes the need for some way of making moral concepts applicable to the world. For Kant, religious claims and narratives serve this purpose, and he attributed a "symbolic" or "analogical" significance to forms of religious representation. Kant's conception of religious notions as symbolic and regulative puts forward again the "Kantian paradox" in a more acute form (I call this new form the "Kantian *religious* paradox"). In deciding the acceptability of *religious* symbols, the philosopher is guided by norms that, according to Kant himself, should be regarded *as issued by God*. Thus, the paradox paves the way for two possible developments: either the subject is regarded as the source, in itself, of norms, playing, so to speak, the role of God (e.g., as happens with Fichte and left Hegelians such as Feuerbach); or the very idea of norms is put into question, as the discovery that norms are human or culturally dependent can lead to the relativistic and skeptical conclusion that "all is permitted" (as happens with Nietzsche).

A number of central contentions of this book might be seen to grow from this point. The first is that Kant's transcendental turn has determined a change in perspective towards the consideration of religious notions in general—a turn that has been assumed by post-Kantian thinkers and that generates an array of common features and problems. The second is that all of the thinkers who are included in the analysis have more in common than is usually conceded in standard accounts. The third and, for our purposes, most important contention is the relevance of the notion of sacrifice. In Kantian terms, sacrifice is an (improper) religious symbol. However, the entirety of Kantian ethics employs a *sacrificial-suppressive* structure, as it is based on the negation of instincts and desires—something that was grasped by both Hegel and Nietzsche. What is more, Kant's theoretical philosophy also implies a sacrificial structure—but there the structure is *kenotic*. My thesis is that Kant's (explicit and implicit) use of the notion of sacrifice is an important theme in the context of the criticisms of German Idealism and subsequent movements in Continental thought. Thus, the kenotic feature of Kantian perspectivism finds different ways of expression in all of the thinkers considered in the book. The first philosopher to have grasped this kenotic feature is Solger, whose intuitions were then fully developed by Hegel. The advantage of such an approach is that it allows an understanding of lines of continuity, not only between Kant and the post-Kantian idealists, such as Solger and Hegel, but beyond this to forms of philosophy that are often considered as *opposing* Kant, such as those of Kierkegaard and Nietzsche.

In the interpretation presented here, kenotic sacrifice represents an important element in the development of the post-Kantian tradition. The kenotic conception of sacrifice on the one hand and perspectivism on the other are strictly interdependent, and one is not conceivable without the other. To put this claim in a slightly oversimplified and crude, and yet (hopefully) effective way: there is no perspectivism without (kenotic) sacrifice. This means that the notion of sacrifice does not merely provide an entry point into the discussion of perspectivism and the letting go of the self in the recognition of the other, but represents a privileged "hermeneutic key" to understand these issues. In other words, sacrifice is an important topic in its own right, one of those that, like the issue of personal identity, become a locus for the intersection of many questions. Of course there can be other approaches to the mentioned issues, but one of the fundamental theses of my book is precisely that addressing perspectivism, the "letting go" of the self, and recognition through an analysis of the notion of sacrifice allows to highlight this web of mutual connections with a clarity that would not be accessible through other approaches.

In the following chapters, the various accounts of sacrifice from Kant to Nietzsche are treated as having laid out an array of interrelated philosophical questions from which philosophers in the twentieth century have drawn. In fact, the reaction of twentieth-century Continental philosophy to the Kantian religious paradox developed from Nietzsche's skeptical standpoint: the *regulative* aspect of sacrifice (as well as of other religious notions), is often rejected while the *symbolic* aspect is overemphasized. However, this solution turns out to be more problematic than the question that generated it because the symbols, once they have been deprived of their regulative status, maintain a merely descriptive value.

In this book I outline the development of the notion of kenotic sacrifice in the post-Kantian tradition, a development that, in my view, is strictly connected with the establishment of perspectivism that in turn arose from

Kant's transcendental move. Clearly this is not meant to be a comprehensive account of all those philosophies in nineteenth-century continental Europe that have taken sacrifice into consideration (not to mention a general account of the idealist tradition). On the contrary, figures and issues have been selected around the theme of the possibility of conceiving sacrifice in a different way, that is, from the point of view of a tradition that had employed the notion of sacrifice as a constitutive element of its own development. Therefore, the selection of these key figures is functional to the treatment of the subject and to the development of my argument.

As previously stressed, this approach relies on results and achievements of recent scholarship in the field which, although sometimes contested within contemporary interpretative disputes, are nonetheless quite well established. I regard my thesis of the centrality of kenotic sacrifice in the post-Kantian tradition as consistent with this interpretative approach (and indeed as strengthening it). I (quite naturally) think of my thesis as recovering an original, important, and yet hidden concern of the post-Kantian philosophers; to the possible objection that my interpretation also arises from my concern with the subject matter, I can at least object by pleading that my interpretation is not intended to force things or to find the presence of the notion of sacrifice at all costs.

Chapter 1 is devoted to covering both Kant's transcendental turn as an essential precondition to the post-Kantian approach to sacrifice and Kant's own account of the notion. Here it is to be remembered that Kant's turn in philosophy's relation to religion had effectively freed philosophical thought from any given religious foundations but had not thereby rendered the role of religious claims and notions philosophically useless. Kant's *Religion within the Boundaries of Mere Reason* removes religious notions from the realm of theoretical reason and references their significance to regulative and symbolic meanings. This allows Kant to maintain that religious notions play a regulative role in human cognition and morality and provides an entry point for features found in the post-Kantians.

Against this background, Kant's position on sacrifice can be appreciated. Kant's explicit treatment of sacrifice is clearly poor; nonetheless, this lack of analysis only becomes a significant issue once it is evaluated in light of the implicit sacrificial structure of Kant's ethics, in which instincts and desires are systematically negated—or *sacrificed*. Thus, the hiatus between Kant's *explicit* and *implicit* use of sacrifice can be regarded as the most powerful symptom of the Kantian religious paradox mentioned above. This hiatus raises a problem that is pressing for post-Kantians: that of maintaining the regulativity of religious notions, specifically the notion of sacrifice, while going beyond Kant's formal grounding (with the problems it entails). I submit that all other thinkers examined in this book consider sacrifice regulatively, but they go beyond Kant's empty regulativity.

The approach to sacrifice outlined in Chapter 2 and exemplified in the work of Karl Wilhelm Ferdinand Solger, is also, I suggest, a Kantian one. Solger is a German Idealist, contemporaneous with Hegel, who has been unjustly underestimated partly because his ideas have been obscured by those of more influential thinkers, such as Schelling and Hegel, and partly because his philosophy has been given a misleading reception. Nevertheless, Solger is a very important figure, because it is with his attempted unification of theoretical and practical philosophy (a problem arising from Kant and another pressing problem for all post-Kantians) that the post-Kantian involvement with the notion of sacrifice starts. This unification represents an early response to Kant's religious paradox: in Solger's philosophy, the notion of sacrifice is the symbolic and regulative expression of double negation (negation of negation) and represents the fundamental structure of the relationship between the finite (human being) and the infinite (God). In Solger's own words, sacrifice is "the highest token" of humans' destination. Thus, Solger introduces the basic concept that will be used by Hegel in his theory of spirit (the double negation), but his use of the notions of privation and negation shows the problematic aspects of his approach (some of which were identified by Hegel himself). Solger's paradoxical non-resolution of the problem of Kant's formality, however, will provide the model for Kierkegaard and some twentieth-century solutions.

Chapter 3 then turns to Hegel to assess his unique solution to the question of sacrifice, which is presented as forged out of an assimilation of the Kantian idea that religious notions play a regulative role in human cognition and morality, in conjunction with the key concept of recognition. As previously mentioned, my treatment of Hegel draws upon the post-Kantian interpretation of Hegel and applies the recognition-theoretic approach to the notion of sacrifice. The first half of the chapter is concerned with the *Phenomenology of Spirit*, an analysis which, I suggest, shows that sacrifice should be considered as a *Darstellung* (namely, the presentation or exhibition of a content that is conceptually present in philosophy). My main argument is that there is, for Hegel, a strict connection between sacrifice and recognition, in the sense that the process of recognition (conceived not only as a social dynamic, but as the organizing principle of Hegel's metaphysics) implies kenotic sacrifice. In fact, there cannot be recognition of the other if the subject does not renounce its own absoluteness, that is, its presumption of absolute objectivity—the God's-eye view. Only if the subject *withdraws* and "makes room" for the other's point of view (at the same time recognizing himself as "relative," that is, as located historically, geographically, etc.), the process of recognition is indeed possible. Therefore, the sacrifice that emerges from this analysis is very different from the "standard" interpretation of sacrifice as the destruction or negation of something for the sake of something else; and the distance of the Hegelian notion of sacrifice from the traditional one can be appreciated only when a post-Kantian interpretation of Hegel's philosophy is embraced. In fact, traditional approaches to Hegel might still regard sacrifice as a necessary step on the way to absolute knowing, that is, for the sake of absolute spirit. Conversely, if a post-Kantian approach to Hegel is used, it becomes clear that sacrifice is the representation of recognition itself, and that absolute knowing is not the God's-eye view, but the set of all the possible points of view as expressions of mutually recognizing individual subjects (whose existence as subjects is dependent upon a joint act of recognition).

Once it is shown that kenotic sacrifice plays an important role in Hegel's recognition-theoretic approach, the explanation of Hegel's interest in the incarnation and the sacrifice of Christ provided in the second half of the chapter follows quite naturally. In fact, in light of the post-Kantian reading of Hegel, it can be argued that Hegel regarded Christianity as the highest form of religion (the "consummate religion") mainly because of its central image of God becoming man. Christ represents the incarnation of the divine and the overcoming of the abstract opposition between the divine and the human. More specifically, Christ represents the concrete expression and realization of kenotic sacrifice. Thus, the incarnation of Christ represents a turning point in the history of spirit, as it provides us with an exemplar on which we can model our normativity. In this light, Hegel's long interest in the tradition of *imitatio Christi* and the replacement of the Old Testament's legislation with the New Testament's regulativity can also be explained.

Chapter 3 concludes with a sketch of some of the consequences for idealist metaphysics of Hegel's idea of a God who renounces his own divinity and becomes human. My main claim here is that Hegel's emphasis on the kenotic significance of Christ's incarnation and sacrifice can be regarded as evidence for the increasing integration of Kantian elements into his metaphysics and theology, and is indicative of his endorsement of social and political freedoms that are characteristic of modernity. That is, modern freedoms are cognate with the existence of a certain *idea* of God and with a different conception of metaphysical knowledge, one that relies on recognition. With the notion of God becoming man, Hegel challenged the Aristotelian goal of philosophy as immutable knowledge of an alleged "ultimate" reality independent from the subject (that idea of "ultimate reality" that was the object of pre-Kantian metaphysics). Thus, the notion of incarnation is conceived not only as an early mythical expression of the dialectic that reveals the progressive incarnation of the spirit, but as the expression of a spirit that advances only insofar as it is willing to *withdraw* and make room for the other—a theme that will be reprised, although in different contexts, both in Kierkegaard and in Nietzsche's critiques of Kant's formal conception of morality.

In Chapter 4, I examine Kierkegaard's attempts to combine the idea of regulativity that is implied in the Kantian conception of religious duties (that ethical duties should be conceived *as if* they were duties toward God) with a peculiar separation between ethical and religious duties (thus claiming autonomy for religion). In the first half of the chapter, I focus on *Fear and Trembling* to argue that Kierkegaard should be regarded as a distinctively post-Kantian philosopher, in the sense that he goes beyond Kant in a way that is nevertheless true to the spirit of Kant's original critical idealism. In fact, Kant's regulativity reemerges as one of the main features of the "knight of faith." Conceived in this way, and beyond Kierkegaard's misunderstandings of Hegel, Kierkegaard's account of sacrifice is not completely incompatible with that of Hegel. Hegel himself accepts the need for religious commitments not mediated by ethics. The most problematic issue is Kierkegaard's claim that sacrifice can escape the necessity of recognition and justification in the social/political realm. Sacrifice as "absolute relation to the absolute" (as it is depicted in *Fear and Trembling*) is a dangerous option from an Hegelian point of view, insofar as it escapes the need for recognition and justification in social and political fora.

The chapter ends with Kierkegaard's diagnosis of the relationship between sacrifice and love as found in *Works of Love*. Here, I analyze Kierkegaard's use of Christ as a tangible model for behavior. Although Kierkegaard's approach to sacrifice can be regarded as a useful "corrective" for some aspects of Hegel's approach, his position is apparently not able to provide a fully developed answer to the problem that Kant's philosophy was meant to answer: that is, the need for some way of making moral and religious concepts applicable to the world. In Kierkegaard, the symbolic dimension of sacrifice is emphasized as a means to express the existential content of sacrifice in opposition to a *concept* of sacrifice as a mere metaphor of an abstract negation. However, Hegel had already been critical of philosophical positions formed on the basis of an "abstract" negation, and a similar critique emerges in Nietzsche's writings.

Against the background of these (partially incompatible) views, Chapter 5 presents how Nietzsche's complex attitude toward the notion of sacrifice can offer a meaningful contribution to a comprehensive theory of sacrifice. In fact, sacrifice in Nietzsche assumes a specific regulative role that is of great importance in handling the opposition between Hegel's connection between sacrifice and recognition and Kierkegaard's emphasis on the need for unmediated sacrifice. To deal with Nietzsche's account of sacrifice, I first distinguish three meanings of the notion that relate respectively to master morality, slave morality, and active nihilism. In master morality, sacrifice is necessarily that of the slaves as a class; in slave morality, sacrifice is necessarily of one's passions and instincts. Given that sacrifice is driven by the will to power, I argue that the meaning of sacrifice in active nihilism oscillates between two approaches, depending on how the will to power is considered. If the will to power is considered as a primordial "impulse" or "impetus," as it often is in the postmodern approach to Nietzsche, sacrifice becomes a radical "sacrifice of the self" and coincides with the suppression of the principle of individuation and the consequent risk of linguistic and rational aphasia. However, if the will to power is considered as a historical and anthropological principle, Nietzsche's account of sacrifice can be regarded as a valuable attempt to provide a solution to the opposition between the Hegelian appeal to recognition and Kierkegaard's need for unmediated sacrifice; and hence, it can also represent a contribution to the analysis of sacrifice in the political context. I show that if the will to power is considered as a historical/anthropological principle, then sacrifice in active nihilism (the sacrifice of the overman) becomes a regulative principle *à la Kant*. As typical of a regulative principle conceived in a Kantian sense, the sacrifice of the overman refuses heteronomy. Sacrifice is nevertheless necessary and serves as a general guideline. Thus, sacrifice is regulative insofar as it is *not* practiced in the name of metaphysical values or according to customs or habits, and insofar as it is guided by responsibility toward mankind. The overman determines what has to be sacrificed relying on his independent will, which only the overman is able to forge, and which is guided exclusively by the responsibility for the good of the species. The strength of Nietzsche's approach consists mainly in the linking of sacrifice with the will to power, which thus grants freedom its independence from morality. If the will to power is considered as a historical and anthropological principle, Nietzsche offers a "hermeneutics of sacrifice" in which the Kantian regulativity no longer appears empty and formal. However, this move introduces other problems, the most important being that the criteria that determine who or what has to be sacrificed are highly subjective and ultimately depend on the judgment of the overman. In other words, the regulativity is not empty in principle, but in practice it reintroduces the same emptiness. Thus

Nietzsche reestablishes an account of Kantian regulativity that is stronger than the one that is sketched in Kierkegaard, but without the resolution found in Hegel.

In the conclusion, the approaches to sacrifice that accrue from Kant's transcendental turn are explored in terms of the need of a theory of sacrifice that takes into consideration both its *regulative* and its *symbolic* meaning. In each approach, the problem becomes that of conceiving of the possibility of a way of thinking in which sacrifice can be thought of philosophically, without turning it into an abstract and fictional reconstruction. Thus, the conclusive thesis of the book is that the philosophical perspectives of the post-Kantian thinkers on sacrifice need to be considered all together to compose a strategy that allows one to fruitfully deal with this notion, with the thoughts of Hegel and Nietzsche playing a major role. I argue that Nietzsche's "hermeneutic" approach can be fruitfully thought of in conjunction with Hegel's theory of recognition to provide a comprehensive theory of sacrifice. In fact, for Hegel too, sacrifice is necessary and serves as a general guideline. Both Nietzsche and Hegel consider sacrifice as a regulative notion and both aim to avoid the emptiness of Kantian regulativity. However, Hegel links sacrifice with recognition. This is an important move, as sacrifice is regarded as not guided by anything external.

Second, Hegel's perspective, based on mutual recognition, avoids the problem of the subjective criteria for sacrifice that was one of the main problems in Nietzsche's account. Finally, and most importantly, kenotic sacrifice assumes a central place in Hegel's philosophy. Recognition is the driving force of the dialectic process, and there is no recognition of another self without renouncing one's own absoluteness. This renunciation, or withdrawal, is precisely what Hegel considers the authentic sacrifice.

Finally, I briefly take into consideration some of the twentieth-century accounts of sacrifice by showing their connections with the philosophical positions examined in the previous chapters. Various directions taken by philosophy regarding the notion of sacrifice are sketched, showing which aspects of the array of post-Kantian alternatives are taken up, and which rejected. Thus, Bataille's notion of sacrifice as pure expenditure (*dépense*) can be seen as combining Hegelian themes, in a way that resembles Solger's account more than Hegel's, with an interpretation of Nietzsche's will to power as a primordial "impetus" or "impulse"; and Derrida's deconstruction can be seen as involving a return to Nietzsche's romanticism in conjunction with Kierkegaard's critique of Kantian ethics. Also, I devote particular attention to René Girard's theory of sacrifice. While Girard's account of sacrifice has a peerless *descriptive* value insofar as it provides a meaningful description of what sacrifice (conceived as suppression) is, it is defective in that it does not provide a *normative* account of sacrifice. I claim that what is missing in Girard's mimetic theory is the consideration of kenotic sacrifice, that notion of sacrifice which is central in the post-Kantian tradition.

In this reading of the twentieth-century approaches to sacrifice, I support two other crucial theses. The first is that kenotic sacrifice is not sacrifice "without reserve"—the kind of sacrifice that emerges from the works of Bataille, Derrida, and Žižek. Postmodern philosophers tend to radicalize sacrifice in an attempt to make the symbolic aspect of sacrifice more meaningful. Conversely, the kenotic sacrifice does not imply the "dissolution" of the self, but rather a "renegotiation" of one's own identity as a result of the withdrawal. The second thesis is that contemporary philosophies of the continental stream overemphasize the *symbolic* aspect of sacrifice while neglecting its *regulative* meaning. It is this neglect, I suggest, that is behind the pervasive miscomprehension of sacrifice in contemporary culture. Sacrificial actions such as those performed by suicide bombers become incomprehensible if the regulative meaning of sacrifice is not taken into account.

I am aware that the decisions that led me to select some figures and issues of the post-Kantian tradition rather than others may be controversial, but I am confident that the results of this study prove them to be judicious. The absence of other figures is justified, in my view, by the fact that I approach sacrifice from a specific angle, that of kenotic sacrifice. Notwithstanding, I make no claim for completeness in my treatment.

An analysis of the role sacrifice plays in the post-Kantian tradition is important for at least two reasons. The first is that, by stressing the kenotic structure of Kantian and post-Kantian thought, this analysis advances our understanding of it insofar as it emphasizes the perspectivism that is intrinsic to this tradition. The second is that such an emphasis should be re-proposed in today's philosophy. Of course, we all know that our individual point of view is not the objective point of view (the God's-eye view), and we all know that we have to withdraw to make room for other points of view. But reflecting on the consequences of this kenotic structure for explicit knowledge about the nature of ourselves is a difficult task, and the very idea that there is something to be discovered here was a huge intellectual step.[32] The post-Kantian tradition can be regarded as a philosophical expression of kenotic sacrifice; it is an attempt to make explicit what everybody "knows" about what it means to recognize other points of view. The philosophical development of this idea is, however, an enormous and complicated task.

In a Vedic hymn (the *Asyavamsya*), it is written that sacrifice is "the navel of the world," meaning that all that exists is made to share in the sacrifice. Although this verse can be regarded as an appropriate poetic expression of the conclusion of this study, I am not so ambitious. If my work can at least show the importance of kenotic sacrifice for the post-Kantian tradition, I will feel I have succeeded.

1

Kant

Sacrifice and the Transcendental Turn

An analysis of the notion of sacrifice in Kant's philosophy has often been neglected in previous literature. Papers and books dealing with this subject matter are very few. Of course, this does not mean that there is a complete lack of interest. After all, Kant explicitly mentions sacrifice while addressing the schematism of analogy in *Religion within the Boundaries of Mere Reason*; therefore, works dealing with Kant's philosophy of religion or "philosophical theology" have sometimes addressed this notion.[1] More recently, Milbank[2] addressed Kant's notion of sacrifice as part of his critique of Kant's practical philosophy.

Furthermore, the issue of sacrifice has been raised in debates surrounding Kant's ethics, usually in relation to discussions of specific questions, such as constructivism,[3] consequentialism,[4] hedonism,[5] charity,[6] supererogation,[7] or security.[8] However, this literature tends to *employ* the notion of sacrifice, either by referring to Kant's use of the term, or by regarding "sacrifice" as the most adequate term to describe the process or dynamics under scrutiny, without wondering what sacrifice *means* for Kant and without raising the problem of its role in Kant's philosophy broadly conceived. Keenan has several references to Kant in his study on sacrifice[9]; but they are mostly connected to readings of Kant made by postmodern thinkers such as Derrida and Žižek, and Kant himself does not feature among the philosophers who are taken into specific consideration in his work.

A recent notable and welcome exception to this lack of specific attention is represented by Axinn's book *Sacrifice and Value*.[10] The main thesis of his book is that sacrifices "create values."[11] Axinn claims that Kant is not a "value realist," and thus reads Kant as an advocate for his central argument: "When what we do is to sacrifice, we create value for ourselves."[12] I find Axinn's view intriguing, and I will address some of his claims shortly.

However, the focus of this chapter is both more general and, at the same time, more specific. It is more general because I will discuss the role of sacrifice in Kant's philosophy in its entirety, including his epistemology and his account of religion. At the same time, it is more specific because I will distinguish between two different meanings of sacrifice, arguing that Kant employs them both, but with a certain degree of ambiguity. The first meaning is sacrifice as suppression, or destruction, of something for the sake of something else. The second meaning is sacrifice as kenosis, or withdrawal.

I will now briefly address Kant's epistemology, arguing that sacrifice as kenosis plays a hidden and yet important role in the development of Kant's transcendental philosophy. Then, I will focus on Kant's practical philosophy, arguing that the notion of sacrifice that is both implied and explicitly analyzed by Kant is mainly *suppressive* sacrifice, although Kant's account is fundamentally ambiguous and ends by being marked with some aporias. Finally, I will consider the role sacrifice plays in Kant's account of religion, showing that Kant's approach, with its achievements and problems, paves the way to various developments of the question of sacrifice in post-Kantian philosophy up to Nietzsche.

Kant's Kenotic Turn in Epistemology

In the *Preface* to the second edition of the *Critique of Pure Reason* (the so-called *B Preface*), Kant wrote:

> Up to now it has been assumed that all our cognition must conform to the objects; but all attempts to find out something about them a priori through concepts that would extend our cognition have, on this presupposition, come to nothing. Hence let us once try whether we do not get farther with the problems of metaphysics by assuming that the objects must conform to our cognition [. . .].[13]

These lines are followed by the famous reference to Copernicus, which made generations of scholars talk about Kant's "Copernican turn" or even "Copernican revolution." And it was indeed a revolution: in fact, from the hypothesis that we should consider the objects of metaphysics as conforming to our knowledge, rather than vice versa—a revolutionary hypothesis in itself—stemmed the even more revolutionary claim that we know the objects not *in themselves*, but *as they are known* by the knowing subject. There is no *absolute objectivity* for Kant, but only *universal subjectivity*, which is due to the fact that we all have the same a priori forms. Put into jeopardy here is the very notion of metaphysics as it was usually understood and practiced in modern philosophy, that is, as the alleged knowledge of the fundamental nature of the world *independent of the knower*. Where did this traditional idea of metaphysics come from?

In Western thought, the philosophical account of God has always been indicative of the knowledge aspired to in philosophy. The Aristotelian God, the immutable and fully actualized "unmoved mover" ("thought thinking itself") was indicative of the goal of philosophy as a metaphysical immutable knowledge of an "ultimate" reality. The mainstream tradition in Medieval and early-modern philosophy did not substantially divert from that image of God, with the addition of the attribute of omniscience as a consequence of the introduction of a personalistic component (the Judeo-Christian omnipotent God). For instance, Thomas Aquinas, in his five statements about the divine qualities, defines God as simple, perfect (lacking nothing), infinite, immutable, and one, that is, without diversification within God's self.[14] In modern philosophy, it is this image of God that has informed the idea of metaphysics, especially in the domain of epistemology, where this image was connected with a conception of metaphysics as expressed by the phrase "God's-eye view." Even for Leibniz, who introduced a perspectival account of knowledge (each monad is a peculiar "point of view" on the world), the main epistemic aspiration is to become God-minded. The distance between the knowledge attainable by the human agent and that attainable by God is represented by a difference in degree (being the "monad of monads," God is able to grasp all the possible points of view on the world), but *not* in kind. Kant broke with this tradition: humans are finite and, as such, can only know phenomena, that is, things as they appear to us. Only God (should he exist) could be able to know things in themselves. In other words, as a consequence of thinking of ourselves as finite, Kant drew an absolute barrier—a difference not only *in degree*, but also *in kind*—between human and divine cognition.

The Aristotelian-Thomistic account of God was clearly dominant in the Middle Ages, and it exerted a major influence on modern philosophy; but it was not, however, the only proposed account of God. Neoplatonic influences led to an alternative, more dynamic conception of God. One of the most notable figures in this tradition is Meister Eckhart. Echkart's triune God, far from being the simple and immutable divinity of the Thomistic tradition, reveals himself through a series of kenotic sacrifices: first the Father pours the totality of his divinity into the Son; and then the Son self-empties of his divinity in the incarnation for the sake of the world.[15]

As already mentioned in the Introduction, Echkart's doctrines had a significant impact on Martin Luther and the Reformation, and his conception of kenosis eventually resurfaced in the thought of the German Christian mystic Jacob Böhme. Significantly, kenotic thinking was common in Pietism, and many of the "radical Pietists" were influenced by the writings of Böhme.[16] In turn, Pietist influences on Kant's thought are often acknowledged, although they are usually regarded as being limited to the impact of the Pietist ideal of ethical purity on the development of Kant's practical philosophy.[17] What if the general approach of kenotic thinking, exemplified in Böhme's thought, lies in the background of Kant's transcendental turn?

The main focus of Böhme's thought is the relationship between the unity of God and the multiplicity of "things" in the universe. A significant aspect of Böhme's theology is that God can have knowledge of himself only through his creation. Böhme writes: "In his depth, God himself does not know what he is."[18] Strictly speaking, God cannot "reveal" himself to anyone (including himself), unless there is someone or something to which the revelation can be made. In a Neoplatonic fashion, God creates the universe by giving "form" to it, thus establishing a subject/object distinction: an observing subject (God), and an object being observed (the created universe). Giving form to the world, God effectively knows it; and by knowing the world, he reveals himself to the world and, at the same time, he reaches knowledge of himself. The explicit kenotic aspect in Böhme's narrative resides in this: God needs to empty himself and to renounce his absoluteness to truly know himself and the universe.

Surely, anyone with a basic knowledge of Kant's philosophy will have grasped some striking analogies between Böhme's theology and the framework of Kant's epistemology. In distancing himself from the metaphysical tradition that had its cognitive ideal in the God of the Aristotelian-Thomistic tradition (a detached account of an independent knowledge of an ultimate reality), Kant's epistemic view is developed in such a way that the "modest" God of the kenotic tradition might be considered its ideal—represented by a concrete and spatio-temporally determined knowledge of the world.

The Kantian "subject" is the human being, rather than God: but once the subject is changed, the similarities are impressive. Like Böhme's God, Kant's cognitive subject can know the external world only by contributing *forms* (the a priori intuitions of space and time, and the categories) to the process of knowledge. And like Böhme's God, Kant's cognitive agent knows his "self" only by knowing external objects: this is the ground of the necessary reflexivity of self-consciousness—that is, the Kantian idea that the capacity to identify external objects as distinct from oneself and the awareness of oneself as a subject are indissolubly connected. However, the most notable analogy, I suggest, concerns precisely the kenotic aspect of Böhme's narrative. Even Kant's cognitive agent has to renounce his/her absoluteness: what has to be renounced is the idea that the world can be known from an alleged God's-eye point of view, free from the spatio-temporal and causal constraints usually limiting the knower in his cognition. Kant's cognitive humility is intrinsically kenotic: we come to accept that we can know the world merely as a set of phenomena (things as they appear to us), and *not* as it is "in itself." In other words, we can know the world only from our finite perspective.

This "modesty" in epistemic aspiration is undoubtedly one of the most characterizing features of Kant's philosophy. It is clearly due to the distance that Kant establishes between the unattainable God's-eye view, which was the goal of traditional metaphysics, and the cognition attainable by a human, finite agent, which is limited by spatio-temporal and causal constraints. Kant effectively moves away from the traditional ideal of the God's-eye view to propose a more modest cognitive ideal, that objectivity which is, after all, only universal subjectivity. This move mimics the process of withdrawal that is at the core of the kenotic thinking: God withdrawing from his absoluteness to make room for the universe; and Christ renouncing his peculiar divine attributes (such as omnipotence, omniscience, etc.) to accept a finite (and thus spatio-temporally determined) condition through the incarnation. However, the transfer of the kenotic dynamic from God to the human beings introduces a new problem, or paradox—one that was already implicit in Leibniz's thesis of the perspectivity of knowledge.[19] If our knowledge is inevitably perspectival (in the sense of spatio-temporally determined), how is it possible for us to become conscious of the perspectivity of knowledge, without *eo ipso* admitting the possibility of reaching a superior, aperspectival standpoint (the God's-eye view), whose possibility seemed to be negated in the definition of knowledge as inevitably perspectival? Clearly the problem does not present itself for God or Christ: for a divine entity, the withdrawal—and the consequent assumption of a perspectival standpoint—are always temporary. For Kant's agent, however, the perspectivity of knowledge is a constitutive condition. Is there any further justification that the restriction of the God's-eye view is not itself stated from a God's-eye view?

Kant's solution to this paradox is simple and quite traditional: it is the understanding (conceptual thought) that frees the thinker from the effects of perspective.[20] *Sensory* intuition is always different because it necessarily depends on spatio-temporal location. However, the content of *thought* is conceptual; and given that the pure a priori forms of the understanding (or categories) are the same for all humans, it follows that its conceptual products are also the same for all humans. The conceptual standpoint is not a God's-eye view; and yet it is aperspectival. However, another problem now arises: which status should be assigned to pure *objects of thought*? According to Kant's famous claim, "Thoughts without content are empty"[21]—the content being sensory intuition. This is why (traditional) metaphysics is, for Kant, "the science of illusion"—because it has the intention of providing knowledge about concepts (such as the soul, or God), of which no empirical (i.e., spatio-temporal) intuitions are possible. Considered from this angle, the *Critique of Pure Reason* has been often interpreted as representing a radical skepticism about metaphysics; and there is no doubt that most of the book pursues this path.

Sometimes, however, Kant seems to suggest that metaphysics is somehow *possible*—not the traditional (pre-Kantian) metaphysics that treated metaphysical objects as if they were natural objects, but a new kind of metaphysics, conceived as that discipline in which reason is concerned *with its own products*.[22] A meaningful example is represented by the ideas of the human soul and of God. Whereas pre-Kantian metaphysics dealt with the human soul and God as if they were natural objects, Kant approached them as products of reasons that hold a peculiar regulative status, that is, as regulative principles that "serve to lead the understanding by means of reason in regard to experience and to the use of its rules in the greatest perfection."[23] In other words, in light of Kant's "strong transcendental idealism," the existence of the objects of metaphysics is different from the existence of natural objects—metaphysical objects have an *ideal* rather than a "naturalistic" existence.

In line with this interpretation, one of the major achievements of the *Critique of Pure Reason* is that knowledge is not "the ultimate orientation to the world"; rather, in Redding's words, "there is a purely conceptual articulated stance not reducible to one of knowing" whose prototypical expression is human morality, which is regarded by Kant as proceeding "from pure conceptual considerations" and as not ultimately resting on knowledge. In short, "metaphysics is reconceived from within a practical point of view."[24]

To recap: apart from any indirect influence that traditional kenotic thinking might or might not have exerted on Kant, kenotic issues play an important role in the development of Kant's project, especially in relation to the central question of metaphysics. Thus, practical philosophy should be the appropriate place within Kant's work to encounter an explicit treatment of the topic of sacrifice. A hypothetical reader with no knowledge of

Kant's ethics, after reading the current section, would undertake the reading of next section with certain expectations about the role sacrifice might play in the practical realm. In such a case, however, he would be mostly (albeit not completely) disappointed.

Kant's Practical Philosophy:
"A Sacrifice Before the Moloch of Abstraction"?

In the practical realm, Kant rejects any heteronomous motive as the foundation of ethics. Moral law can only be grounded in the *form* of will. Kant does not assign a specific content to will and recommends that we choose potentially universalizable maxims as the basis of our morality. In other words, according to Kant's formal conception, humans should behave *as if* maxims were universally applicable.

Kant's modesty, which is a distinctive element of his epistemology, does *not* extend to his practical philosophy. As emphasized at the end of previous section, metaphysics can be reconceived from within a practical point of view because human morality is regarded by Kant as proceeding from *pure conceptual* considerations. The kenotic dynamic, identified in the previous section in relation to Kant's cognitive humility, is driven by the negation of the possibility to step out of spatio-temporality and causality. In the practical realm, the possibility to step-out of spatio-temporality and causality is reestablished; actually, this possibility represents the precondition of that freedom from natural necessity that Kant wants to reestablish in the practical, noumenal realm. Indeed, the moral law is given "as a fact of pure reason of which we are conscious a priori and which is apodeictically certain" (KpV, 47/66). Kant also argues that we have a duty to the moral law itself (on which our duties to others depend) prior to having duties to others.

An evidence of the *absolute* standpoint in the Kantian foundation of morality is his repeated insistence that duties "be regarded as commands of the supreme Being" (KpV, 5: 129/164). Kant invites the moral agent to listen to moral commands *as if* they were spoken by the voice of God. That is, the categorical imperative should be regarded as a duty toward God. Kant's insistence represents an attempt to solve the paradox that, according to Pinkard, is implied in the Kantian idea of self-legislation—the idea that one has to be bound by laws of which one is also the author.[25]

Therefore, there is only *one* autonomous and objective moral law, which is absolute and must not be determined by spatio-temporal and causality issues. Because there is no necessary agreement between will and reason, morality is a duty, and hence implies some violence against our sensible inclinations and desires. The first time the word "sacrifice" (*Aufopferung*) occurs in the *Critique of Practical Reason* is precisely in the context of affirming the necessity to negate desires that might lead the moral subject to deviate from the moral law; such a negation is, in Kant's own words, a sacrifice:

> For if a rational creature could ever get to the point of fulfilling all moral laws completely *gladly*, this would be tantamount to meaning that there would not be in him even the possibility of a desire stimulating him to deviate from them; for, overcoming such a desire always costs the subject [some] sacrifice [*Aufopferung*] and hence requires self-constraint, i.e., inner necessitation to what one does not do entirely gladly. (KpV, 84/108)[26]

The understanding of sacrifice that emerges from this passage—which is not limited to it, but rather informs the entire Kantian ethics—is very far from the kenotic dynamic that we have seen at work in the previous section. The notion employed is rather that of sacrifice as suppression of something (instincts, desires, inclinations) for the sake of something else (moral law).

If the hypothetical reader I mentioned at the end of the previous section was now disappointed, he would be in good philosophical company. Hegel, for instance, maintains that Kant's conception of morality is formal and empty;[27] and the second chapter of the *Phenomenology of Spirit* is harshly critical of the "abstract negation" of desires, in which the desire is not overcome but only abstractly denied. From a different angle, and even more explicitly, Nietzsche thunders against the Kantian suppression of desires for the sake of the "impersonal" duty, something that he defines as "a sacrifice before the Moloch of abstraction."[28] Additionally, Nietzsche saw in Kant's practical philosophy a regression to the idea of "a real world" (the metaphysical idea of a world conceived as what is there independently of the knower), a move that Nietzsche stigmatized as the last consolation of metaphysics.[29]

As regards to recent scholarship, Milbank focused precisely on Kant's use of the notion of sacrifice, which in his view drives the entire Kantian theory of ethics "into irresolvable aporias."[30] In fact, sensory inclinations "must be sacrificed," Milbank remarks, "even in the case where a sensory inclination happens to coincide with duty." The point raised by Milbank is indeed an important one and deserves to be analyzed in detail.

When addressing sacrifice, Kant often considers it as a possible moral motive and usually in association with the topic of heroism. A first reference to sacrifice as a moral motive can be found in the *Groundwork*:

> It is indeed sometimes the case that with the keenest self-examination we find nothing besides the moral ground of duty that could have been powerful enough to move us to this or that good action and to so great a sacrifice [*Aufopferung*]; but from this it cannot be inferred with certainty that no covert impulse of self-love, under the mere pretense of that idea, was not actually the real determining cause of the will; for we like to flatter ourselves by falsely attributing to ourselves a nobler motive, whereas in fact we can never, even by the most strenuous self-examination, get entirely behind our covert incentives.[31]

Even great sacrifices (including the sacrifice of one's life) are not necessarily moral for Kant, as they can involve pride alongside duty. This is clearly a serious concern for Kant because we find the same remark in two different places in the *Critique of Practical Reason*:

> Actions of others which have been done with great sacrifice [*Aufopferung*] and, moreover, solely on account of duty, may indeed be praised under the name of *noble* and *sublime* deeds, yet even this only insofar as there are indications suggesting that they were done entirely from respect for one's duty, not from bursts of emotions. (KpV, 85/110)

And again:

> More decisive is the magnanimous sacrifice of one's life [*die großmütige Aufopferung seines Lebens*] for the preservation of one's country; and yet there remains some scruple as to whether it is indeed so perfectly a duty to dedicate oneself to this aim on one's own and without having been ordered to do so, and the action does not contain the full force of a model and impulse for imitation. (KpV, 158/198)

If one considers Kant's rejection of any heteronomous moral motive, which is the foundation of his ethics, these concerns are understandable. And yet, Milbank touches on an important point when he wonders: "How is one ever to know that sacrificial motives are pure?"[32] Clearly, one cannot; and yet, we cannot simply get rid of our attraction for sacrifice because sacrifice and heroism are *symbols* that grant us access to the otherwise inaccessible purity of duty. In Milbank's words:

> How is one to discriminate within oneself, if only a feeling of love of self-sacrifice registers the law, and yet *even this feeling* contaminates the purity of duty and is only valid in so far as this feeling constantly negates itself, sacrificing even the love of sacrifice? If this sacrifice even of sacrifice is, still, nevertheless sacrifice, how to distinguish a diminution of love of sacrifice and denial of self, from a subtle increase of love of sacrifice and affirmation of self?[33]

Milbank's discussion of sacrifice is functional to his critique of Kant's account of radical evil as "an original possibility constitutive of freedom as such," something that makes of Kant's philosophy "only an alternative theology" (and not a good one, in Milbank's view). However, Milbank's opinion of Kant aside, his analysis has the merit of showing some aporias and problems embedded in Kant's discussion of sacrifice as a moral *symbol*. In fact, the need for symbols (including religious symbols) in Kant's conception of morality is connected to the issue of sacrifice, and I will devote the next section precisely to this topic. Before that, however, it is appropriate to consider another recent reading of Kant's notion of sacrifice, that proposed by Axinn.

Axinn offers a much more positive interpretation of Kant's use of sacrifice. The main thesis of his book is that "we don't find the values, and then sacrifice for them: our sacrifices produce them."[34] By arguing that Kant is not a value realist, he comes to the conclusion that, through the emphasis on suppression of the individual's personal desires, Kant has effectively clarified the process of formation of values. I do not dispute Axinn's claim about a general relationship between sacrifices and values (which is something that is beyond the scope of this chapter); what I wish to explore here are: (a) the implications of such a reading for Kant's philosophy, and (b) whether Kant can be legitimately regarded as supporting such a claim. In fact, these two aspects are related to each other. Let us assume that Kant is effectively not committed to value realism: this means that *we* create the values to which we are bound. This is the paradox identified by Pinkard,[35] to which Kant found no other solution than a repeated insistence that moral commands should be listened to as if they were spoken by the voice of God. The position that Axinn attributes to Kant—that values effectively depend on us, they are *made* by us[36]—might be attributed much fittingly to some post-Kantians—first of all, Hegel. It is Hegel who, through the notion of recognition, made values dependent on human activity (most notably, sacrifice);[37] and after him, the so-called left Hegelians considered the distribution of the activity of the constitution of norms over the species to be a better solution to the Kantian paradox. It might be objected that an understanding of values as objects having an *ideal* (and thus, human-dependent) rather than a *naturalistic* existence was already implied in a reading of Kant along the lines of "strong transcendental idealism" (according to Redding's definition).[38] However, this objection on the one hand reminds us of a fundamental ambiguity in Kant, who constantly oscillated between weak transcendental idealism and strong transcendental idealism; and on the other, confirms my previous claim because it is precisely on the 'strong transcendental idealism' reading that post-Kantians have drawn to develop post-transcendental forms of idealism. Significantly, the Kantian passage that Axinn cites in support of his argument is from the *third* critique—the *Critique of Judgment*.[39] Once a certain tension running through the formulation of transcendental idealism (as articulated in the *Critique of Pure Reason*) has been acknowledged, it seems safe to say (with Redding) that the general trajectory of Kant's journey "was towards conceptions that are [. . .] closer in spirit to the type of idealism developed by those coming after him, such as Fichte, Schelling and Hegel."[40]

Finally, even assuming that Kant's understanding of sacrifice is positive, as Axinn maintains and that Kant can be interpreted as establishing a strong relation between sacrifices and values (with sacrifices effectively *producing* values), what is the notion of sacrifice that emerges from this interpretation? It is the traditional meaning of sacrifice as suppression of something for the sake of something else. "Why would a rational person sacrifice in this sense, give away more than is expected to be returned?" Axinn asks, and continues: "My response: to gain nonmonetary value." We are certainly very far from the conception of sacrifice as kenosis that is at work in the development of Kant's perspectivism. Effectively, most of the references to sacrifice in Kant's practical philosophy seem to be related with such an interpretation of sacrifice as the suppression of something to gain something else in exchange. This might even raise the doubt that perceiving the presence of a kenotic conception of sacrifice in the development of Kant's perspectivism could be the result of an overinterpretation.

Sometimes, however, Kant shows an understanding of sacrifice that goes precisely in the *opposite* direction—that is, in the direction of a *kenotic* interpretation of sacrifice. In *The Metaphysics of Morals*, in the context of the discussion of the relationship between freedom and the states, Kant writes:

> One cannot say: the human being has sacrificed [*Aufgeopfert*] a *part* of his innate outer freedom for the sake of an end, but rather, he has relinquished [*Verlassen*] entirely his wild, lawless

freedom in order to find his freedom as such undiminished, in a dependence upon laws, that is, in a rightful condition, since this dependence arises from his own lawgiving will. (MS, 316/127)

Here we have precisely the opposition between sacrifice as *suppression*—the human being as *suppressing* a part of his freedom for the sake of the state—and sacrifice as *kenosis*—the human being as *relinquishing*[41] his freedom. The human being does not relinquish his freedom for the sake of something else, but to have his freedom reestablished in that dependence upon laws that sees the moral/political subject in a mutual and constant relationship with his fellow citizens.

A kenotic understanding of sacrifice is even more evident in another passage, which is worthwhile to quote in full:

> [. . .] I ought to sacrifice [*Opfer machen*] a part of my welfare to others *without hope of return* [*ohne Hoffnung der Wiedervergeltung*] because this is a duty, and it is impossible to assign specific limits to the extent of this sacrifice. How far it should extend depends, in large part, on what each person's own happiness, one's true needs, would conflict with itself if it were made a universal law. Hence this duty is only a *wide* one; the duty has in it a latitude for doing more or less, and no specific limits can be assigned to what should be done. The law holds only for maxims, not for specific actions. (MS, 393/197; emphasis added)

The key point here is that the happiness of others is an end *that is also a duty*; however, it is first of all *an end in itself* (MS, 393/196–197), and it is for the sake of others' happiness that I am required to sacrifice a part of my welfare. The dynamic described here looks more like a withdrawing of my welfare to "make room for others," rather than a *suppression* of my welfare. That the sacrifice at stake is different from the sacrifice mentioned above is evident from the concern suddenly expressed by Kant. Others' happiness is not primarily a duty, but it is a duty only insofar as it is an end in itself; which implies the problem of the extent to which sacrifices have to be performed to make other people happy. The law has, therefore, only a *regulative* value: it tells us that we must promote the ends of others, but does not provide any indication of *how much* we should sacrifice for the sake of others' happiness.[42]

In conclusion, it appears that there is a certain tension running through Kant's account of sacrifice. The general orientation of Kant's employment of sacrifice in his practical philosophy seems consistent with the meaning of sacrifice as suppression of instincts and desires for the sake of the moral role. However, Kant's account of sacrifice in the context of his practical philosophy is not without a certain degree of ambiguity because sometimes the kenotic meaning of sacrifice seems to resurface, especially in connection with the central issue of the regulative nature of the moral law. At stake is the viability of Kant's *formal* conception of morality. The formality of the moral law is that which makes it universally applicable; and yet, it generates the need for some way of making moral concepts concretely applicable to the world. Religion and, to some extent, beauty serve this purpose. We should therefore analyze the role sacrifice plays in Kant's account of religion, with the goal of exploring if in that realm a solution to the fundamental ambiguity mentioned above can be found.

Symbolic and Regulative Value of Sacrifice

The role of religious notions and narratives in Kant's moral theory is often underestimated. Standard accounts tend to regard religious representations as mere metaphors or, at best, as useful symbols that serve to illustrate some moral content. From Kant's perspective, it is suggested, religious representations have more or less the function of pictures in old novels: they embellish the pages, but ultimately it would not make any difference if they were omitted from the text. If one considers them in the light of the Kantian need for some way of making moral ideas applicable to the world, however, a very different picture emerges.

First, Kant's discounting of any religious *foundation* from either the theoretical or the practical realm does not mean that he dismisses the content of revealed religion as irrelevant in general, or that he discounts the idea of God in particular.[43]

Regarding the latter, it has already been recalled that Kant invites the moral agent to listen to moral commands *as if* they were spoken by the voice of God. In other words, moral duties should be regarded as *theonomous* duties—that is, duties toward God: "Since all religion consists in this, that in all our duties we look upon God as the lawgiver to be honored universally" (RGV, 6:104/137). And a few pages later, Kant reinforces the claim: "Religion is (subjectively considered) the recognition of all our duties as divine commands" (RGV, 6:154/177).

Regarding the former, Kant considers religious claims and notions as symbolic *presentations* or exhibitions (*Darstellungen*) of the moral law. They are not mere "metaphors": the need for such *presentations* is, conversely, deeply rooted into the need for a way of making moral concepts concretely applicable to the world. In fact, in the *Critique of Practical Reason*, Kant notes "special difficulties" in dealing with the application of the moral law—difficulties that do not present themselves in the realm of theoretical reason. As pointed out by Redding,[44] the problem of applying categories (pure concepts) to the contents of intuition was solved by Kant through the introduction of "schemata" (rules that connect pure concepts with sensible data). In the realm of practical reason, however, we deal with "the morally good," and "the morally good as an object," that is—in Kant's own words—something supersensible

> so that nothing corresponding to it can be found in any sensible intuition; hence the power of judgment under laws of pure practical reason seems to be subject to special difficulties which are due to [the fact] that a law of freedom is to be applied to actions as events that occur in the world of sense and thus, to this extent, belong to nature. (KpV, 68/90)

The problem for Kant is to find something equivalent to schemata for practical reason, that is, transitional forms to be used to apply the pure principles of practical reason to experience. These forms are identified by Kant in symbolic presentations or exhibitions (*Darstellungen*). In fact, whereas a pure concept can be *schematized*, moral ideas can only be *symbolized*.[45] Religious notions and narratives are an essential component of a set of symbolic notions that, for Kant, is necessary to make moral ideas applicable to the world.[46]

Therefore, for Kant, religious symbols (both notions and narratives) are transitional forms, or analogical *presentations* (*Darstellungen*), that must be used to apply the pure principles of practical reason to experience, insofar as they can serve as models for our behavior; in other words, they play a *regulative* role in the application of moral ideas to the world. It follows that religious notions and narratives, far from being mere metaphors or symbols *in a weak sense*, are rather an *essential* component of Kant's practical philosophy.

However, not *all* religious notions or narratives can be accepted as moral symbols and can thus serve as models. In *Religion within the Boundaries of Mere Reason*, Kant distinguishes between "the natural religion," whose main characteristic is that "every human being can be convinced [of its truth] through his reason," and "a learned religion," whose main characteristic is that "one can convince others only by means of erudition" (RGV, 6:155/178). In natural religion, theology conforms to morality, whereas in learned or revealed religion, morality conforms to theology. The relationship between natural religion and revealed religion is visible in the image of the concentric circles included in the Preface to the 1794 edition: revealed religion, represented by the wider circle, includes natural religion ("the pure religion of reason"), which is in turn represented by the narrower circle. What is implied in this image is that the criteria according to which it is decided that some claim is acceptable within the sphere of natural religion are set by the philosopher ("as purely a teacher of reason"), who is guided by the consistency of the a priori principles of practical reason.[47] It follows that only those religious contents that are compatible with potentially universalizable moral maxims can be regarded as having symbolic and regulative status.[48]

As in the realm of practical philosophy, even in the realm of religion (understandably, as in Kant's view these two realms are strictly related to each other), Kant's standpoint is grounded by a restated possibility to step out of the constraints represented by spatio-temporality and causality (similar to what happens in his practical philosophy): if the philosopher is correctly guided by the consistency of the a priori principles of practical reason, he will be able to decide which religious claims are acceptable within the sphere of natural religion, and which are not. If they are not acceptable, they have to be rejected.

What about sacrifice as a religious symbol? With reason as a guide, the philosopher should conclude—as Kant does—that sacrifice is an *improper* symbol. Firstly, *self-sacrifice* is an improper symbol because, as we have already seen, it is not necessarily moral inasmuch as it can involve pride alongside duty. Secondly, Kant has serious concerns about the way *sacrifice* is addressed in the Bible—most notably, God's request to Abraham to sacrifice his son Isaac (the "binding" of Isaac, or *Akedah*). Kant thinks of morality as *prior* to the content of any religion; as already stressed, only religious content that is compatible with potentially universalizable moral maxims can be regarded as having symbolic and regulative status. This is clearly not the case with the *Akedah*. Kant writes:

> If something is represented as commanded by God in a direct manifestation of him yet is directly in conflict with morality, it cannot be a divine miracle despite every appearance of being one (e.g., *if a father were ordered to kill his son who, so far as he knows, is totally innocent*). (RGV, 6:87/124; emphasis added)

The claim that the whole of *Religion within the Boundaries of Mere Reason* "was designed to denounce Abraham and banish such acts of reason-blind faith from the sphere of religion"[49] is exaggerated. However, there is no doubt that Abraham's willingness to sacrifice his own son due to a direct command from God represented a serious concern for Kant. This is further evinced in a passage from *The Conflict of the Faculties*, in which Kant condemns Abraham without appeal:

> Abraham should have replied to this supposedly divine voice: "That I ought not to kill my good son is quite certain. But that you, this apparition, are God—of that I am not certain, and never can be, not even if this voice rings down to me from (visible) heaven."[50]

The sacrifice that Abraham is willing to perform definitely falls outside the realm of religious symbols that Kant considers acceptable. After all, the relationship between moral duties and the idea of God is grounded for Kant on the priority of morality over religion: what Kant suggests is to listen to moral commands as if they were spoken by the voice of God, and *not* to listen to an alleged voice of God as if it were legitimate in itself (which is what is apparently happening in the *Akedah*[51]).

As in the practical realm, in the religious sphere Kant seems to conceive sacrifice in its suppressive meaning, and in general terms he does not seem to think that sacrifice might play a *positive* role. Once again, however, Kant's account of sacrifice in the context of his approach to religion is not without a certain degree of ambiguity because the kenotic meaning of sacrifice resurfaces (almost inevitably, one might add) when Kant comes to examine the symbolic and regulative value of the figure of Jesus Christ.

The figure of Christ is regarded by Kant as the religious symbol *par excellence*. In *Religion within the Boundaries of Mere Reason*, Kant refers to Christ as the "prototype [*Urbild*] of moral disposition in its entire purity," maintaining that that prototype "has *come down* [*herabgekommen*] to us from heaven" and has taken up humanity "by *descending* [*herablasse*] to it," and concluding that "this union with us may therefore be regarded as a state of *abasement* [*Erniedrigung*] of the Son of God" (RGV, 6:61/80). In this paragraph, Kant employs the classic kenotic vocabulary, and the second half is almost a direct quote from Philippians 2:8 which, as we know, is the first text where the term *kenosis* is used in connection with a sacrificial dynamic.

Later on in the text, Kant refers to the "schematism of analogy" involved in the representation of Christ and comments,

> It is plainly a limitation of human reason, one which is ever inseparable from it, that we cannot think of any significant moral worth in the actions of a person without at the same time portraying this person or his expression in human guise, even though we do not thereby mean to say that this is how things are in themselves for we always need a certain analogy with natural being to make supersensible characteristics comprehensible to us. (RGV, 6:65/107)

We must, Kant claims, have exemplars on which we can model our behavior. Thus, the claim that "Jesus is the son of God" can be interpreted as a symbolic way of expressing the ethically exemplary nature of Jesus. The fact that Jesus's behavior can be considered exemplary means that it serves as a model for our own behavior; the scriptural representation of Christ is peculiarly *regulative*. Christ represents the prototype of a pure moral disposition, one willing to undergo the greatest sacrifice (sacrifice until death) to be morally perfect. Thus the Scriptures, Kant writes, attribute to God,

> the highest sacrifice [*Aufopferung*] a living being can ever perform in order to make even the unworthy happy ('Therefore hath God loved the world, etc.'), although through reason we cannot form any concept of how a self-sufficient being could sacrifice something that belongs to his blessedness, thus robbing himself of a perfection. We have here (as means of elucidation [*Erläuterung*]) a *schematism of analogy*, with which we cannot dispense. (RGV, 6:65/107)

In this passage, all Kant's ambiguity about the role of sacrifice as symbol is concentrated. Christ is recognized as the prototype of pure moral disposition, and his willingness to self-sacrifice is acknowledged as an essential component of his perfection. The concerns raised in the context of the discussion of the *Akedah* are obviously absent here; similarly absent is any skeptical consideration about the possible involvement of pride alongside duty in Christ's moral motive. To some extent, Kant's positive consideration of Christ's sacrifice might be culturally contextualized within the Lutheran tradition, where *kenosis* was often linked to the dreadful and paradoxical abasement of the most high. However, this cultural contextualization alone could not explain the philosophical relevance that Christ's sacrifice assumes in Kant's philosophy. Christ's willingness to sacrifice himself "in order to make even the unworthy happy" appears to be a regulative symbol [*Darstellung*], or schema, for that willingness to sacrifice part of one's welfare to others "without hope of return" that Kant introduced in the *Metaphysics of Moral* (MS, 393/197), which I discussed in the previous section. The example of Christ seems to suggest that we not consider the duties to others as dependent on the moral law itself (as in the standard account of Kant's practical philosophy), but the happiness of others (including the happiness of the unworthy ones) as *an end in itself*. In short, Christ, as an exemplar, seems to invite us to sacrifice ourselves, to withdraw our welfare and to (so to say) "make room for others" for the sake of their happiness.

At the same time, after claiming that we must represent God's love toward the world in terms of self-sacrifice and that Christ, who is the concrete personification of this love, must serve as an exemplar for our moral behavior, Kant suddenly stresses that to suppose that an omnipotent being could sacrifice his absoluteness and divinity ("robbing himself of a perfection") is absurd, even nonsensical.[52] Additionally, it is not clear if Christ's willingness to sacrifice himself for the happiness of everyone else should be considered as having a strong regulative value (thus concretely guiding our moral behavior), or merely as an unachievable ideal of perfection. Clearly, behind this issue lies the question whether or not Kant is a theological realist (meaning by theological realism the idea that there is a transcendent divine reality). Kantian scholars are greatly divided on this issue.[53] According to some, Kantian religion is substantially the result of Kant's attempt to graft Lutheran Pietism into his rationalism.[54] Others considers Kant a theological realist who advances a rationalistic faith that has nothing to do with the "mystic" idea of a kenotic God that was an important motor in the development of German idealism.[55] In addition, there are several other more moderate positions that lie between these two extremes. While an in-depth analysis of this issue is beyond the scope of this chapter, it is worth pointing out that, in light of Kant's strong transcendental idealism, his claims about religion in general, and God in particular, should not be interpreted in terms of pre-Kantian metaphysical realism or unrealism.[56]

Let us recap. It is possible to argue that there is a kenotic dynamic embedded in Kant's epistemology and that kenotic issues play an important role in the development of Kant's metaphysical project. Metaphysics is reconceived by Kant from within a practical point of view; and in the practical realm, a substantial tension runs through Kant's account of sacrifice. While the entire Kantian ethics seems to be dominated by a suppressive sacrificial conception (suppression of instincts, desires, and inclinations for the sake of the moral law), sometimes the kenotic meaning of sacrifice seems to resurface, especially in the context of Kant's reflections on the happiness of others as an end in itself, for the sake of which the moral agent is required to sacrifice his or her welfare. However, a moral ideal simply holds a *regulative* status. The need for some way of making moral ideals applicable to the world, which is a concern running through the entirety of Kant's philosophy is particularly evident here, as it seems difficult to provide any indication of how much we should sacrifice for the sake of others' happiness—it does not express the extent to which the kenotic process must be carried on. Religious notions and narratives are supposed to serve as transitional forms (symbols, or *Darstellungen*) to be used to make moral ideals applicable to the world. However, sacrifice is regarded by Kant as an improper symbol—both the unacceptable scriptural sacrifice of the *Akedah*, and self-sacrifice, which can always involve pride alongside duty. And yet, Kant recognizes in Christ the prototype of pure moral disposition, identifying in his willingness to self-sacrifice and to give up some of his divine perfections the highest symbol of morality. Although the idea of a God "robbing himself of a perfection" sounds like an absurdity to Kant, the figure of Christ, in his essential kenotic attitude, is clearly indicated as an exemplar for our moral behavior. Nevertheless, these reflections seem to remain partially undeveloped.

It might be argued that Kant grasped the importance of including a kenotic dynamic in practical philosophy, but he was somehow unable or unwilling to integrate it into the formal grounding of his ethics. Clearly, the rigid structure of his ethics, at the core of which lies the primacy of duty to the moral law itself (with respect to which our duties to others are merely secondary), made it very difficult for him to emphasize the kenotic aspect of interpersonal relationships, and thus that aspect remained confined in the context of his reflections on the happiness of others as an end in itself. This tension, however, effectively provides an entry point for features that can be found in the post-Kantians.

First, Kant's perspectivism is a legacy that can be traced through the post-Kantians, obviously finding different ways of expression in various thinkers—the German Idealists, most importantly Hegel, but also Kierkegaard and, obviously, Nietzsche.

Second, the hiatus between Christ as a moral *Darstellung*, and the lack of explicit attention to the kenotic dynamic, is a symptom of a problem that is pressing for post-Kantians: maintaining the regulativity of religious notions (including sacrifice), while going beyond Kant's formal grounding (with the problems it entails). At a more general level, this hiatus is also the symptom of the "Kantian paradox" diagnosed by Pinkard, which in the context of religious symbols presents itself in an even more acute form (the "Kantian religious paradox" that I referred to in the Introduction).

Third, the difficulties experienced by Kant in integrating the kenotic dynamics into the formal grounding of his thought are dealt with, from different angles, by several post-Kantians. Significantly, the "nonsense" of a God "robbing himself of a perfection," and giving up his own divinity to become human was precisely the direction pursued by the German Idealist Solger, who built his entire philosophy around the idea of a God sacrificing himself first in the creation, and then in the incarnation (more on this in the next chapter). Hegel too, in his philosophy of religion, elaborated on this idea, considering Christianity "the highest form of religion" largely because of its central image of God becoming man, thus renouncing his divinity and absoluteness. Furthermore, the kenotic dynamic also plays a role in Hegel's critique of Kant's formal conception of morality. As argued by Pippin,[57] Hegel strongly relies on the idea that establishing moral and ethical relations with others does not involve a suppressive sacrifice, or abstraction from our particular ends, but rather their rational "realization." This realization happens through the recognition of the other person, which presupposes a kenotic withdrawal. Therefore, the next two chapters will be devoted to Solger (Chapter 2) and Hegel (Chapter 3), respectively.

2

Solger's Sacrificial Dialectic

Sacrifice as Double Negation

Karl Wilhelm Ferdinand Solger (1780–1819) is usually considered a theorist of aesthetics and romantic irony. Nevertheless, the essay written by Hegel in 1828 as an extensive review of *Solger's Posthumous Writings and Correspondence*[1] represents a challenge for the classic interpretation of Solger. In fact, the main focus of Hegel's essay is not Solger's aesthetics, but the theoretical framework of his work, constituted by Solger's negative dialectic between the finite and the Infinite. Despite several criticisms, the text shows that Hegel clearly held Solger in great esteem. This high regard cannot be merely explained by the fact that Hegel was appointed at the University of Berlin in part thanks to Solger's efforts.[2]

Dealing with Solger's thought is definitely not easy given that, as Kierkegaard stresses (quoting Hotho) in *The Concept of Irony*, "he has developed his point of view with a philosophical clarity difficult to comprehend [*schwer begreifbarer philosophischer Klarheit*]."[3] And yet, Solger represents a milestone in our journey toward the notion of sacrifice, as it is with Solger's attempted unification of theoretical and practical philosophy (a problem that, as we have seen, raised from Kant) that the post-Kantian involvement with the notion of sacrifice starts. In order to appreciate Solger's theory of sacrifice, it is essential to go through the fundamental theoretical dynamic of his thought. I am going to do that by referring mainly to his *Posthumous Writings*.[4]

Solger assumes that the Infinite (or God) is originally *absolute* [*Das Absolute*], as it is literally not *qualified* or *diminished* in any way. Nevertheless, such an Infinite is a pure theoretical hypothesis, as the Infinite (God) exists exclusively *via negationis*, that is, only when it limits itself in the finite.[5] It follows that the Infinite, that is, the Absolute, denying itself reality by creating the finite, inevitably loses its absoluteness[6]—that is to say, it alienates itself from itself. In fact, the Infinite is infinite as it is absolute; if it loses its absoluteness, it loses the very attribute that makes it what it is. In other words, such self-limitation of God is also a radical self-negation, because "losing the absoluteness" and "self-annihilating" are the same thing for the Absolute.

The movement of God's self-alienation, in keeping with the Idealistic tradition to which Solger belongs, is not presented as a deed that happened in time and space, but rather as a timeless act or movement constituting the structure of reality as it is grasped by the finite. This movement should not be confused with *emanation* as it is usually understood in Neoplatonic philosophy. In Neoplatonic philosophy, the highest principle, the One, overflows merely because of its nature, and without a conscious act. The One contains an "excess of being" that allows it to emanate the finite without any privation or diminution. The finite world is therefore usually understood in Neoplatonic philosophy as an emanation or a pale reflection of the One. In the emanationist process the One preserves its absolute status, whereas everything else is finite and is ontologically dependent on the One. Plotinus's metaphor of water represents this process very clearly: "Imagine a spring that has no source outside itself; it gives itself to all the rivers, yet is never exhausted by what they take, but remains always integrally as it was."[7] The One always remains unaffected and loses nothing by giving away.

By contrast, for Solger, the movement bringing the finite to reality is not an emanationist process, but a conscious act of *creation* (*Schöpfung*, NS, 171)—a creation which happens, as mentioned above, *via negationis*. First, the Infinite (God) creates the finite (world) by losing its own absoluteness, and thus suffers an ontological diminution. Second, once the Infinite has created the finite, the finite is no longer ontologically bound to the Infinite—that is, the finite is ontologically independent from the Infinite and thus it is never referred to by Solger as a "pale reflection" of the Infinite. If one were to apply Plotinus's metaphor of water to Solger, then one would imagine a spring that gives itself to the rivers and in doing so *is* exhausted, while the rivers persist independently.

Therefore, Solger uses the notion of creation to refer to the absolutely undeducible (as it cannot be deduced from anything else) and gratuitous (as it is not naturally determined) act that constitutes the essence of reality. With this act the Infinite (God) gives itself up to the reality of the finite. This is clearly a *kenotic* process: God creates the world by withdrawing and, consequently, *denies* itself in denying its own absoluteness.[8]

If the Infinite (God) creates the finite (world) by denying itself, then the product of this act (the finite world) is the negation of God or, to use a more literal translation from the German, the "nothing of God."[9] The German expression (*Das Nichts Gottes*) better captures Solger's account in which the finite (world) is *non-being* in relation to the *being* of God. Nevertheless it paradoxically follows that positiveness inheres in the primary act of creation: the finite (and thus also every finite being) is the place where the Infinite (God) manifests itself. Therefore, the creation of the finite (world) is at the same time God's radical negation *and* its manifestation and revelation. This is coherent, as it is only in the very creation of a Godless world that God "manifests itself" in the world. By annihilating itself, the Infinite (God) creates the finite (world), which is nonbeing. It is the fact that the finite world is *nonbeing* (in the sense that it is the "nothing of God") that allows the being (of God) to manifest itself. The Infinite (God) creates the finite (world) by denying itself; the finite thus is the nothing of God. If the finite is the negation of the Infinite, the Infinite too is the negation of the finite. This double negation is expressed by the theological category of "revelation," that is, as a self-affirmation that is a *negation of the negation*.[10]

This is Solger's vision of reality from the point of view of the Infinite: a paradoxical vision. The vision from the point of view of the finite—the human being's point of view—is equally paradoxical. Although we do not have a complete and organic exposition of Solger's philosophical system, a continuous alternation of these two points of view can be noted in the *Posthumous Writings*—an alternation that is strongly reminiscent of the framework of Hegel's *Phenomenology of Spirit*.[11]

As stated earlier, the finite has an ontological consistency because the Infinite (God) has denied itself to let the finite be, and thus the finite is the nothing of God. Solger writes: "when we become aware of the eternal and of the truth in ourselves, we do nothing but dissolve this appearance in its nothing."[12] In other words, when the human being realizes that the finite is real because the Infinite (God) has denied itself, then our finitude (the "appearance") can be thought of as it truly is, that is, nothing (of God). This awareness is not just a passive realization of a fact, but requires an active process of self-negation from the finite (human being). In fact, if the finite is the nothing of God, then the annihilation of the finite is the affirmation of God.

This conception could lead one to associate Solger with mysticism.[13] Nevertheless Solger's approach is fundamentally different. In the traditional Christian Western mysticism (in Meister Eckhart for example) the finite eliminates its finitude in order to let the infinite, which is inside it, emerge.[14] This conception assumes that finite beings are *emanations* of God. This, in turn, implies that such emanations, as they are reflections of God, maintain (and are indeed constituted by) a divine element—the "little divine spark,"[15] as Meister Eckhart calls the part of the human soul where God is prominent and alive. Whatever the ontological distance that separates the Infinite and the finite, the human being can reestablish a connection with God thanks to the presence of a divine element within the human being. Conversely, for Solger the finite is neither an emanation nor a pale reflection of God, because it is ontologically independent. There is no divine spark in the finite (neither in the world nor in the human being), as God has given rise to the finite through its self-alienation. Finite and Infinite are the real opposites of each other, as the one *completely negates* the other as its nothing ("*das eine das andere gänzlich als sein nichts aufhebt*," NS, 172): in fact, each one of them plays the role of the being in relation to the other, determining it as nothingness. To reestablish a connection between the Infinite and the finite is possible only through an active acceptance of their reciprocal negation. For the Infinite (God), this means that the timeless act of self-negation and creation is also *revelation*, insofar as the non-being of the finite (world) requires a manifestation of the being of God. In the same way, for the finite human beings this means that their ontological independence (which constitutes them as the nothing of God) requires an act that corresponds to God's manifestation. In other words, the reestablishment of a connection with the Infinite (God) requires from the finite (human being) another self-negation as total and unconditioned as the one that has created the world. Finite and Infinite "must hold each other in equilibrium" ("*müssen einander das Gleichgewicht halten*," NS, 248).[16] The equilibrium, expressed by the theological category of salvation, is established through a negation of the negation (double negation).[17]

It can also be said that the equilibrium between finite and Infinite is a contrasting (*kontradiktorische*) but not contradictory (*widersprüchliche*) equilibrium. It is *contrasting* because there is an unresolved dialectical tension between finite and Infinite. At the same time, this identity is not *contradictory* because the dialectical tension of the terms finds a solution when the equilibrium is realized through the self-negation of the Infinite (God) and the corresponding self-negation of the finite (human being).

It is important to underline that the process described by Solger and briefly summarized in the present section is a dialectic without *Aufhebung*.[18] Solger's dialectic is not triadic like the Hegelian one, but it is *dual* as the contradiction remains open. It could be said that it is a *kenotic* dialectic: the moment establishing this dialectic is the self-negation of God. In a strict philosophical sense, this process corresponds to a dialectical thought centered on the negation of the negation,[19] whose outcome is not a positiveness which has negated the preceding moments, but a consciousness of the negativity of the relationship between the Infinite and the finite. Therefore, the main aim of philosophical knowledge is to reach this consciousness.

Knowledge and Tragic Dialectic

From the overview of Solger's metaphysics included in the previous section, it seems possible *prima facie* to distinguish two moments: (1) the Infinite (God) denies itself and creates the finite (world); and (2) the finite (world) denies itself and opens itself to the Infinite (God).

Nevertheless this distinction rises from the only point of view that is accessible to the human being: the point of view of the finite. *Sub specie aeternitatis* the process is unique and eternal: the Infinite (God) continuously denies itself; in doing so it makes the finite real, and at the same time the finite (world), by denying itself, lets the Infinite (God) reveal itself in the negation of the negation. Moreover, if the whole process is considered in its simultaneousness, it appears that the unconditioned being does not really exist (as we already anticipated), but is a pure theoretical hypothesis. In fact, Solger assumes that the Infinite (God) is originally absolute insofar as it is not qualified or diminished in any way. However, this originality refers to an ontological status never really held by the Infinite (God), as it is real only when it loses its absoluteness, and thus denies itself by creating the finite (world), which is its own nonbeing. Therefore the (finite) human being cannot ever know the absolute (God) because, properly speaking, the Infinite (God) is not real, except when it limits itself, loses its absoluteness, and lets the finite be. But the finite is nothing—it is nonbeing in relation to the being of God. As already noted, the theological category of "revelation" corresponds for Solger to the philosophical category of the double negation (negation of the negation).[20] An alleged knowledge of the Absolute, of the Infinite (God) in itself (*an sich*), does not make sense as it would imply our non-reality (NS, 166). If the Absolute were real, there would be no finite (world), and vice versa. Insofar as it is finite, human reason cannot grasp the Infinite (God) in itself (*an sich*), since the finite is real only because the Infinite (God) has renounced and denied its absoluteness, that is, its "*an sich*." The cognitive process can happen only through the double negation. Therefore, real knowledge is not an overcoming of the finitude but a radical, though ironic, acceptance of the finitude.

I use the term "ironic" to define the acceptance of the finitude that constitutes "the real knowledge" for Solger. An account of the notion of irony in Solger's aesthetics is now required to show that Solger's aesthetics, and particularly the notion of irony, is grounded in his metaphysics.

In the *Lectures on Aesthetics*, Solger claims that classic tragedy, considered the highest form of art, is the expression of the opposition between the human and the divine. Such opposition is aesthetically represented through the encounter of beauty and irony. Tragedy represents the suffering of the hero and his struggle with destiny.[21] The culmination of tragedy is the death of the hero. It is precisely at the point of death that the hero experiences a fleeting understanding of the universe and the equilibrium between the Infinite and the finite. This understanding is named by Solger "the divine idea" (*göttliche Idee*).[22] Through this experience, the hero becomes reconciled to his destiny and to the divine forces that have determined it. This understanding represents beauty. The fact that this understanding happens only at the point of death represents irony. Beauty and irony are the main features of the tragic outcome.[23]

Therefore, the process represented in the tragedy is an ironic dialectic.[24] Solger writes:

> In the tragic, the idea manifests itself as existence through annihilation [*Vernichtung*]: in fact, as it removes itself as existence, it exists as idea, and both are the same thing. The succumbing of the idea as existence is its manifestation as idea.[25]

The divine idea, namely, the understanding of the equilibrium between the Infinite and the finite, comes into existence at the point of death only through the annihilation of the hero's life. It is not possible to have that understanding without the death of the hero. The hero constituted the embodiment of the idea (the idea *as* existence), but the idea as such can manifest itself only through the break of the temporary union between the idea and its embodiment (that is, through the hero's death).

What is shown by the tragedy—the ironic dialectic—is the aesthetical representation of Solger's fundamental metaphysical dynamic, or (which is the same for Solger) the narrative of that dynamic from the point of view of a finite human being. A connection with the Infinite (God), here represented by the divine idea, requires the negation of the finite (human being), here represented by the hero. However, Solger does not simply say that the succumbing of the hero is the manifestation of the idea. He says that "the succumbing of the idea as existence is its manifestation as idea." This claim can appear obscure. In order to clarify its meaning, it is necessary to identify the sense of the ironic dialectic beyond every possible equivocation and misunderstanding.

First, Solger's dialectic implies a notion of irony that is clearly different from Romantic irony: "Romantic irony is based on an absolute individualism, psychological subjectivism [. . .] Solger defends his own concept of irony against this mere play with moods."[26] For example, Friedrich Schlegel, following Fichte, claims that the finite, which has been posited by the absolute I, needs to be denied in order to realize a dialectical overcoming of the finitude. Schlegel's irony is, as he says, "self creation, self-limitation and self-destruction."[27] Solger's view is different in many respects: the I is not absolute, the finite is not posited by the I and, most of all, there is no dialectical overcoming of the finite.

Second, Solger's ironic dialectic cannot be strictly associated with Neoplatonism. In Neoplatonic philosophy, and particularly in Christian Neoplatonism, the finite world is only appearance (the "true world" is the infinite, divine reality); thus it is considered necessary to unveil the appearance *as* appearance and to negate what is mortal and finite in man in order to let what is eternal and infinite in him surface. However, for Solger, the negation concerns not only what is mortal and finite in man but, just as much, what is highest and noblest, that is, that part of the finiteness which maintains an ontological connection with the Infinite (a *connection* that is not *dependence*).

The sense of the ironic dialectic represented in the tragedy is placed by Solger neither in the negation of the finitude (Romanticism) nor in the painful unveiling the appearance *as appearance* (Neoplatonism), but "in the self-position of the Idea conceived as the negation of the negation."[28] Reviewing *Lectures on Dramatic Art and Literature* written by August Wilhlem Schlegel,[29] Solger writes:

> We see the heroes ruined [*irre*] for what is noblest and most beautiful in their purposes and their feelings, and not only because of their outcome, but also as regards their sources and worth: what thus lifts us up is the destruction of the best as such, yet not merely by way of taking refuge in an infinite hope.[30]

It is not just the succumbing of the hero, but the succumbing *of the idea embodied* in the hero, that allows the manifestation of the idea. The idea succumbs *as existence*, that is, as embodied in the hero, and without its succumbing the idea could not manifest itself *as idea*. In other words, the emphasis is not on the negation of the finite human being (represented by the tragic hero), but on "the destruction of the best as such." Put differently, the idea is denied *as idea* when it is embodied (first negation). The idea is denied *as existence* when its embodiment is annihilated (second negation). Hence, the idea manifests itself through a double negation (negation of the negation).

This process is nothing else but the aesthetic representation of Solger's dual dialectic described in the first section. The Infinite (God) denies itself as absolute when it creates the finite (first negation). The finite (world) then denies itself (second negation). The Infinite (God) manifests itself through this double negation. As Kierkegaard writes, commenting on Solger's thought, "Solger actually turns the existence of God into irony: God continually translates himself into nothing, takes himself back again, translates himself again, etc."[31]

Solger's Sacrifice

As shown by the aesthetic representation of the tragedy, the reestablishment of a connection and an equilibrium between the Infinite (God) and the finite (human being) requires not just the annihilation of the finitude, but (paradoxically) the annihilation of that part of the finitude which maintains an ontological connection with the Infinite ("the best as such"). Solger explains:

> Thus Oedipus in Sophocles' tragedies does not succumb merely because of the fragility of man's normal existence, of the violence of external and casual circumstances, but because of what is noblest in man, considered in a twofold sense. He is simultaneously guilty and innocent, since he committed unconsciously a terrible atrocity. Here human nature enters into a contradiction with itself that is unresolvable in existence. The idea must incontestably desist, but only as idea; if it lowers itself to appearance, it must fall into an inexplicable contradiction with itself. Guilt and innocence are irreconcilable, and he in whom they are joined will be annihilated. No excuse erases awareness of this horrible act, but this revulsion cannot, in its turn, efface the recognition of our innocence. Man as a phenomenal entity is thus condemned to an irreconcilable contradiction, which will terminate only with the end of existence.[32]

We pointed out that the metaphysical process described by Solger is dialectic without *Aufhebung*, a dialectic whose outcome does not include any conciliation or synthesis. The absence of a synthesis appears even clearer if Solger's aesthetics is taken into consideration. The human being, insofar as it is finite, is destined to irreconcilable contradictions between the finite and the Infinite. However, the reestablishment of the equilibrium between finite and Infinite (*redemption* or *salvation*, in religious terms) is possible through the double negation. Both the first and the second negations can be described as *sacrifice*.³³

Tragedy aesthetically expresses the irreconcilable tension between the finite and the Infinite together with the paradoxical outcome of this tension, consisting in the contrasting (*kontradiktorische*) equilibrium of the double negation. Solger writes:

> We know that our succumbing is not the consequence of a chance, but of the fact that existence cannot support the eternal, to which we are destined, and we consequently know that *the sacrifice [Aufopferung] is the highest token of our superior destination*. Thus, what in the tragedy raises and corroborates is in the ruin itself, not the waiting for a better fate, an idea already edging towards the religious. We have to deal here with existence and with the manifestation of the divine in existence. Here the question concerns solely the present being [*Dasein*], considered not, however, in its fortuitousness, but in its essence [*wesen*]. Precisely in the moment of ruin lies the most consoling elevation, because the ruin is nothing but the semblance of the divinity manifesting himself in this annihilation.³⁴

There are several aspects of this quotation that it is worthwhile to stress. First, the succumbing of finite human beings is not the consequence of a chance, but the consequence of the disproportion between the finite and the Infinite ("the eternal"). Second, what is "sacrificed" or "given up" in the tragedy is not the mere existence of "the present being" (the death of the hero as a human being, "in its fortuitousness"), but "its essence," that is, "the highest part." The *divine idea* (the fleeting understanding of the equilibrium between the Infinite and the finite) can manifest itself only through this process of giving up "the best in itself," whose annihilation paradoxically constitutes the reestablishment of the equilibrium.

Tragedy is the aesthetical representation of the ironic dialectic. But the ironic dialectic is not exclusively the drive of aesthetics; it is also, and more fundamentally, the drive of Solger's metaphysics. Solger claims that God "sacrifices Himself up and destroys Himself in us because we are nothing" (NS, 603). This affirmation can be complemented by another longer quotation:

> We are for this reason insignificant manifestations because God has assumed existence in us ourselves and has thereby separated Himself from Himself. And is this not the highest love that He

> has placed Himself into nothingness, so that we might exist, and that He even sacrificed Himself and annihilates His nothingness, has killed His death, so that we do not remain a mere nothing but return to Him and may exist in Him? (NS, 511)[35]

Here Solger explicitly calls sacrifice the ironic dialectic considered not from the aesthetic, but from the metaphysical point of view: the Infinite (God) denies itself as absolute to create the finite (world). Furthermore, Solger is implicitly referring here to the sacrifice of Christ. The sacrifice of Christ is explicitly mentioned in another passage:

> Our entire relationship to Him [God] is continuously the same which is established for us in Christ as a type. We should not only remember it, not therefore merely derive reasons for our behaviour, but we should experience and realize this event of the divine self-sacrifice in us, what takes place in each and every one of us that has happened for the whole human race in Christ. It is not merely a reflex of our thoughts, what we have of it, but the most real reality. (NS, 603)

The relationship between the Infinite and the finite is connected with the figure of Christ "as a type." Again, Solger is not primarily interested in a religious discourse here. Christ represents the Infinite (God) in its self-negation and self-sacrifice. He also represents the equilibrium between the Infinite and the finite, an equilibrium that can be realized only through the self-negation of the finite (Christ dies as man). The Infinite (God) and the finite (world) reach an equilibrium (the revelation that makes possible, and theologically coincides with, the salvation) only through the double self-negation (self-sacrifice). Therefore "what has happened in Christ," that is, the self-sacrifice (the reestablishment of the equilibrium between the finite and the Infinite) should be realized "in each and every one of us." The meaning of the sacrifice of Christ is not simply the negation of the finitude, but the negation of "the best as such," that is, the negation of that part of the finitude which maintains an ontological connection with the Infinite.

Tragedy is precisely the aesthetical representation of this ironic dialectic. As the idea is constrained to become concrete, but in this negation manifests itself *as idea*, so Christ is destined to become man and in this *sacrifice* he manifests himself as truly God. As Solger writes in *Lectures on Aesthetics*, "the suffering is represented as suffering of a god."[36] Even when the finite succumbs, what is sacrificed is not what is limited (the finite) but precisely what goes *beyond* the limit (the Infinite). Theologically speaking, we could say that, for Solger, he who suffers on the Cross is not the man, but God. Also, the reestablishment of the equilibrium between the Infinite and the finite lies not in the overcoming of the opposition between the finite and the Infinite in a superior *Aufhebung*, but in a sacrifice whose fundamental meaning is the acceptance of the finitude. As Solger states, "The consolation [*Beruhigung*] is the tragedy itself."[37]

To recap: for Solger the aesthetic category of the tragic is the representation of the ironic dialectic that grounds reality. The drive of the ironic dialectic is the double negation, or double sacrifice. This does not mean a shift into the religious sphere. Rather, it means that sacrifice, conceived as the process of giving up, has for Solger an important philosophical meaning.

Negation and Privation

The most problematic aspect of Solger's philosophy lies in the relationship between logical, ontological, and theological categories. The problematic relationship between the logical and the ontological is a central point for an understanding of Solger's philosophy, and I will deal with it shortly. Regarding the relationship between the ontological and the theological, it is true that Solger often presents his thought through what seems to be a religious discourse more than a philosophical one. For example, he makes use of theological categories such as "God," "creation," "redemption"—and sacrifice. The relationship between ontological and theological categories is much less clear than in other philosophers of the idealistic tradition, such as Kant and Hegel. Kant removes religious notions and claims from the realm of theoretical reason and references their significance to regulative and symbolic meaning. Hegel explicitly establishes a coincidence between logical and ontological categories, and then introduces the theological categories as representations of these. Conversely, for Solger there is not such a sharp distinction between ontological and theological categories. Solger blends the ontological and theological vocabularies. This lack of distinction is not peculiar to Solger alone within the German Idealistic tradition. For instance, the alleged strangeness of Schelling's 1809 essay "Philosophical Inquiries into the Nature of Human Freedom" mostly stems from this apparent confusion between theological and ontological categories. However, it is through Schelling's analysis of theodicy that the epoch-making distinction between being as ground of existence and as existence is eventually posited. As it was for Schelling, it seems that a sharp distinction between ontological and theological categories is not a central interest for Solger. The use of such a distinction would turn out to be inevitably artificial for Solger. It is much more useful to focus on Solger's arguments.[38]

We have said that, according to Solger, the Infinite (or God) is originally absolute [*Das Absolute*], as it is not *qualified* or *diminished* in any way. The Absolute, denying itself reality by creating the finite, inevitably loses its absoluteness. In fact, if the Absolute loses its absoluteness, it loses the very attribute that makes it what it is. In other words, such self-limitation of God is also a radical self-negation.

Before continuing, it is necessary to explain why, when I claim that the Absolute "denies itself reality," I use the "reality predicate" instead of the more often used "existence predicate." In fact, Solger's move of double negation cannot be understood without a general understanding of how the notion of existence is conceived in Neoplatonic philosophy, which constitutes an important part of Solger's philosophical background. The Neoplatonists do not use the "existence predicate" in the way we typically think of it.[39] In modern or contemporary philosophy, we think of the existence predicate as only having two values ("existence" and "non-existence": *either* A exists, *or* A does not exist). Conversely, the Neoplatonists think of it as *scalar*: being comes in degrees. To mark this sense of existence apart from the more familiar one, let us call it "reality." Within this system, the most real is "the One," and everything else is lower down the reality tree. Accordingly, for Solger, the Infinite (God) is originally *absolutely* real, but loses this *absolute* reality when it creates the finite (world). This Neoplatonic ontological conception is implicitly assumed in Solger's philosophy, as it allows both the Infinite (God) and the finite (existent things) to have nonbeing. When Solger uses *existieren* (the German equivalent of "to exist"), the term does not coincide with our "exist."

It could be objected that Solger's view is contradictory. In fact, it has been said that Solger's metaphysical view lies in the affirmation that the Infinite (God) denies itself to create the finite (world). It has also been stressed that this view is different from the traditional Neoplatonic account insofar as the creation of the finite (world) implies (together with the ontological independence of the finite) a radical self-negation of the Infinite. And yet, we are then told that the Infinite (God) manifests itself in the finite (world). This is a contradiction in the ordinary sense—in fact, how is it possible that God manifests itself if it previously *denied* itself? The reader could feel disorientated, and could be tempted to dismiss Solger's reasoning as simply lacking in basic rationality, in the way that a person attending a play who sees a character unquestionably dead in the first act then reappearing on the stage without any explanation could understandably be tempted to leave the theatre. However, an explanation for this contradiction can be provided. It is connected with Solger's notion of irony and it will be considered in the next section.

Both the self-negation of the Infinite (God) and the negation of the finite (human being) can be described as *sacrifice*. The claim that double negation can be described as "double sacrifice" is not intended to suggest that Solger uses sacrifice as a specifically religious concept, or that the double negation hides (or is grounded in) a religious belief. On the contrary, the notion of sacrifice deserves philosophical attention as a regulative and symbolic notion, and Solger's account of the double negation represents an interesting way of thinking about sacrifice philosophically.

The term sacrifice (*Opfer* or *Aufopferung*) does not occur very often in Solger's work but, when it does, it does not seem to be chosen by Solger arbitrarily. We have seen that Solger defines sacrifice [*Aufopferung*] as "*the highest token of our superior destination.*"[40] It is interesting to note that the quotation does not feature the German term *Opfer*, but *Aufopferung*, which commonly indicates the process of giving something up. As already stated, the term *Opfer* is commonly used to refer to a specifically religious concept, originally meaning the act or practice of destroying or renouncing something in order to receive something more valuable in exchange. However, Solger is clearly not interested in this concept of sacrifice, which is expressed in the "waiting for a better fate," an idea that—as it is explicitly stated by Solger—"shifts" in the sphere of the religious. The notion of sacrifice that interests Solger is precisely that of *giving something up without receiving anything in exchange*. Sacrifice for Solger is either unconditioned or it is nothing at all.

In *Posthumous Writings* Solger claims that God "sacrifices Himself up and destroys Himself in us because we are nothing" (NS, 603). In the light of this claim, the consideration of sacrifice as "*the highest token of our superior destination*" appears more understandable. The self-negation of the finite (human being) is a repetition of the original self-negation of the Infinite (God), and a reestablishment of the equilibrium between the Infinite and the finite (*salvation*, to use the theological term) can happen only through this double negation. If this account is connected with the claim that "Our entire relationship to Him [God] is continuously the same which is established for us in Christ as a type,"[41] it is clear that this relationship is essentially based on self-sacrifice.

Solger and Hegel

Now, let us focus on Hegel's critique of Solger. An analysis of what Hegel writes in his review of *Solger's Posthumous Writings* has two related aims: to emphasize that Hegel understood that Solger's philosophical system implied the centrality of the notion of sacrifice as expression of the double negation, and to show what distinguishes the philosophical approaches of Hegel and Solger on *privation* and *negation*—which is a central issue for a discussion of the notion of sacrifice.

Hegel praises Solger for having understood the truth of the "disintegration" of all forms, both forms of existence and forms of thought, in the concept—"the most abstract speculative apex"; from this point of view, Hegel claims, there is "no difference" between his own philosophy and Solger's philosophy. However, Hegel continues, "the development of this concept and the necessity for it is yet another matter," and Solger "did not see his way clear about insight into this."[42] Hegel's text is rich and complex,[43] but his concern can be unpacked by identifying two main issues. First, Solger's discourse appears too "formal" to Hegel: Solger uses representations that "do not deal with content." The way in which Solger deals with representations such as "mysticism," "inner life," and "sacrifice," implies a separation of concept and reality that "cruelly anatomized the living insight" (ironically, the same criticisms raised by Solger himself against Schlegel).[44] In other words, he remains at the level of what Hegel calls "reflective understanding"—a subjective way of thinking (I will come back to this at the end of this section). Second, Solger employs, in Hegel's view, "undeveloped categories," because, as already noted, Solger blends ontological and logical categories: "just as disadvantageous as for philosophizing itself as for the discourse and understanding is that admixture of such concrete representations as God, sacrificing oneself, we human beings, knowing, evil, etc., with the abstractions of being, nothingness, appearance, and the like."[45] As a result, Solger's philosophy remains stuck, according to Hegel, in a kind of picture-thinking.

Both these aspects of Hegel's criticism of Solger are important but, for our purposes, the latter—that is, the relationship between logical and ontological categories—is particularly relevant, and therefore it deserves to be addressed separately. For now, however, let us focus on Hegel's comments about Solger's use of the double negation as sacrifice.

Hegel quotes Solger extensively and, interestingly, he focuses on the passage where Solger states that God "sacrificed Himself and annihilates his nothingness." Hegel then writes:

> I notice, first of all in general, that the logical concept, which constitutes the foundation for all speculative knowing, is found in this idea, the 'sole genuine affirmation, namely' (it is the eternal divine activity which is represented) comprised as the negation of negation.[46]

Hegel here recognizes and emphasizes the core of Solger's thought, which is constituted by the negation of the negation. Hegel appreciates Solger's way of understanding the dialectic process, which leads one to consider negation as the fundamental framework. Furthermore, Hegel grasps the link between the ontological and logical category of double negation ("this abstract form") and the figure of Christ ("its most concrete shape taken in its highest reality"). Hegel sees that Solger's interest in Christ is not primarily religious, but philosophical. In fact, Christ expresses "the unity of the divine and human nature" insofar as this unity is "brought to consciousness for the human being."[47] Nevertheless, Hegel is not happy with Solger's blending of ontological and theological categories, with "the transition from the abstraction" of the ontological category of the double negation "to this abundance of content" assumed in the sacrifice of Christ. He writes:

> In that transition which, philosophically carried out, will be a long pathway, many difficulties and contradictions result to be resolved. Already in the lecture cited such things become manifest. One time, we are postulated in it as nothingness (which is the evil), then again, the harsh, abstract expression about God is used that He annihilates Himself, that He is thus the one who postulates Himself as nothingness, and this furthermore, so that we may exist, and thereupon the nullity in us ourselves is called the divine, insofar as we, namely, perceive it as nullity.[48]

Hegel is disappointed by the contradiction that has been stressed in the previous section—how is it possible that God manifests itself if it previously denied itself?

From a logical point of view the contradictions that emerge in Solger's thought derive from a particular conception of the terms finite (human being) and Infinite (God) as opposite and mutually exclusive: when denying one the other must be affirmed and there is no third possibility. Strictly speaking, this is a *mutual negation*. Nevertheless Solger insists that, despite this conceptual contradiction, both the Infinite (God) and the finite (human being) are real (but again: one is real as the nothingness of the other).

Hegel criticizes in detail this contradiction which is at the core of Solger's thought: the finite, which is "nothingness of God," in order to reestablish a connection with the Infinite (God)—which has become nothingness for letting the finite be real—must in turn annihilate itself.

It is necessary to note that this contradiction is, partially at least, conscious, as it forms the foundation of Solger's ironic dialectic—a dialectic where the synthesis is completely absent and the opposition between the finite and the Infinite remains unresolved. According to Solger, the ironic dialectic is grounded in a contradiction because this contradiction, as illogical as it may be, is the drive of reality itself. Furthermore, this contradiction takes "its most concrete shape [. . .] in its highest reality" (to use Hegel's words) in the figure of Christ: the Infinite (God) denies its absoluteness by becoming finite (human being), and with its sacrifice manifests itself as the true God. Moreover, the contradiction prevents any reconciliation between the finite and the Infinite. In fact, the reestablishment of the equilibrium between the finite and the Infinite is not a reconciliation, for, in the double negation, finite and Infinite remain real opposites of one another. Solger thinks of the opposition *without synthesis* as the fundamental framework of reality. According to Hegel, Solger is wrong, as he does not recognize the necessity of an *Aufhebung*: he has not reached the proper essence of the dialectic.[49]

In order to clearly identify what distinguishes the philosophical approaches of Hegel and Solger, and hence to grasp the deep reasons for Hegel's criticism and final refutation, two intersecting questions in Solger's thought need to be taken into consideration.

The first problem concerns the notions of *privation* and *negation*. It has to be noted that there are no unanimously accepted definitions for such notions.[50] To introduce the analysis of these notions, which will serve the purpose of this chapter, two preliminary considerations are necessary.

First, the use of the notions "privation" and "negation" by Solger, as well as by the Neoplatonists and by Hegel, does not belong to the *propositional logic* originally introduced by the Stoics and currently considered, in its post-Fregean version, as the logic *par excellence* (that is, a logic in which the objects are propositions). Rather, the use of "privation" and "negation" by these authors belongs to the *term logic*, also called *traditional* logic, originally introduced by Aristotle, (that is, a logic in which the objects are terms), and which remained the dominant form of logic until the advent of modern predicate/propositional logic in the late nineteenth century.

Second, it is important to recall that for Aristotle, who is followed in this respect by both Solger and Hegel, there is no separation between ontology and logic. A consequence of this lack of separation is that in the

Aristotelian term logic the division between negation and privation is not neat, as the same division is supposed to work also in the ontological realm, where the separation is obviously harder to draw.[51]

Consider negation. Traditional term logics have two forms of negation: one can negate the term predicated of a subject in a sentence, or "one can deny, rather than affirm, the predicate of the subject."[52]

Now, consider privation. Aristotle examines the notion of privation in the Fifth Book of *Metaphysics*.[53] He identifies four subtypes of privation, but a common definition can be used for all of them: privation is the absence of an attribute in something capable of possessing it. The second subtype is particularly interesting for our purposes: "We speak of 'privation,'" Aristotle writes, "if, though either the thing itself or its genus would naturally have an attribute, it has it not." The example provided by Aristotle is that of "a blind man" who is deprived of sight "in contrast with his own normal nature." In this respect, "privation is negation from some defined genus."[54]

The Neoplatonic conception of the One is perfectly compatible with this Aristotelian idea of "privative negation" that implies the privation of what is being negated. The One cannot be deprived of its absoluteness during the process of emanation, because such a privation would be a negation of its most fundamental attribute—the very attribute that makes it what it is. In other words, to deprive the One of its absoluteness is equivalent to negating the One as such, because a non-absolute One is inconceivable for Neoplatonic philosophy. For the Neoplatonic One, privation is negation: the One is not deprived, and hence it is not negated.[55]

The form of negation that is characteristic of Hegel's philosophy is determinate negation (*bestimmte Negation*), which is the core of the method adopted in Hegel's *Logic*. This is the fundamental dynamic of Hegel's *Logic*: thought posits a category, then realizes that this category collapses because it generates a contradictory negation (the so-called *determinate negation*), and thus seeks a more complex category which is able to make sense of that contradiction. Traditionally, Hegel's determinate negation is associated with Spinoza's famous claim that "*omni determinatio est negatio*." However, the determinate negation can be more easily and perhaps better connected to Hegel's use of Aristotle's term logic.[56] Thus, for Hegel, there is no radical negation, only determinate negation. With this connotation of negation as determinate negation, privation becomes secondary to determinate negation.[57] Consider the case of the *Phenomenology of Spirit*: during the dialectic process the consciousness suffers privation (for instance, the feudal nobility is deprived of its independence). However, this privation is a determinate negation and is sublated in a superior and more complex form of consciousness (the absolute monarchy). "The negation coming from consciousness," Hegel writes, "supersedes [*aufbewahrt*] in such a way as to preserve and maintain what is superseded, and consequently survives its own supersession (PG 188/114)." Unlike the Neoplatonists, Hegel does not consider the absoluteness as an a priori, but rather as the final outcome of the dialectic process. It follows that privation (as secondary to determinate negation) and (radical) negation do not coincide: on the contrary, privation is necessary for the development of the absoluteness of the spirit. For Hegel's spirit, privation is not negation: it is deprived, but not negated.

Solger, in his use of term logic, is closer to the Neoplatonists than to Hegel. In fact, Solger shares with the Neoplatonists the belief that for the "supreme being" (Neoplatonists' One and Solger's God) privation is negation, as to deprive God of its absoluteness is equivalent to negating God as such. However, *unlike* what happens in the Neoplatonic view, for Solger God *is* deprived of its absoluteness during the creation of the finite (world), and *thus* is negated (it becomes nothingness). For Solger's God, privation is negation: it is deprived, and hence it is negated.

The second problem, which is connected with the previous one, concerns the relationship between concept and reality, between *logical* and *ontological* categories. The Infinite (God) is deprived of its own absoluteness during the creation of the finite (world), and thus is negated—"it postulates itself as nothingness," to quote the expression used by Hegel to describe the process of double negation. But Solger then claims that the Infinite (God) manifests itself in the finite (world). As mentioned in the previous section, if we take the categories "infinite" and "finite" in their *logical* meanings—as concepts—this is clearly a contradiction. However, this logic is not applied by Solger to the Infinite (God), as its ontological reality *ironically* transcends the logical categories. Irony, for Solger, is precisely the tension between concept and reality emerging from the double negation of finite and Infinite—in other words, the fact that the coincidence between logical and ontological categories does not apply to God. Kierkegaard is shown to have perfectly understood this problem, when he affirms that "Solger actually turns the existence of God into irony."[59]

This picture is not acceptable for Hegel. First, Solger's reasoning derives from his conception of finite and Infinite as opposite and mutually exclusive: in denying one, the other must be affirmed and there is no third possibility. According to Hegel, the distinction between finite and Infinite is an *abstract* distinction and thus not acceptable. This is even less acceptable if the distinction is conceived as *mutually exclusive*. Second, Solger's argument produces a separation between concept and reality. According to Hegel the reflective understanding, considered as falsifier, produces this separation. This is the definition given by Hegel of "reflective understanding":

> In general it stands for the understanding as abstracting, and hence as separating and remaining fixed in its separations. Directed against reason, it behaves as ordinary common sense and imposes its view that truth rests on sensuous reality, that thoughts are only thoughts, meaning that it is sense perception which first gives them filling and reality and that reason left to its own resources engenders only figments of the brain. In this self-renunciation on the part of reason, the Notion of truth is lost; it is limited to knowing only subjective truth, only phenomena, appearances, only something to which the nature of the object itself does not correspond: knowing has lapsed into opinion.[60]

In Hegelian terms, Solger has fallen prey to the dreams created by the reflective understanding: he has separated concept and reality, a separation which is a false abstraction, whereas reason is, according to Hegel, characterized by the identity between concept and reality. Despite what Kierkegaard writes in the *Concept of Irony* (where he presents Solger as "a sacrifice Hegel's system demanded"[61]), if Solger's thought is an example of reflective understanding, then his thought *is* integrated and overcome in Hegel's system, and specifically in Hegel's *Logic*, where the understanding's grasping the finite and Infinite is dialectically undermined.

Broadly speaking, the distinction between concept and reality makes Solger's thought irreconcilable with Hegel's thought. In fact, this distinction, as it appears clearly from the outcome of Solger's thought, means not only to accept the contradiction as the framework of reality, but also to renounce every possible elevation or sublation (*Aufhebung*).

Sacrifice as Salvation

It is now time to take position about the relative importance and merits of Solger's philosophy. Although not free from discursive gaps (called "undeveloped categories" by Hegel and "absence of intermediate determinations" by Kierkegaard), Solger's thought leads to an interesting issue. As shown above, the opposition of finite and Infinite is not overcome in a superior *Aufhebung* and the insolubility of such opposition is not an impotence of thought in Solger, but rather the keystone of philosophy. Conversely, for Hegel, this opposition is the outcome of reflective understanding that has not been dialectically overcome.

A comparison between Solger and Hegel is particularly interesting as it clearly shows an alternative that the so-called Continental philosophy has faced, and often followed, in the last century. It has been shown that Solger's ironic dialectic is grounded in a contradiction because this contradiction, as illogical as it may be, is the drive of reality itself. In this valorization of irrationality, the central problem of philosophy becomes the way in which one conceives dialectic. For Hegel, dialectic is primarily the transfer from alterity to identity. Conversely, for Solger, dialectic is the transfer from reason "to its other," from the *same* to the *other*. This way of conceiving dialectic is usually attributed to Kojève, who then influenced Sartre, Merleau-Ponty, and many others.[62] It was Solger, I suggest, who opened this path long before Kojève did. For a long time it has seemed difficult to find the peculiarity of Solger's thought and to distinguish it from Hegel's because several interpreters of Hegel have followed Kojève, who misunderstood Hegel by attributing to him a conception of dialectic that is much more characteristic of Solger than of Hegel.

To conclude, consider the relevance of the notion of sacrifice in Solger's thought. The outcome of his philosophy leads to a notion of sacrifice that is considered as redemption from the nothingness of the finite existence, a redemption which is not a synthetic overcoming of the negation but which reveals its redeeming significance in the negation. Sacrifice thus becomes the *profound structure* of the relationship between the finite and the Infinite. Salvation takes place in sacrifice: a salvation that is coessential with the experience of nothingness.

Solger sees in the continuing sacrificial exchange "the true mysticism," a superior mysticism that grasps the whole reality without involving a "conceptual" thought. Nevertheless he affirms the identity of content between philosophy and revelation and argues that neither can subsist without the other (NS, 120–121), and thus even the revelation cannot be simply left to religious experience, but must be thought of philosophically. Furthermore, salvation cannot be thought of philosophically, except as sacrifice. In other words, the reestablishment of a connection between the Infinite (God) and the finite (human being), which is idealistically considered as the main outcome of philosophy, is the philosophical translation of the theological category of "salvation." Salvation is realized, according to Solger, through the double negation (sacrifice).

It would be a mistake to underline in this argument only the religious aspect. The more relevant aspect is instead the philosophical one. As mentioned above, Solger opened a way for dialectic to be conceived as the transfer from the *same* to the *other*. For Solger, philosophy should not renounce reason, but accompany reason toward its failure, its "wreck." This conclusion is not acceptable in Hegelian terms simply because, according to Hegel, if the conception of dialectic as transfer from alterity to identity is applied, Solger does not get as far as reason: he remains at the level of reflective understanding.

The philosophies of Solger and Hegel have completely different and opposite purposes,[63] and corresponding different conceptions of the negative. In particular, Hegel's theoretical aim basically consists in recomposing the unity of finite and Infinite. The negative is the drive of the dialectic process and it is necessary in order to reach a superior sublation (*Aufhebung*).[64] On the contrary, Solger's thought is structured on a rupture (or an unresolved tension) between finite and Infinite. For Solger this rupture is itself salvation, because it expresses the paradoxical, ironic and tragic, "superior destination" of man. To communicate the meaning of this salvation, Solger employs a symbolic language that inevitably remains at the level of picture-thinking. Conversely, Hegel thinks that this rupture is unsustainable; as we are going to see in the next chapter, sacrifice plays a role in Hegel's reconciliation between the finite and the infinite.

3

Hegel

Sacrifice and Recognition

Sacrifice in the *Phenomenology of Spirit*

The word "sacrifice" (including its derivatives) occurs 57 times in the *Phenomenology of Spirit*. Such a frequency leaves very little room for the possible objection that the choice of the word is arbitrary—especially for someone like Hegel, who was very careful about terminological choices. It is interesting to note that the German term *Opfer* (sacrifice) occurs only 5 times, whereas there are 23 occurrences of *Aufopferung*. Moreover, the other 29 occurrences are derivatives of *Aufopferung*. As already remarked, first in the Introduction and then in relation to Solger, the term *Opfer* is commonly used to refer to a specifically religious concept, originally meaning the act or practice of destroying or renouncing something in order to receive something more valuable in exchange, whereas the term *Aufopferung* commonly indicates the process of giving something up, with an emphasis on reflexivity—sacrifice as *self-sacrifice*. The reflective dimension of sacrifice will appear clear in the episodes of the *Phenomenology* that I am going to analyze in the present and following sections. At a general level, it can be noted that, as Hegel himself states, the whole *Phenomenology* "can be regarded as the path of the natural consciousness which presses forward to true knowledge; or as the way of the Soul which journeys through the series of its own configurations as though they were the stations appointed for it by its own nature, so that it may purify itself for the life of the Spirit, and achieve finally, through a completed experience of itself, the awareness of what it really is in itself" (PG, 77/49).[1] The "series of configurations" through which consciousness passes are related, such that each new configuration will grow out and resolve the problems affecting the preceding one. In other words, as already stated in the comparison with Solger's notion of privation, the drive of Hegel's philosophy is the determinate negation (*bestimmte Negation*).

On these grounds, the notion of sacrifice in the *Phenomenology* can be considered in an *extensive* and in a *specific* sense. In the extensive sense, sacrifice can be regarded as a metaphoric notion used to describe the process of determinate negation at the phenomenological level. Each pattern of consciousness faces the fact that something of itself has to be negated—or *sacrificed*—in order to allow a new configuration to grow out and to make sense of the problem of the previous pattern.[2] However, the notion of sacrifice can also be considered more specifically. Among the various forms that the determinate negation can take (including difference, opposition, contradiction, etc.), sacrifice can be considered as a specific form of determinate negation phenomenologically conceived, in which recognition plays a central role. Three episodes of the *Phenomenology* in particular show the specificity of the notion of sacrifice: the unhappy consciousness, the virtue and the way of the world, and the noble consciousness.

The first occurrence of the term *Aufopferung* is found in the two concluding paragraphs (§229 and §230) of the section entitled "Freedom of self-consciousness: stoicism, skepticism, and the unhappy consciousness." This stage immediately follows the master-slave stage. The independence sought by the master through control over the slave has been internalized by the Stoic, and independence and self-mastery are at issue. In an attempt to achieve independence from the external world, the Stoic tries to withdraw from engagement with it. Then, Hegel considers the unhappy consciousness. One of its main features is the renunciation or surrender (*Aufgeben*) "first of its right to decide for itself, then of its property and enjoyment" (PG, 229/137). The outcome of this process for the consciousness is, Hegel claims, "the certainty of having truly divested[3] itself of its "I," of its self-sufficiency. Hegel writes:

> Only through this *actual* sacrifice [*Aufopferung*] could it demonstrate this self-renunciation. For only therein does the *deception* vanish which lies in the inner acknowledgement of gratitude through heart, sentiment and tongue [. . .].
>
> But in the sacrifice actually carried out, consciousness, having nullified the *action* as its own doing, has also *in principle* obtained relief from its *misery*. [. . .] But that sacrifice made by the unessential extreme was at the same time not a one-sided action, but contained within itself the action of the other. (PG, 229–230/137–138)

The unhappy consciousness tries to unite itself with the unchangeable ("that which is both authoritative and unobtainable for the 'unhappy consciousness'"[4]) and disavow its own activity. The deception implied in the unhappy consciousness is that in the very act of thanking the unchangeable for the gifts that the latter has bestowed on it (namely, the agent's abilities and skills), and thereby showing itself to be the passive recipient of those gift, the unhappy consciousness is nonetheless *active*. The alleged passivity turns out to be a strategy whose aim is to achieve independence. This strategy is then overcome, and subsequently the pursuit of independence takes a new form. As Pinkard explains, it takes the form "not of trying to bend other subjects to one's own projects, nor in completely disavowing one's own subjective point of view in favor of a forever distant, 'God's-eye' objective point of view, but in fusing the two points of view into a unity."[5] In other words, absolute independence turns out to be what needs to be sacrificed—not through the alleged passivity, but through the recognition of the other. Sacrifice is the conscious overcoming of that deceptive passivity, and the negation of absolute independence through recognition.

Another important step for the consciousness in its struggle for universal recognition is the opposition between "Virtue and the way of the world," which is the title of a section of the fifth chapter. Consciousness, in the virtue phase, wants to subordinate individuality to the "discipline of the universal; the intrinsically true and good" (PG, 381/228). Conversely, the "way of the world" can be thought of as all those doctrines or standpoints that want to subordinate "true and good" to individuality. In Hegel's words, "Virtue's purpose is [. . .] to reserve again the perverted 'way of the world' and to make manifest its true essence. [. . .] This faith virtue proceeds to rise to sight, without, however, enjoying the fruits of its labor and sacrifice [*Aufopferung*]" (PG, 383/230). However, virtue cannot win. Virtue and the way of the world have something in common: they both regard natural inclinations as the fundamental motive for human behavior. If this were right, then there would be no merit for the virtuous agent in its struggle with the way of the world, as all its sacrifices would be just expressions of its natural inclinations.[6] Virtue's aim is "bringing the good into actual existence by the sacrifice of individuality [*Aufopferung der Individualität*]"; however, this rejection of individuality is based on the inclusion of culturally and historically determined standpoints into a specific (normative) account of nature—an account according to which humans should naturally follow the good. It is clear that, given the premises, the defense of individuality by the egoistic supporters of the way of the world is much more convincing. Thus, virtue is destined to fail.[7]

Again, the notion of sacrifice is used to describe a conscious attempt to resolve the problem affecting a particular phenomenological stage. And again, sacrifice is meant to be sacrifice of something peculiar to the subject (in this case, individuality) without getting anything in return ("without enjoying the fruits of its labor and sacrifice"). However, the aim that virtue wants to realize through its sacrifice—the subordination of individuality to the "discipline of the universal"—turns out to be an illusion: its purpose is too abstract, and cannot be realized in the concrete reality.

A third, pivotal moment for the understanding of the notion of sacrifice in the *Phenomenology* is found in the section entitled "Culture and its realm of actuality." Hegel is showing how consciousness is moving from impersonal reason to "a form of reflective social practice," that is, "spirit."[8] One of the stages of this process is represented by the feudal aristocracy. At stake once again is the subordination of individuality to the universal; however, unlike what happens with virtue in its opposition to the way of the world, here the purpose is intended to be not abstract, but concrete—the purpose being the achievement of a reflective *social* practice. "This consciousness," Hegel writes, "is the *virtue* which sacrifices [*aufopfert*] the single individual to the universal, thereby bringing this into existence—the *person*, one who voluntarily renounces possessions and enjoyment and acts and is effective in the interests of the ruling power" (PG, 503/306). The aristocracy considers the good of others as its only concern; from its own point of view (or, as Pinkard puts it, "according to the story that the aristocrat tells himself"[9]), aristocracy sacrifices itself for the sake of the good by putting honor and service above itself. However, Hegel does not regard this as a real sacrifice. In fact, self-consciousness "has only given that power [the state power] its mere being, has only sacrificed its *outer existence* to it, not its *intrinsic being* [*Ansichsein*]" (PG, 505/307). In fact, there is no agreement within aristocracy as to what public interest really is, and these disagreements inevitably jeopardize its unselfish self-image.

> The sacrifice of existence [*Die Aufopferung des Daseins*] which happens in the service of the state is indeed complete when it has gone as far as death; but the hazard of death which the individual survives leaves him with a definite existence and hence with a *particular self interest*, and this makes his counsel about what is best for the general good ambiguous and open to suspicion. (PG, 506/307)

This contradiction leads to the rise of absolute monarchy. Aristocrats accept to submit to the king, provided that he recognizes their privileges and status.[10] This dynamic is historically represented by the move of the court to the Palace of Versailles willed by Louis XIV. The old sacrifice of one's life (allegedly) done for the sake of the good now becomes the sacrifice of one's independence for the sake of the nation: the state power achieved through "the sacrifice of action and thought by the noble consciousness," is "an *independence that is self-alienated*" (PG, 512/311). However, honor is the identity-conferring commitment of aristocracy; once the nobles have been deprived of the possibility to prove their honor on the battlefield, they need some other means to recognize each other as nobles. Battles and duels are now replaced with "the brandishing of a sophisticated wit and the wielding of the sneering *bon mot*,"[11] that is, with language; and this linguistic activity becomes the essential means to create a new mutual recognition within aristocracy.

In this phenomenological stage, the notion of sacrifice is introduced to refer first to another attempt to subordinate individuality to the universal, and then as a conscious strategy aiming at resolving an internal contradiction (the unity of the nation). Further, sacrifice is perceived by the agent (self-consciousness in this specific phenomenological stage) as a self-sacrifice that gets nothing in return (it is meant to be performed for the sake of the good). The self-image of the sacrifice as unselfish has proven to be an illusion, but the sublation (*Aufhebung*) of aristocracy in the unity of the nation has been achieved, thus paving the way for the use of language as a social and political instrument of mutual recognition. Language is "self-consciousness, *qua independent separate individuality*" and "exists *for others*" (PG, 508/308): it is essential for the generation of that form of *reflective social practice*, which is the spirit.

So far we have addressed three phenomenological stages in order to show that sacrifice is a specific form of determinate negation. Three common features have been identified. First, sacrifice is a conscious negation. Second, it is a self-sacrifice (sacrifice of something peculiar to the agent) that is regarded by the agent (the consciousness in that particular phenomenological stage) as a self-limitation that does not get anything in return. Third, sacrifice, although it is supposed to be *decisive*, can include a deceptive illusion—either the sacrifice is not *effective* and does not reach its goal (as happens for virtuous consciousness), or the agent turns out to be less disinterested and more *selfish* than it seems (as happens for noble consciousness). This analysis has shown that Hegel does not regard the sacrifice depicted in these phenomenological stages as a *real* sacrifice. This seems to suggest that for Hegel a real sacrifice should be *effective* and *unselfish*. Given the premises, this characterization seems reasonable: after all, the agent should not expect any return (otherwise, its act would not be a sacrifice at all, but rather an *investment*). Furthermore, if sacrifice is indeed a form of determinate negation, it should be effective, that is, it should solve the problem affecting a specific phenomenological stage.

Hence, the question arises: Does sacrifice in the *Phenomenology* necessarily include an illusion (in the sense that sacrifice conceived as "giving up oneself without getting anything in return" is a self-illusion),[12] or is a real (effective and unselfish) sacrifice possible? The answer to this question lies in the sections of the *Phenomenology* devoted to the Enlightenment and to the development of religion.

"Pure insight," "Faith," and "Religion"

In the modern world of the seventeenth and eighteenth centuries, the old aristocratic ethos is perceived as groundless, and needs to be replaced by something else. The two movements arising in the modern world are described by Hegel as "pure insight" (the Enlightenment) and "faith" (an alienated form of religion).[13] The main feature of the Enlightenment is the assumption that knowledge must rely on self-sufficient and detached reason alone. On these grounds, the general attitude of the *philosophes* towards sacrifice is negative:

> Enlightenment finds it foolish when the believer gives himself the superior consciousness of not being in bondage to natural enjoyment and pleasure by *actually* denying himself natural enjoyment and pleasure [. . .]. Pure insight finds both to be of no purpose as well as wrong: the purpose of showing oneself to be free of pleasure and possession is not served by denying oneself pleasure and giving away a possession; in the opposite case, therefore, it will declare the man a fool who, in order to eat, has recourse to actually eating. (PG, 556/339)

Pure insight finds sacrifice "foolish" because, as Hegel clarifies some lines below, it finds it wrong to give something away [*wegzugeben*] "without receiving anything in return" (PG, 556/339). In other words, Enlightenment rejects sacrifice precisely insofar as it is conceived as unselfish, that is, when it does not get any profit in exchange. The genuineness of sacrifice is not at stake here. Pure insight does not seem to be concerned with a possible self-deception of faith regarding the absence of personal interest; in fact, the *philosophes* reject sacrifice precisely insofar as they consider it useless. Although the criticism advanced by pure insight is clearly considered weak by Hegel, there is an internal contradiction in the religious consciousness: in fact, faith itself—despite its claims—"recognizes this reality of possessing, holding on to, and enjoying property" (PG, 669/247). Because of this contradiction, "this service of sacrifice [*Aufopferung*] of natural impulses and enjoyments has no truth. Retention occurs *along with* sacrifice [*Aufopferung*]; the latter is merely a *sign* [*Zeichen*], which performs real sacrifice [*wirkliche Aufopferung*] in only a small degree, and is therefore in point of fact only a *representational thought* [*vorstellt*] of the sacrifice" (PG, 569/347).[14]

In this respect, the Enlightenment has a positive content: the extirpation of error—the error being the fact the sacrifice performed by religious consciousness is only represented [*vorstellt*]. The *philosophes* are right in criticizing that, but are wrong in affirming that sacrifice is senseless (it is not senseless because, as it will be shown, sacrifice plays a role in the development of consciousness). Conversely, religious consciousness is right in affirming that sacrifice is necessary, but wrong in performing sacrifice "in only a small degree."

From here, two important points can be drawn. First, the representation of sacrifice is not the real or actual sacrifice. Second, faith (as opposition of pure insight) is not immune from that deceptive illusion which has been previously identified as a characteristic feature of other phenomenological stages dealing with sacrifice, such as virtuous consciousness and noble consciousness. In other words, although sacrifice is perceived by the agent as a selfless sacrifice that does not receive anything in return, this turns out to be a deceptive illusion. I will return to the first point later in the chapter. With regard to the second point, it puts forward again the question, "Is a real (effective and unselfish) sacrifice possible?" The answer to this question can be found in the seventh chapter of the *Phenomenology*, which is devoted to an analysis of religion. In this respect, the account of the cult [*Kultus*] and Hegel's treatment of the figure of Christ are particularly relevant.

The cult is the self-consciousness of the practical life,[15] and aims at recomposing the unity of nature and spirit. In cult, the agent recognizes the unessential aspects of human life vis-à-vis nature. At the same time, however, the agent also recognizes the unessential aspect of nature to itself. In the cult, the agent is really willing to sacrifice something without receiving anything in return. As Hegel writes, "the act of the Cult itself begins with the pure *sacrificial dedication* [*Hingabe*][16] of a possession which the owner, apparently without any profit whatever to himself, pours away or lets rise up in smoke" (PG, 718/434). It does not matter if what is sacrificed is an animal, or just fruits: in fact, the object of sacrifice is just a sign, or a symbol [*das Zeichen*] of a god. At this point, Hegel provides a very meaningful explanation of the significance of the act of sacrifice, which is worthwhile to quote in full, as it is fundamental for our purposes:

> The sacrifice [*Aufopferung*] of the divine substance, in so far as it is an act, belongs to the self-conscious aspect: that this actual deed be possible, the divine Being must already have *in itself* [*an sich*][17] sacrificed itself. [. . .] The unity which has resulted from overcoming the individuality [*Einzelnheit*][18] and separation of the two sides is not merely a negative fate, but has a positive significance. It is only to the abstract being of the underworld that the sacrificial offering is wholly surrendered, and thus the reflection of possessions and being-for-self into the universal is distinguished from the self as such. At the same time, however, this is only a small part, and the other act of sacrifice is merely the destruction of what cannot be used, and is really the preparation of the offering for a meal, the feast that cheats the act out of its negative significance. At that first sacrifice [*Opfer*], the person making the offering [*der Opfernde*] reserves the greatest share for his own enjoyment, and from the latter sacrifice, what is useful, for the same purpose. This enjoyment is the negative power which puts an end both to the divine Being and to the individuality, and it is at the same time the positive actuality in which the objective existence is transformed into self-conscious existence, and the self has consciousness of its unity with the divine Being. (PG, 718/435)

Commenting on this paragraph, Pinkard points out two important issues, which I will explain in the light of my previous reflections on sacrifice. First, it appears, prima facie, that sacrifice in the cult is simply a loss. However, it also has a positive meaning; in fact, "the act of sacrifice is a kind of reflection on what is of absolute value in the world: not the purely contingent aspects of individual life nor the contingent effects of nature but the essential and abiding aspects of divinity in its quasi-human form."[19] The sacrifice that does not receive anything in return (this time for real) is recognition of "the underlying universal essence of nature and spirit."[20]

Second, by participating in the cult, the persons performing the sacrifice necessarily agree on that for which they are going to give up something (without receiving anything in return); in other words, they agree on their recognition of something higher than mere contingent aspects of individual life—such as values and beliefs. Pinkard writes: "By making themselves into participants without whose participation the god could not appear, the members of the cult create the 'social space' in which it will be possible for them to acknowledge their own determining power in the way in which things are conceived. They no longer take themselves to know the divine immediately but only in terms of the shared activity between the divine letting itself come to presence before them and their activity of calling forth the divinity."[21] Therefore, it can be argued that the sacrifice that happens in the cult, through which the self develops "consciousness of its unity with the divine Being," gives an important contribution for the self-constitution of human beings as free, rational and able to generate identity-conferring values and commitments.

This contribution clearly is a gain—but this gain appears in all its clarity only *retrospectively*. I will come back to this distinction in the next section. Now, it is important to note that the sacrifice that is performed in the cult is still not the most genuine sacrifice. In fact, as Hegel claims, "Spirit has not yet sacrificed itself as *self-conscious* Spirit to self-consciousness, and the mystery of bread and wine is not yet the mystery of flesh and blood" (PG, 724/438). In fact, in the cult, the *performer* is a self-conscious agent, but the *object* of sacrifice is not. Only with the figure of Christ, self-consciousness, as Hegel writes, "surrenders itself consciously" (PG, 749/453). Through the incarnation, God sacrifices something peculiar to himself, that is, his own divinity and absoluteness. In other words, Hegel takes seriously the idea of a God "robbing himself of a perfection," which had sounded absurd to Kant (RGV, 6:65/107).

In the person of Christ, who sacrifices *himself* by becoming human and accepting death, both the *subject* and the *object* of sacrifice are fully conscious of the act. Hegel's idea that Christianity is the highest form of religion largely relies on this central image of God becoming man, that is, on the overcoming of the abstract opposition between the divine and the human.[22] The idea of God emerging from the last chapters of the *Phenomenology* is far from that of the Aristotelian God (immutable, pure being of perfected, fully actualized intellect). Conversely, God "must learn that to *be* a God is to be marked by the same fallenness into objectivity and material affectability: God *must* become man"[23] and sacrifice himself by renouncing his own absoluteness. To the extent that in the sacrifice of Christ both the subject and the object of sacrifice are fully conscious of the performed act, it becomes the exemplar of the real (effective and unselfish) sacrifice.

The analysis carried on in this section has confirmed that the notion of sacrifice, as it is presented in the *Phenomenology*, is a specific form of determinate negation that has three fundamental features. This is important because these three features effectively represent the three characteristics of kenotic sacrifice.

First, sacrifice has to be performed consciously. Second, it needs to be considered as a selfless sacrifice that does not expect anything in return. Third, its genuineness (its being a real and actual sacrifice) depends on its capacity to be effective (to reach its proposed goal) and unselfish (to not *really* expect anything in return, beyond any possible self-deception). In this respect, the sacrifice that is performed in the cult is close to being a real and genuine sacrifice. In the cult, the agent deprives itself of something, but the object of sacrifice is external (animal, fruits, bread and wine). We can speak of a genuine sacrifice only when the object of sacrifice is something *essential* to the subject, that is, something that constitutes the subject, as happens with Christ's renunciation of his divine absoluteness. These considerations are important achievements for the formulation of a theory of sacrifice, and in fact even a thinker definitely not sympathetic to Hegel such as Kierkegaard will come to the same conclusions, as we will see in the next chapter.

Sacrifice as *Darstellung* and Recognition

Two (related) questions are still open. The first concerns the relationship between sacrifice in the different phenomenological stages and the sacrifice of Christ as an exemplar. The second, already introduced at the beginning of the previous section, is the definition of the status that should be assigned to the notion of sacrifice in the *Phenomenology*.

Sacrifice has been previously defined as a conscious act of the agent (virtuous consciousness, noble consciousness, religious consciousness, etc.) in a particular phenomenological stage. It has been stressed that, *from the point of view of each pattern of consciousness*, the sacrifice is meant to be effective (able to solve the problem affecting that phenomenological configuration) and unselfish (not receiving anything in return). But this perception always implies a certain degree of self-deception: apart from the case of Christ, the sacrifice performed by all the other agents previously taken into consideration turns out to be not effective (for the purpose of the agent) and/or not completely unselfish. However, the point of view of the consciousness in a specific phenomenological stage is not the only possible perspective; there is another point of view, and it is the point of view of the (absolute) spirit. We are already familiar with a similar dynamic, insofar as Solger's philosophy is also characterized by a continuous alternation between the point of view of the Infinite and the point of view of the finite. However, Hegel's philosophy is intrinsically retrospective.[24] In fact, only from the point of view of the spirit, is it possible to: (1) recognize the self-deception of the consciousness; and (2) conceive a real (effective and unselfish) sacrifice.

Before proceeding further, it is important to clarify that the traditional view, according to which the Hegelian spirit is regarded as a bizarre supra-individual conscious being, has turned out to be poorly substantiated in the light of the analyses that have been conducted in the last few decades. While the non-traditionalists[25] differ among themselves on several issues, they usually agree that Hegel's spirit should not be regarded as a super-entity like, for example, Newton's God. "The point of view of the spirit" is not the God's-eye point of view, but (to use Redding's definition) a "configuration of mutually recognizing individual subjects" whose existence as subjects is dependent upon a joint act of recognition[26]—or, to use Pinkard's more concise definition, a form of reflective social practice.[27] If this account is accepted, speaking of "the point of view of the spirit" is not weirder than speaking of "the point of view of the Church" or (even more appropriately) "the point of view of the legislator."[28]

The point of view of the spirit on sacrifice is clearly expressed by Hegel at the very end of the *Phenomenology*:

> The self-knowing Spirit knows not only itself but also the negative of itself, or its limit: to know one's limit is to know how to sacrifice oneself [*aufzuopfern*]. This sacrifice [*Aufopferung*] is the externalization in which Spirit displays [*darstellt*] the process of its becoming Spirit in the form of free contingent happening [. . .]. (PG, 807/492)

The only real (that is, really effective and unselfish) sacrifice is the sublation [*Aufhebung*][29] of all of the (not really effective and/or unselfish) sacrifices performed by the becoming spirit (the consciousness in its development) in the various contingent phenomenological phases. *Aufhebung* is, in Hegel's own words, "at once a *negating* and a *preserving*" (PG, 113/68). All the contingent sacrifices are preserved but, at the same time, negated. Sacrifice is a form of determinate negation insofar as the contradictory negation, represented by the fact that all the contingent sacrifices are not *completely* effective and/or unselfish (which is clearly a contradiction for a sacrifice that is supposed to get nothing in return), is sublated in the real and actual sacrifice, represented by the willingness to renounce one's own absoluteness.[30] Using a more narrative language, it could be said that, as in the sacrifice of Christ all the sins of humanity are remitted, so sacrifice from the point of view of the spirit is the overcoming of all the contingent and specific sacrifices, and of all the related self-deceptive illusions. To be completely clear, it has to be stressed that even the sacrifice of Christ is a phenomenological moment, and as such is not inherently different from all the other sacrifices performed by the other patterns of consciousness—except for the fact that in the sacrifice of Christ the real effectiveness and unselfishness of sacrifice is displayed, which is the reason why it can be *retrospectively* considered the exemplar of sacrifice.

To better understand in which sense the sacrifice of Christ is the exemplar of sacrifice, it is now appropriate to turn to the definition of the status of the notion of sacrifice in the *Phenomenology*. One could be tempted to consider sacrifice as a *Vorstellung*, for Hegel's analysis in the context of religion is characterized by a massive use of this term. *Vorstellung*, usually translated into English as "representation,"[31] is the "consciousness as a representational system" and "is based upon and constituted by the dichotomy between subject and object."[32] More simply, *Vorstellung* is a picture-thinking,[33] or a memory-like image (as well as the faculty producing it), whose content is perceived as external by the consciousness. However, to define sacrifice as a *Vorstellung* would be highly inaccurate. First, Hegel's use of *Vorstellung* in the context of religion, and particularly when he addresses Christianity, is mainly due to the fact that Hegel fundamentally refers to the mode of presence of Jesus to the community of believers: in fact, Christ can only be "present" as memory—that is, he can persist only in an internalized form as a subjective content among his followers.[34] The notion of sacrifice as such is not affected by this consideration. Second, the dynamic of sacrifice is not limited to religion but, as it has been shown in the previous sections, is a process that plays a role in phenomenological stages that do not imply religion directly (such as virtuous or noble consciousness). Third, and most important, Hegel himself makes a meaningful distinction and clarifies that sacrifice is *not* a *Vorstellung*. Consider the passage of the *Phenomenology* analyzed in the previous section, where Hegel stresses the deceptive nature of the sacrifice performed by "faith" in its struggle with "pure insight." The sacrifice performed there, Hegel claims, "is merely a *sign* [*Zeichen*], which performs real sacrifice [*wirkliche Aufopferung*] in only a small degree, and is therefore in point of fact only a *representational thought* [*vorstellt*] of the sacrifice" (PG, 569/347). Therefore, the partial sacrifice performed by the consciousness in that particular phenomenological stage (as well as, it can be argued, the sacrifice performed by the consciousness in all the other particular phenomenological stages) is only a *Vorstellung*—but clearly, the real sacrifice is something else. These partial sacrifices are deceptive precisely because they are just signs—in other words, they are merely represented (*vorgestellt*). It can also be said that they remain in the sphere of *Vorstellung* precisely because they are deceptive: their deceptive nature prevents them from going beyond that sphere (as they can only be represented) and thus from becoming real sacrifices.

Again, Hegel himself clarifies what the real sacrifice (or the sacrifice from the point of view of the spirit, as I argued above) really is. In the very last passage in which the term "sacrifice" appears in the *Phenomenology* (previously quoted in this section), Hegel considers sacrifice in relation to "the self-knowing spirit," and states: "This sacrifice [*Aufopferung*] is the externalization in which Spirit displays [*darstellt*] the process of its becoming Spirit in the form of free contingent happening [. . .]" (PG, 807/492). Therefore, sacrifice is a *Darstellung*. This term, usually translated into English as *exposition*, *display*, or *presentation*, is an account of something in its peculiar movement, and is the authentic modality in which philosophy unpacks its content. *Darstellung* implies an intrinsic reference to the method of philosophy; in fact, if the development of truth cannot be grasped irrespectively of those cultural products within which humans see their own existence patterns reflected, as Hegel maintains in the second section of the chapter on spirit, "then our method cannot be a universal, apriorist analysis of the relation of certain concepts in abstraction from their historical situation," but must be "embedded in that historicality [. . .] of the actual development of the concept."[35] More simply, the *Darstellung* is a presentation of a content that is presented in philosophy as a concept (*Begriff*). The real sacrifice, or the sacrifice from the point of view of the spirit, *displays* sacrifice in its peculiar movement through the various stages of the phenomenological history and in its actual development. To define sacrifice as *Darstellung* leads to an explanation of the twofold connection between sacrifice and recognition. But first, it should be stressed that the process of recognition requires a willingness to renounce one's own absoluteness. This renunciation can indeed be named *sacrifice* in the kenotic sense, of which Christ is, as we have seen, considered by Hegel as the prototypical expression.

The most straightforward connection between sacrifice and recognition directly emerges from the analysis carried on in the previous two sections: recognition is essential to understanding the notion of sacrifice in the *Phenomenology*. In fact, there is no sacrifice without (a certain degree of) recognition, in the sense that the recognition of the other is a necessary precondition of self-sacrifice. In the case of the unhappy consciousness, the sacrifice connected with its deceptive passivity turns out to be not actual, because it does not imply the renunciation of absolute independence and, thereby, the recognition of the other. The sacrifice of the feudal nobility is fundamental for the generation of a social linguistic activity as the essential means to create a new mutual recognition—self-consciousness now exists, as Hegel says, "for others" (PG, 508/308)—thus paving the way for the spirit. This process then develops through the cultural experience of the cult, where the individuals not only recognize each other in the "social space" built around the ritual sacrifice, but also agree on the recognition of common values and beliefs. As Brandom states, "to sacrifice is not a matter of biology, but of culture":[36] and culture, in Hegelian terms, is not possible without recognition.

Moreover, there is another connection between sacrifice and recognition: sacrifice is the *Darstellung* of the process of recognition. Consider the section of the *Phenomenology* on forgiveness and reconciliation (PG, 665–671/403–409). Here the acting consciousness, or "beautiful soul" (historically represented by the Romantic movement) is imagined as confessing its being contingent (that is, historically located) to a judgmental agent who, although initially "rejects any continuity with the other" (the "hard-hearted judge" refuses to consider itself equally contingent), eventually forgives the beautiful soul. Both the beautiful soul and the hard-hearted judge "display (*darstellt*) the power of the Spirit";[37] and "the forgiveness which it extends to the other is the renunciation of itself [*Verzichtleistung auf sich*]" (PG, 669/407). This "reciprocal recognition [*ein gegenseitiges Anerkennen*] is absolute Spirit" (PG, 670/408); and later on, at the very end of the section, Hegel defines it as "God manifested in the midst of those who know themselves in the form of pure knowledge" (PG, 671/409). What the judgmental consciousness has to give up in the act of mutual concession and forgiveness is the immediate identification with the absoluteness of God's law: as Pinkard puts it, the hard-hearted judge eventually grasps that "there are no truths that can be taken as metaphysical anchors independently of social practice," and thus he becomes "aware of the contingency of his own beliefs."[38] This dynamic involves the type of acceptance of one's fallen condition and estrangement from immediate union with God that Hegel sees in Jesus.[39]

Consider the sacrifice of Christ, which can be taken as the exemplar of the genuine (current and real) sacrifice. What is peculiar to the sacrifice of Christ is the fact that the *subject* sacrifices something *essential* to himself—that is, something that *constitutes* the subject. Christ is God (the absolute Being): in becoming human, he sacrifices his divine absoluteness. Thus, the self-sacrifice of Christ displays [*darstellt*] the sacrifice of one's own absoluteness. Now, consider recognition: of course there is no recognition of another self without renouncing one's own absoluteness. In this sense, the self-sacrifice of Christ is not only the exemplar of the genuine sacrifice:

it can also be considered as the *Darstellung* of recognition. The reciprocal recognition between the beautiful soul and the hard-hearted judge is realized through the abandonment of the latter's initial standpoint, which was the rejection of "any continuity with the other" (PG, 667/405). Similarly, but most fundamentally, God recognizes humanity by renouncing his own absoluteness and accepting his continuity with humanity, and it does so through the incarnation of Christ. Both the "forgiveness and reconciliation" episode and the story of Christ display the sacrifice of one's own absoluteness; the latter is just more radical than the former (it goes "as far as death"), and hence it can be considered the most meaningful exemplar of the real and genuine sacrifice.[40]

What is missing in the unhappy consciousness, or in the religious consciousness (as opposed to pure insight), is precisely this renunciation of one's own absoluteness, which, alone, constitutes the essence of real sacrifice—and of real recognition. From the point of view of the (absolute) spirit, the real and genuine sacrifice ultimately leads to a gain from giving up one's absoluteness: it *displays* the process of recognition (but again: this gain can appear in all its clarity only *retrospectively*). The genuine sacrifice (sacrifice of one's absoluteness), insofar as it is the *Darstellung* of recognition, contributes to the self-constitution of human beings as free, rational, and able to generate identity-conferring values and commitments.

There is no sacrifice without recognition, and there is no recognition without sacrifice. These two connections are, in fact, two perspectives on (or two ways of expressing) the same dialectic reality, since sacrifice, conceived as a *Darstellung*, is an account of a process that can be referred to, in the form of concept (*Begriff*), as recognition. To acknowledge the fact that the notion of sacrifice expresses a process that is presented in conceptual terms in philosophy proper does not mean to dismiss sacrifice as "overtaken" by a more conceptual expression of its content: indeed quite the opposite. In fact, according to Hegel, ideas always need to turn into sensibilized forms in order to be applied. Religious notions and symbols are effectively sensibilized forms. Therefore, a survey of the notion of sacrifice in Hegel's philosophy would not be complete without an analysis of the use of this notion in the context of Hegel's philosophy of religion.

Sacrifice and Incarnation in Hegel's Philosophy of Religion

There is little evidence in previous literature of a connection between recognition and sacrifice. This is partly because the interpretative standpoint that emphasizes the importance of recognition for Hegel's philosophy has not yet addressed Hegel's philosophy of religion. This lack is probably also due to the influence of Georges Bataille's essay "Hegel, la Mort et le Sacrifice."[41] Bataille sees sacrifice merely as destruction or suppression. However, this is only one aspect of the Hegelian conception of sacrifice. As it is clear from our analysis of the *Phenomenology of Spirit*, there is another, and even more important, aspect. It is the kenotic sacrifice, or sacrifice as *withdrawal*. According to Williams, while the *Phenomenology of Spirit* proceeds by a process of skeptical self-subversion ("Hegel shows that certain shapes of consciousness self-destruct and subvert themselves"[42]), the *Encyclopedia of the Philosophical Sciences*, by contrast, proceeds constructively ("Here Hegel emphasizes the affirmative relationships based on reciprocal recognition"[43]). The apex of the process of reciprocal recognition as it is depicted in the *Encyclopedia* is represented by the notion of *Freilassen*, that is, "an affirmation of the other in his singularity and difference";[44] it is a *withdrawal*, which is also *liberation* from one's perspective to embrace other perspectives.[45]

The distinction between suppressive and kenotic sacrifice is not limited to the *Phenomenology* and the *Encyclopedia*, but extends to the *Lectures on the Philosophy of Religion*, where the presentation (*Darstellung*) of this dynamic in sacrificial terms appears more clearly. To appreciate the depth of this distinction, it is useful to turn to the section of Hegel's 1827 *Lectures* devoted to the Cultus. Here, Hegel distinguishes three forms of the Cultus: devotion (*Andacht*), external sacrifice (*Opfer*), and interiorized sacrifice.[46] Introducing the second form (external sacrifice), Hegel writes:

> Negation exists within devotion and even maintains an outward configuration by means of sacrifice. The subject renounces something or negates something in relation to itself. It has possessions and divests itself of them in order to demonstrate that it is in earnest. On the one hand this negation is accomplished in a more intensive fashion only through the sacrificing or burning of something—even through human sacrifice; on the other hand the sensible enjoyment [of the sacrifice], for instance the eating and drinking, is itself the negation of external things. Thus from this negation or from the sacrifice one advances to enjoyment, to consciousness of having posited oneself in unity with God by means of it. The sensible enjoyment is linked directly with what is higher, with consciousness of the linkage with God. (Rel, 194)

This account of external sacrifice substantially mirrors the picture of the "sacrificial dedication" (*Hingabe*) that is featured in the *Phenomenology*, but in the *Lectures on the Philosophy of Religion* the fundamental characteristics of this form of sacrifice are stressed more explicitly. Sacrifice appears when negation enters into the act of devotion, and it consists in the suppression, or negation, of something external to the subject. The enjoyment resulting from this sacrifice is an expression of a reestablishment of the unity between nature and spirit. This form of sacrifice is external and is never interiorized, not even when performed on the subject itself, as happens, for example, in acts of self-mortification, in which sacrifice as suppression remains, as Hegel writes later in the *Lectures*, "the abstractly negative" (Rel, 300). A further confirmation of this reading comes from Hegel's analysis of the myth of Prometheus. In Greek mythology, Prometheus is regarded as the one who taught humans to perform sacrifices. When he sacrificed to Zeus for the first time, he presented two sacrificial offerings, one consisting of beef hidden inside an ox's stomach, and the other consisting of bones wrapped in "glistening fat." The god was caught in the snare and chose the latter, thus establishing the usual procedure for future sacrifices, where humans keep the meat to be eaten and burn the bones as a sacrificial offering. Prometheus, Hegel remarks, "still belongs among the Titans," that is, pre-human creatures, "for the very reason that these skills are only to satisfy the human needs—they have no ethical authority, they are not laws" (Rel, 338). External sacrifice always turns out to be "utilitarian" destruction or suppression of something for the sake of something else, be it the satisfaction of needs, the benevolence of the gods, or a simple manifestation of power.[47]

External sacrifice is not, however, the highest form of the cult. The third and highest form is represented by the interiorized sacrifice, whereby one not only destroys external things but also gives up one's own subjectivity. Hegel writes:

> The third and highest form within the cultus is when one lays aside one's own subjectivity—not only practices renunciation in external things such as possessions, but offers one's heart or inmost self to God and senses remorse and repentance in this inmost self; then one is conscious of one's own immediate natural state (which subsists in the passions and intentions of particularity), so that one dismisses these things, purifies one's heart, and through this purification of one's heart raises oneself up to the realm of the purely spiritual. This experience of nothingness can be a bare condition or single experience, or it can be thoroughly elaborated [in one's life]. If heart and will are earnestly and thoroughly cultivated for the universal and the true, then there is present what appears as ethical life. To that extent ethical life is the most

genuine cultus. But consciousness of the true, of the divine, of God, must be directly bound up with it. (Rel, 194)

What happens when sacrifice is interiorized? First, sacrifice becomes self-sacrifice (*Aufopferung*), not in the form of self-suppression or self-mortification, but as an offering of the "inmost self." When one "lays aside one's own subjectivity," she senses "remorse and repentance." As we know from *The Philosophy of Right*, subjectivity is, for Hegel, "a one-sided form" and "pure certitude of itself in contrast with the truth"[48]: it is a (false) presumption of objectivity.[49] In the previous state, there was no distinction between subjectivity and objectivity: in the external sacrifice, the relation with the divine is immediate, and the subject is concerned only with his purported achievement (satisfaction of needs, gods' benevolence, etc.).[50] Once the subject has given up her own subjectivity, she becomes conscious of her finitude (her "nothingness" in relation to the divine) and dismisses her passions and intentions. If this is not a one-time experience, but a recurring and cultivated habit, then it becomes the condition for the emergence of a proper ethical life, and the foundation of metaphysical knowledge ("consciousness of the true, of the divine, of God").

Therefore, the main distinction between external sacrifice and interiorized sacrifice consists in this: external sacrifice is *suppressive* ("the abstractly negative"); conversely, interiorized sacrifice is *kenotic*. We know that the notion of kenosis resurfaced in the thought of the seventeenth-century mystical thinker Jacob Böhme. Significantly, Böhme is one of the two figures (the other being Francis Bacon) Hegel addresses in the section "Modern Philosophy in its First Statement" of his *Lectures on the History of Philosophy*: it is "through him," Hegel claims, "that philosophy of a distinctive character first emerged in Germany."[51] One of most original features of Böhme's theological account is that God can change and, most importantly, can suffer—and, in fact, *does* suffer.

Therefore, it might be suggested that it is a Böhmian conception of kenosis that is at work in the interiorized sacrifice. The importance of the notion of kenosis in Hegel's thought, as well as Böhme's influence in this respect, has already been stressed in previous literature, most notably by O'Reagan in his *The Heterodox Hegel*.[52] Nevertheless, O'Reagan, consistently with his interpretative approach, contextualizes the emphasis on kenosis within an analysis of the mystical features of Hegel's theology, and recognition does not appear to play a significant role in his account of Hegel's philosophy of religion (or absolute spirit broadly conceived).

As shown by the Hegelian passages analyzed above, there cannot be a recognition of the other if the subject does not preliminarily renounces its own absoluteness, that is, its presumption of considering its subjectivity as absolute objectivity. Only if the subject withdraws and "makes room," as it were, for the other's point of view (thus recognizing itself as relative, i.e., as located historically, geographically, etc.), is the process of recognition indeed possible.

Because the kenotic sacrifice is the representation of the act that effectively establishes the process of recognition, it is also the condition for the *existence* of self-consciousness.[53] It has been said that, in the context of Hegel's *idealist* metaphysics, human beings *themselves* must be regarded as products of reason. Hence, our own *identity* (as human beings) is constituted through the process of *withdrawing*.[54]

Therefore, the next section will be devoted to an analysis of the philosophical value of the incarnation of Christ in light of the outcomes that result from this reading.

The Incarnation of Christ

Once it is assumed that kenotic sacrifice plays an important role in Hegel's account of absolute spirit, it becomes easier to explain Hegel's interest in the incarnation and sacrifice of Christ. Let us focus on the philosophical value of the incarnation of Christ in light of the outcomes that result from the interpretation carried on so far.

It is well known that in his youth Hegel shared with some of his contemporaries (such as Schelling and Hölderlin) a significant enthusiasm for Greek mythology and gods. From the *Phenomenology* onward, however, he incorporated a more conventional Christian theological outlook. This change is partly due to the development of a methodological approach that assumes that, to analyze a cultural subject (say, religion), it is a better philosophical strategy to start from existing beliefs and symbolic features rather than moving from an abstract[55] standpoint and, like Kant, speculating what religion should be. This attitude of speculation, in Hegel's view, can be associated with that of a Scholastic philosopher who declared that he will not go into the water "until he has learned to swim" (Rel, 95). Nevertheless, this methodological approach alone cannot explain either Hegel's idea that Christianity is the highest form of religion (the "consummate" religion) or Hegel's increasing interest in the incarnation of Christ. In fact, these two elements are connected. One feature that the Greek gods have in common with the Jewish God (at least as it is presented in the Bible) is that they do not experience suffering as a human would. They feel (human) feelings, such as jealousy and anger, but they do not suffer, they do not die, and (perhaps most importantly) they do not fail. From this point of view, the Christian god is very different: it is a God who becomes fully human.[56] Therefore, it can be argued that Hegel regarded Christianity as the highest form of religion precisely because of its central image of God becoming man. But again, why is this image so important for Hegel?

Here, we should remember that Hegel is concerned with God as the subject of a philosophical analysis. In other words, his philosophy of religion is a *philosophy* of religion:[57] he is not interested in advancing a religious account, but in analyzing god qua object of human reason. Furthermore, Hegel is an *idealist*. Therefore, when he takes into consideration Christian doctrines, he is also interested in their regulative and symbolic value. The centrality of the incarnation of Christ in Hegel's philosophy can be fully grasped only if its function as model of the kenotic sacrifice is taken into consideration.

The figure of Jesus Christ in Hegel's philosophy clearly represents the incarnation of the divine and the overcoming of the abstract opposition between the divine and the human. This overcoming can be realized only through a sacrifice that consists in a *withdrawal*. Effectively, in becoming human, God sacrifices his own divinity and absoluteness and accepts all human limitations, including being geographically and historically located. Considered as such, the notion of incarnation is not only an early mythical expression of the dialectic that reveals the progressive incarnation of the spirit. It is also the symbolic and regulative expression, portrayed in the form of historical narrative, of a content conceptualized in philosophy. This content is the process of kenosis between self and other, which is essential for recognition. In fact, if recognition is, first and foremost, the subject's withdrawal and renunciation of its own objective point of view, what can better symbolize this process than a god who becomes human and renounces the *God's-eye* point of view?

The death of Christ is therefore the highest expression of this kenotic sacrifice, as it shows that God has indeed withdrawn from his absoluteness and has fully accepted human nature—he has accepted it until death. Hegel writes: "'To sacrifice' means to sublate the natural, to sublate otherness. It is said: 'Christ has died for all.' This is not a single act but the eternal divine history: it is a moment in the nature of God himself: it has taken place in God himself" (Rel, 470). The sacrifice of Christ is not merely "a single act," but it shows that the Christian God is not an immutable, always already actualized being; conversely, he is a "being in becoming."[58]

Thus, Christ sublates "the natural" by withdrawing from the "supernatural," accepting the natural and overcoming it through his kenotic sacrifice. This overcoming is what Christ's followers are required to remember in the Eucharist. Furthermore, the representation of the Christian God in the internalized mode of memory also has an ethical significance. This should not come as a surprise—after all, even the passage in Philippians, which is the original source of the kenotic tradition, presents some immediate ethical implications: Christians are required to follow Christ's example by sacrificing themselves. Here, the sacrifice of Christ is assumed to be a paradigm for a sacrifice conceived as a withdrawal or a "making room" for others. When Hegel claims that Christ should be the normative paradigm for the church (qua community of Christ's followers),[59] he is not simply retaining some elements of the well-established tradition of the *Imitatio Christi*. In fact, Hegel's reception of this tradition appears more meaningful once it is considered in light of the kenotic sacrifice. In Hegel's view, the incarnation of Christ represents a turning point in the history of spirit, as Christ becomes the exemplar of the kenotic sacrifice, on which we humans can model our normativity. One of the novelties of the Christian church consists in its willingness to perform a twofold withdrawal: the first, in which each individual gives up her subjectivity (previously perceived as absolute objectivity) to establish the intersubjectivity of the community; and the second, in which the community gives up its inner spirituality (the traditional spiritual component of a religious community) to engage with the world. As Hodgson comments, "Hegel traces a movement from heart to church to ethical life, a movement that points to freedom as the *telos* of world history. The freedom of the *basileia* community passes into social and political freedom."[60]

There is a strict interrelation between the affirmation of Christianity, with its central image of the incarnation as the kenotic sacrifice of Christ, and the rise of the age of modern freedoms. The immortal Greek gods symbolize an idea of freedom as being untouched by human frailty and weakness. The angry and jealous God of the Old Testament, then, that absolute lawgiver and judge who looked at the world from the God's-eye point of view, represents the negation of freedom for the sake of a "legal morality." Finally, the Christian God, who accepts human finitude until death and represents a model for the kenotic sacrifice, is cognate with modern freedom. Hegel is explicit in saying that it was through Christianity that the idea of freedom came into the world.⁶¹ Modern freedom does not consist in keeping distance from otherness, but rather, by a full acceptance of otherness, in a process that is realized through a withdrawal of one's personality (*in Aufgeben seiner Persönlichkeit*). This is what love consists in: "a self-conscious activity, the supreme surrender [of oneself] in the other."⁶² As Hegel writes in the section of the 1827 *Lectures* entitled "The Idea of Reconciliation and Its Appearance in a Single Individual," "The other-being, the finitude, the weakness, the frailty [*Gebrechlichkeit*] of human nature is not to do any harm to that divine unity which forms the substance of reconciliation. [. . .] the self-positing and sublating of otherness is love or spirit" (Rel, 453–454).⁶³ Modern social and political freedoms are therefore associated with the idea of kenotic sacrifice that is represented by the incarnation of Christ, that is, with the renunciation of the God's-eye view and the withdrawal of one's own personality, or point of view, to *recognize* other personalities and points of view.

Some Consequences of Kenotic Sacrifice on Hegel's Metaphysics

For Hegel, religious belief systems are to be understood as nonconceptual presentations of a content that is conceptually presented in philosophy. Therefore, just as a proper understanding of Hegel's metaphysical view is relevant for appreciating his conception of the nature of religious experience and representation, so too his particular views about the incarnation of Christ and the kenotic sacrifice shed light on how his metaphysics is to be interpreted. In Hegel's own words, "Philosophy is only explicating *itself* when it explicates religion, and when it explicates itself it is explicating religion" (Rel, 78–79).

The image of God emerging from Hegel's account of Christianity represents a radical challenge to the traditional view of the immutable and fully actualized Aristotelian God, which was indicative of the goal of philosophy as a metaphysical knowledge of an ultimate reality, and which Kant had started to jeopardize. Hegel's emphasis on the figure of Christ, that is, God emptying itself of its divine attributes (such as omnipotence and omniscience)⁶⁴ to become human (that is, historically and geographically located), suggests a conception of metaphysical knowledge different from traditional pre-Kantian metaphysics. The organizing principle of an idealist metaphysics is the reciprocal recognition of different finite points of view. As the image of the Aristotelian immutable god was consistent with an account of metaphysics as knowledge of an ultimate reality (what is there "anyway"), Hegel's image of the kenotic Christian God (who renounces the

God's-eye view) is consistent with an account of metaphysics as knowledge of ideal objects dependent on human recognition.

Hegel's turn to Christianity and his emphasis on Christ's incarnation and sacrifice can be regarded as evidence for the increasing integration of Kantian elements into his metaphysics as well as being indicative of his endorsement of the peculiarly kenotic dimension of sacrifice. This endorsement is clear from the last few lines of Hegel's passage on the interiorized sacrifice quoted above. After having said that "ethical life is the most genuine cultus" but that "consciousness of the true, of the divine, of God, must be directly bound up with it," Hegel adds: "To this extent philosophy [too] is a continual cultus. [. . .] It is part of knowing the true that one should dismiss one's subjectivity" (Rel, 194). This quotation seems to suggest that a fundamental component of metaphysical knowledge (idealistically conceived) consists in the dismissal of subjectivity. As already mentioned, subjectivity is nothing else but the false presumption of objectivity ("pure certitude of itself in contrast with the truth"[65]), and this is precisely what has to be given up to gain real metaphysical knowledge.

The idea of God, as it is presented in Hegel's philosophy of religion, is the image of an idealistic standpoint in the domain of epistemology and metaphysics. It also has a peculiar *normative* value, as it appears from Hegel's appeal to the tradition of *Imitatio Christi*, and therefore it has an *ethical* significance: human subjects are required to imitate Christ in his sacrifice/withdrawal. Does this mean that the function of the idea of God in Hegel's philosophy is merely that of an epistemological and ethical metaphor?

This question is anything but new, as it was at the root of the split that developed between the so-called "right Hegelians" and "left Hegelians" after Hegel's death. As is known, the right Hegelians represented the theist faction of Hegel's followers, whereas the left Hegelians (such as Strauss and Feuerbach) turned Hegel's thought into a "humanist" critique of theism. Hegel's approach to religion, they claimed, should be interpreted as implying a conception of God as a human projection. Addressing this dispute is obviously beyond the scope of this book. Some general remarks along the lines of an interpretation of Hegel as a *post-Kantian* philosopher are, however, useful in the context of our analysis.

We have seen that Kant's account of the categorical imperative implies a repeated insistence that moral commands should be listened to *as if* they were spoken by the voice of God. That is, the categorical imperative should be regarded as a duty toward God. Kant's insistence represents an attempt to solve the paradox that, according to Pinkard, is implied in the Kantian idea of self-legislation (the idea that one has to be bound by laws of which one is also the author).⁶⁶ Feuerbach and the other left Hegelians considered the distribution of the activity of the constitution of norms over the species to be a better solution to the Kantian paradox—however, by considering the norms not universal and immutable (as for Kant), but historically and culturally determined, they paved the way for the Nietzschean solution, that is, the will to power considered as the individual capacity to autonomously create new values independent of customs and social habits. Some recent interpretations of Hegel seem to suggest that Hegel too should be regarded as employing the left-Hegelian strategy—that is, a conception of norms and concepts (including religious notions and symbols) regarded as mere human creations and considered only for their instrumental value.⁶⁷ From this point of view, Hegel's approach should be taken as meaning that values and norms are *merely* cultural and social reflections. In respect to religion, the claim that the idea of God has no existence external to reason should be taken as meaning that it exclusively has a *social* function. This interpretation effectively turns Hegel's account into a kind of *instrumentalism* or *expressivism* (although a socially based rather than individualistic form of expressivism), with the concept of God conceived as a merely useful instrument whose worth is measured by how effective it is in explaining social phenomena.

Regarding norms and values in general (but including religious representations), Paul Redding has recently suggested that from an Hegelian point of view they cannot be regarded "as merely the cultural reflections of a particular finite society" and that their representations "are afforded a type of necessity" that "is part of the status they have *as* norms."⁶⁸ As I said, it is beyond the scope of this book to develop a full treatment of this issue, and I think much has still to be done to clarify Hegel's account of God. Nevertheless, it is (relatively) undisputable that for Hegel the idea of God plays a crucial normative role, meaning that the *content* of this idea is significant for the lives of individuals (subjective spirits) insofar as it is regulative of their interactions and constitutive of their identities not only at the social, but also at the psychological and existential level. What is the peculiar content of the Christian idea of God?⁶⁹ Hegel clearly takes the incarnation of Christ to be at the heart of Christianity, and the incarnation expresses the kenotic sacrifice of God. The kenotic sacrifice is the expression of a spirit that advances only insofar as it is willing to *withdraw* and make room for the other. As such, the Christian idea of God represents not only a normative idea in ethics (the "imitation of Christ" mentioned above); it also has a regulative impact on philosophy itself insofar as it enhances a perspectival standpoint. Kant suggested considering the idea of God as a representation of the systematic unity of knowledge toward which we aspire—as if there were a single unified body of knowledge. To posit the idea of a God who, insofar as he accepts becoming human (i.e., historically located), is affected by the same partiality in perspective that we as humans suffer, is to undermine the traditional idea of (metaphysical) knowledge as "the omni-comprehensive point of view," and to replace it with an idea of knowledge as an expression of all different (and even contrasting) points of view.

Furthermore, Hegel stresses that Christ became the "perfect [*vollkommenen*] man" because "He suffered, sacrificed himself, negated his naturalness and thereby elevated himself above it." Hegel also emphasizes that the renunciation of his "naturalness" is something "which is to come to pass in the subject," that is, in us as humans.[70] In the philosophical register, this call might be regarded as an invitation to renounce the natural or naturalistic domain and to focus on the recognitively based structure of norms and values.

To recap: in Hegel's view, psychological subjects ("subjective spirits") are embodied within forms of finite life that are shaped by normative and action-guiding narratives that carry strong affective charges. These narratives constitute religion. Conceived in this way, religious narratives and notions regulate the interaction of subjects, and they contribute to those core commitments that are constitutive of moral identity. In this context, the notion of kenotic sacrifice plays a hidden and yet fundamental role. Expressed by the incarnation and the death of Christ, the kenotic sacrifice significantly shapes both modern moral identity and modern post-Kantian metaphysics. Kenotic sacrifice (giving up something of one's own identity to make room for other points of view and perspectives) is significant not only because of its capacity to express a philosophical concept (mutual recognition) in an emotionally affecting and motivating representation, it also necessitates a historically located will to realize and improve a (potentially universal) recognitively based structure of norms and values.

In short, kenotic sacrifice can be considered as the Hegelian most adequate strategy to develop one's consciousness, a development that, in turn, is made possible by the process of mutual recognition. There is no doubt that there is, for Hegel, a strong connection between ethics and religion. The extent to which this connection turns into a dependence of religion on the ethical (mutual recognition), however, has been, and still is, an object of dispute. From this angle, a reaction against the risk of turning faith into a mere statement of social fact rather than a personal and existential commitment was inevitable. Kierkegaard well represents this reaction—and interestingly, his reaction is associated with an account of sacrifice that has striking similarities, as well as important differences, with Hegel's account.

4

Kierkegaard

Sacrifice and the Regulativity of Love

Sacrifice in *Fear and Trembling*

In order to address Kierkegaard's account of sacrifice, it seems quite straightforward to start from that which, among Kierkegaard's books, has indubitably engendered the largest number of interpretative disagreements, heated debates, and philosophical conflicts—namely, *Fear and Trembling*.

According to the traditional understanding of his philosophical thought in general, and of *Fear and Trembling* in particular, Kierkegaard is regarded as having taken up aspects of Kant's philosophy "only to reject Kantianism as a whole."[1] In light of a deeper analysis, however, Kierkegaard can be regarded as a post-Kantian philosopher. It is beyond the scope of this book to provide an overall comparison between Kant and Kierkegaard;[2] what I want to argue here is that Kierkegaard has a Kantian approach to the regulativity of religious symbols, but he is disappointed with Kant's use of those symbols exclusively for ethical purposes. As I am going to show, *Fear and Trembling* can be regarded as evidence of this disappointment. This is relevant, because sacrifice is, for Kierkegaard, an important religious symbol.

Traditional interpretations often paint Kierkegaard as an advocate of the superiority of faith over knowledge in the theoretical realm and as a supporter of the divine command ethics in the practical realm. In short, he would be an apologist for Christian conceptual truths and a champion of irrational faith against abstract reason (a position that would have a positive value for some and a negative value for others). However, these conclusions turn out to be surprisingly poor if the Kantian approach to regulativity is taken into account.[3]

Kierkegaard does not consider the idea of God to be a cognitive object. It is clear in the second chapter of the *Postscript* that Kierkegaard "comes to the same skeptical conclusion as Kant"[4] with respect to traditional arguments for the existence of God. Kierkegaard shares Kant's distinction between knowledge and faith and thinks that rational knowledge of God is impossible.[5] Thus, Kierkegaard may be seen as expressing the same "cognitive humility" found in Kant.[6] In *Point of View Regarding my Work as an Author*, Kierkegaard explicitly claims that "the purpose of his authorship was not to raise the question of the truth of Christianity, but rather to cause men to inquire how they could become Christians."[7] Kierkegaard, like Kant, believes that religion must be approached through *practical* and not theoretical reason.[8] Therefore, it is on *the ethical* that we should focus to analyze the role of religious symbols in *Fear and Trembling*.

An interpretation that assumed a unitary account of the ethical in Kierkegaard's work would be dangerous, as each pseudonym represents a distinct existential standpoint.[9] One might, however, appeal to the distinction made by Vigilius Haufniensis (Kierkegaard's pseudonymous author) in the Introduction to *The Concept of Anxiety*. There, a distinction is made between "first ethics" and "second ethics." First, or secular, ethics "is the ethical that is contrasted with the aesthetic in *Either/Or*,"[10] whereas second, or "Christian," ethics turns particularly on the consciousness of sin and is fully developed in *Works of Love*.

The reader should not forget that the purported author of *Fear and Trembling* is Johannes de Silentio—a fictional character who "does not have faith" (FT, 28)—and not Kierkegaard himself. Most Kierkegaard scholars, such as Philip L. Quinn, agree that the ethics at issue in Kierkegaard's *Fear and Trembling* is "the secular ethics of his own time":[11] that is, first ethics. Although this claim can be considered disputable, here I will take it as sufficiently persuasive.[12] It is also important to stress that the distinction between moral and religious behavior that the reader finds in *Fear and Trembling* is drawn by *Johannes*, for whom ethics is simply first ethics.

What seems problematic to Johannes de Silentio, the fictional author of *Fear and Trembling* (and perhaps to Kierkegaard himself), is Kant's formal conception of morality (indeed, all post-Kantians, including Hegel and Nietzsche, recognize this as a problem). According to Kant's formal conception, humans should behave "as if" maxims were universally applicable. Conversely, in the context of the discussion about tragic heroes in *Fear and Trembling*, it is suggested that "there is an historical and cultural component to what is 'ethical.' Ethical duties are not derived from some timeless rational principle [. . .], but from the concrete customs of a people."[13]

Kierkegaard's philosophical relationship with *Religion within the Boundaries of Mere Reason* is extremely complex and is certainly more complex than

Kierkegaard scholarship typically concedes. It is beyond the scope of this book to pursue this in detail;[14] however, some points need to be stressed for our purposes.

First, *Fear and Trembling* is clearly critical of the Kantian reduction of (natural) religion to moral philosophy.[15] If, as Kant writes, "religion is (subjectively considered) the recognition of all our duties as divine commands" (RGV, 6:154/177), then all duties can be ultimately understood as duties to God.[16] For Kant, revelation is unnecessary in principle, or, in Johannes's words, "God becomes an invisible, vanishing point . . . his power is to be found only in the ethical, which fills all existence" (FT, 59). The risk of reducing religion to moral philosophy is what leads Johannes to draw a strong distinction between (and often to contrast) *ethical* behavior and *religious* behavior.

Second, Kant's approach to sacrifice is highly reductive, and Kierkegaard is acutely aware of this. As we know, the sacrifice that Abraham is willing to perform definitely falls outside the realm of religious metaphors and symbols that Kant considers acceptable.

In short, the position expressed in *Fear and Trembling* is often marked by disappointment in Kant's reduction of religion to moral philosophy and in his consequent rejection and expulsion of all religious symbols that cannot serve as models for moral behavior. Kant's account of religion is extremely complex and cannot be simply described as a reduction of religion to morality[17]—conversely, as already stated, religious symbols are an essential component of Kant's philosophy. From this angle, it might well be that Johannes's (or even *Kierkegaard's*) take on Kant is, to some degree, ungenerous; but even in this case, Green's claim that "Kant's treatment of Abraham in his *Religion within the Limits of Reason Alone* and *The Conflict of the Faculties* may have provided the stimulus for *Fear and Trembling*"[18] seems plausible.[19] In fact, the text in its entirety may be regarded as a defense of the irreducibility of religion to morality and a revaluation of the *Akedah* as a symbol of faith, although (or, better yet, because) Abraham's willingness to sacrifice Isaac violates any moral code.

Although this reading stresses the importance of Kant to the development of Kierkegaard's philosophy, it is not in itself incompatible with traditional interpretations of *Fear and Trembling*, which maintain that Kierkegaard aims to dismiss ethics in favor of an irrational (or, at best, a nonrational) account of faith. However, this is only half of the story. I submit that *Fear and Trembling* remains true to the spirit of Kant's critical philosophy, while at the same time trying to go beyond Kant. More specifically, the *Akedah* is regarded in *Fear and Trembling* as a symbolic and regulative notion and the Kantian approach to religious notions is preserved and transformed in an attempt to amend Kant's formal conception of ethics and religion.

In the next section, I will draw a comparison with Hegel and specifically with his theory of recognition. In the final section, I will explore the *regulative* value of sacrifice as it emerges from *Fear and Trembling*.

Kierkegaard, Hegel, and Recognition

Traditional Kierkegaard scholarship has often superficially characterized Kierkegaard's relationship to Hegel as one of mere frontal opposition. Scholars such as Jon Stewart and Merold Westphal have done much to correct this misleading perception. Kierkegaard held Hegel in great esteem and was massively influenced by his thought, especially in his early work. Furthermore, even in his maturity, Hegel's extraordinary philosophical quality is not a matter of discussion for Kierkegaard.

As is well known, Hegel maintains that Kant's conception of morality is formal and empty because it requires that norms be considered universally applicable. Johannes de Silentio seems to be equally critical of Kant's formal conception of morality. In the context of the analysis of the actions of the "tragic heroes," Johannes's claim that "everyone" can understand them implies that those actions are considered acceptable according to a moral code that is valid in a specific place and time (an example is Jephthah's promise to sacrifice the first creature he saw on returning from the battle, as pointed out by Evans and Walsh[20]). For Johannes, ethical duties cannot be derived from timeless rational imperatives. When Johannes speaks of "the universal," he refers to "the concrete universal of the social order."[21] In this respect, *Fear and Trembling* seems to suggest that *first* ethics (which, we should not forget, has value in itself) needs to be conceived not as a set of timeless rational principles, but as an ethical order or substance that takes into consideration and even relies upon historical and cultural components such as customs and social roles. This is what Hegel calls *Sittlichkeit*.

The idea that, should ethics be considered as *first* ethics, then morality cannot be considered formally *à la Kant*, but needs to take into consideration social and cultural components, seems to be confirmed by Judge William, Kierkegaard's pseudonymous author of the second part of *Either/Or*. Most of Judge William's reflections are compatible with (or are even expressions of) Hegel's *Sittlichkeit*.[22]

Johannes de Silentio and Judge William clearly express specific existential standpoints, and their position cannot be *tout court* equated with Kierkegaard's. In addition, this does not mean that Kierkegaard *and* his fictional authors think of Hegel's *Sittlichkeit* as a perfectly adequate conception of the ethical life. Many clues are disseminated in Kierkegaard's pseudonymous and non-pseudonymous works suggesting that he disagrees with Hegel regarding the inclusion of religion within the ethical as *Sittlichkeit* and regarding the dependence of religion on human recognition. A short story included in the *Postscript* is meaningful in this respect. When the husband is imagined wondering whether he can really call himself a Christian, his wife addresses him as follows:

> How can you not be a Christian? You are Danish, aren't you? Doesn't the geography book say that the predominant religion in Denmark is Lutheran-Christian? You aren't a Jew, are you, or a Mohammedan? What else would you be, then? It is a thousand years since paganism was superseded; so I know you aren't a pagan. Don't you tend to your work in the office as a good civil servant; aren't you a good subject in a Christian nation, in a Lutheran-Christian state? So of course you are a Christian.[23]

Of course, this story does not do justice to Hegel's theory of recognition, which is not limited to the realm of ethics because it plays an important role in his (idealistically conceived) metaphysics. I will return to Hegel's "original" account of the relationship between recognition and religion later in this section. For now, it is sufficient to focus on this relationship as it was understood by the Danish right Hegelians. After all, it is reasonable to believe that it is against this version of Hegel's thought that he was reacting. (The question of whether or not he viewed it as an accurate understanding of Hegel's thought is not prominent here).

Hegel's philosophy of spirit starts from the notion of *Sittlichkeit* and therefore, quite understandably, with a discussion of religious and civic law. We know that most right Hegelians saw society as the embodiment of the divine. Johannes seems to be concerned with the consequences of such a view when he refers to a generation that "presumptuously wants to occupy the place that belongs only to the spirit who governs the world" (FT, 108). Commenting on this passage, Evans convincingly argues, "Johannes sees the combination of Hegelian ethics and Hegelian philosophy of history to be fatal for an understanding of genuine religious faith. If my society is itself the concrete embodiment of the divine, then *Sittlichkeit*, ethical participation in those social institutions by accepting 'my station and duties,' is at the same time true religion. It makes perfectly good sense to think of faith as common social possession."[24] In other words, Hegel's account of the relationship between recognition and religion might be seen as generating a sense of the inevitability of faith as a product of history, which in turn causes "the degeneration of the Christian religion in the objective thinking of Christendom."[25] Considered as such, the Hegelian approach might present the risk of turning faith itself into a mere statement of social fact rather than a personal and existential commitment.

In short, Kierkegaard does not like the idea of religion as something *mediated*, whether it is mediated through *ethics* or through *concepts*. First, Hegel's understanding of religion via the notion of recognition sounds to Kierkegaard like mediation through ethics (the idea that religion cannot be thought of but *through ethics*) and therefore like an absolutisation of the ethical; religion becomes *relative* with respect to ethics (FT, 61).

Second, Hegel maintains that "the conceptual form of philosophy" deals with the idea of God "in a more developed way" than is achievable in religion as a representational form.[26] In other words, Hegel's philosophy, as read by Kierkegaard, requires that religious *Vorstellung* (representation) be mediated through philosophical *Begriff* (concept) in order to be grasped in a fully developed way. Conversely, Kierkegaard wants to preserve the immediacy of faith, conceived of as a relationship with God that is not and should not be conceptually mediated.

The story of the *Akedah* perfectly serves Kierkegaard's purposes. Kierkegaard wants to show that religion is derived neither from rational knowledge nor from ethics. That religion is not derived from rational knowledge is something that Kant and Hegel would agree on without hesitation. However, Kierkegaard wants to stress that religious symbols cannot be mediated through either concepts or ethics. Abraham's willingness to sacrifice his son cannot be mediated through ethics because it would be condemned under any moral code; and it cannot be mediated through concepts because, as an expression of Abraham's personal, immediate, and absolute relationship with God, is not expressible via rational thought or words (hence the repeated claim that Abraham "cannot speak" and "cannot be understood").[27] Nonetheless, Kierkegaard has his fictional author Johannes hold up Abraham's willingness to sacrifice Isaac as an exemplar of faith. The sacrifice that Abraham is willing to perform is neither a mere metaphor nor a concept. It is a direct *symbol of faith* that does not require any ethical or conceptual mediation. In other words, the *Akedah* is meaningful because it has an *analogical* relation with the idea of faith that Kierkegaard, via Johannes, wants to advance, that is, an immediate and absolute relationship with God—the analogy residing in Abraham's willingness to sacrifice Isaac and, even more importantly, in his belief that he will eventually get Isaac back, while everything seems to suggest otherwise. In this way, the sacrifice of Abraham becomes a symbol of faith.

Now, consider Hegel's position with respect to both the charge of mediating religion through ethics and the charge of mediating religion through concepts. Regarding the latter, Hegel claims that "there may be religion without philosophy, but there cannot be philosophy without religion, because philosophy includes religion within it."[28] This claim is usually regarded as suggesting that philosophical knowledge can and should replace religion, and Kierkegaard seems to accept this interpretation. However, to claim that Hegel advocates abandoning religion in favor of philosophy is definitely an oversimplification, especially in light of the "revisionist" reading of Hegel that has been established during the last two decades.[29] To be fair to Hegel, and to assess Kierkegaard's criticism, it is useful to briefly address Hegel's original account.

To acknowledge that religious narratives are symbolic representations (*Vorstellungen*) of a content that is presented in the conceptual language of philosophy (*Begriff*) does not mean to dismiss them as overtaken by concepts. Indeed, quite the opposite is true. According to Hegel (who shares Kant's concern as mentioned in the previous section), ideas must always be sensibilized to be applied, "and it is this type of symbolically or analogically expressed idea that formed the traditional picture of God."[30] This is the reason why Hegel finds it necessary for religion and philosophy to coexist. We already recalled Hegel's claim that "Philosophy is only explicating itself when it explicates religion, and when it explicates itself it is explicating religion" (Rel, 78–79).[31] Hegel's account of self-consciousness is strictly interdependent with his idea of God, understood as a regulative ideal and the source of norms.

If one considers not only *Fear and Trembling* but also the rest of Kierkegaard's work, then it is difficult to avoid concluding that Kierkegaard misunderstands Hegel's general account of religion to some degree. Hegel does not mean to invalidate religion in suggesting that religious notions express content that is also presented in philosophy in the form of concepts. Kierkegaard tends to underline the "inadequacy of the concept"[32] to express religion (although Hegel would probably respond to this objection by saying that the concept is not an abstract and static logical notion. It is the most adequate conception of the world as a whole and the process of conceptual change. Therefore, from a Hegelian point of view, it is Kierkegaard who has a restricted conception of what *reason* is).

Now, consider the charge that Hegel mediates religion through ethics. It is undeniable that Hegel's understanding of religion incorporates the notion of *recognition*. However, this does not directly indicate that religion is mediated through ethics because Hegel makes much wider use of the dynamic of recognition than would be the case if he limited it to the realm of ethics. A quick reading of Hegel's *Philosophy of Right* shows that Hegel recognizes an individual's right to perform religious acts that have no ethical significance. He is even willing to allow for behavior that is in open contradiction to the norms of the social community and the state.[33] However, there are limits; the right of the individual conscience must stop "as soon as it comes into conflict with the law."[34] Therefore, Hegel would easily accept the contemporary knight of faith depicted in *Fear and Trembling*: the man who looks like a "tax collector," who "enjoys and takes part in everything," and who "does not do even the slightest thing except by virtue of the absurd" (FT, 33–34). What Hegel cannot accept from an ethical and political point of view is Abraham's willingness to kill his own son. As Stewart stresses, Abraham "must be persecuted since the state cannot permit the universalisation of individual acts of faith and conscience that encroach on the rights of others."[35] In other words, from a Hegelian point of view, the most problematic aspect of an account that interprets the sacrifice of Abraham as the symbol of faith, resides in Johannes's claim that Abraham's behavior does not need to be justified in the sociopolitical realm.

To recap: Kierkegaard's account of sacrifice as a direct symbol of faith is not completely incompatible with Hegel's approach to religion. In fact, Hegel himself accepts the need for religious commitments that are not mediated by ethics (although a certain degree of mediation is unavoidable for Hegel). The social and political dimensions of sacrifice remain the most problematic issues; from a Hegelian point of view (as well as in the great majority of moral theories), the teleological suspension of the ethical is too dangerous because it removes the need for recognition and justification in social and political arenas.

Kierkegaard is well aware of this danger. His fictional author Johannes is *fascinated* by Abraham, but he is also *appalled* by him. As Sylviane Agacinski notes, "Faith is not necessarily madness, but it always might be. In this respect, Kant and Kierkegaard were in agreement: where reason gives out, madness may always take over. Hence the terror that Abraham strikes into us, and our trembling before his crime."[36] It should be added that here the paths of Kant and Kierkegaard seem to diverge inexorably: Hegel and Kant are in accord with regard to this issue. However, it might be true that Kierkegaard does not wish to depart so completely from Kant. The extent to which he can be regarded as effectively departing from Kant depends on how the role of the *Akedah* in *Fear and Trembling* is interpreted. What does it mean to claim that Abraham's willingness to sacrifice Isaac is the symbol of faith, an exemplar on which we should model our own behavior? How literally should we read Johannes's invitation to take Abraham as a model, and how *real* this sacrifice is meant to be? Traditionally, this question (call it the *reality of sacrifice* problem) is answered in one of two ways.

The first possible answer is that Abraham's obedience to God should be considered a mere metaphor for faith, which is understood as the abandonment of the believer to the will of God. However, once it has been accepted that Johannes does not support divine command ethics, the interpreter is left wondering why it is necessary to turn to such a paradoxical and appalling story to make a point that could have been more appropriately made with other narratives or biblical episodes.[37] Furthermore, the insistence on the episode in itself makes it difficult to regard its use as merely metaphorical.

The second possible answer is that *Fear and Trembling* should be read literally. After all, this is precisely what Johannes invites the reader to do. He asks the reader to resist the temptation of a metaphorical reading (FT, 64). Of course, it is not always necessary to prepare to assassinate one's own son to be faithful to God—the tax collector does not do any such thing and yet is a knight of faith. The claim (and hence the ultimate meaning of the book) may instead be that one should be ready to go this far if required. According to this interpretation, Kierkegaard's account of sacrifice would be absolutely incompatible with the views of Kant and Hegel. Still, it remains unclear why it is it necessary to use such a paradoxical and appalling story when Johannes makes very clear, by describing the tax collector, that one can be a knight of faith without doing anything extraordinary.

I think that the second answer confers *too much* reality to the idea of sacrifice, whereas the first answer *too little*. I suggest that there is a third option. It has been said that according to Kant, some religious notions are symbols, that is, *moral* exemplars capable of serving as models for our own *moral* behavior. Insofar as they are *symbolic*, they are also *regulative*. Kierkegaard wants to maintain (and indeed, to strengthen) the symbolic meaning of religious notions but insists that they do not just symbolize morality; they symbolize faith first and foremost.

Kierkegaard thinks of sacrifice as a direct symbol of faith—that is, a symbol of a faith that is not mediated through ethics. Therefore, the *Akedah* can also be regarded as regulative, as a model not for our *moral* behavior but rather for our *religious* behavior. In other words, it can be regarded as regulative of one's personal relationship with God, which is what faith consists of. This reading resolves, in my view, some of the most problematic aspects of *Fear and Trembling*.

Regulativity of Sacrifice

The feature of *Fear and Trembling* that is both the source of most problems and one of the reasons for its longevity is the multiplicity of interpretative levels that it allows. This problem is even further worsened by the opening motto, an episode from Livy's *History of Rome* in which the king Tarquinius sends his son a secret message that the recipient understands but the messenger does not. This opening suggests the presence of a hidden message not made explicit in the text.

According to Green, *Fear and Trembling* contains "multiple levels of meaning," each with "its own significance."[38] The first level of meaning contains "a call to strenuous, lived commitment to Christian Faith." The second "develops the psychology of faith and love." The third "explores the question of the norms that should guide the conduct of a committed Christian." The fourth addresses the question of "how the individual believer can be saved from sin." For our purposes, we should focus on the third and fourth levels.

Consider the third level of meaning suggested by Green. There are, of course, many different interpretations of the notion of normativity in *Fear and Trembling*. The book has been traditionally regarded as an attack on Kantian ethical absolutism, "ethical philistinism," and the Hegelian notion of *Sittlichkeit*, or as supporting divine command ethics. Some interpretations are more convincing than others, but none of them is *completely* convincing.

However, critics such as Robert Perkins and Alastair Hannay have suggested a different way of reading the normativity presented in *Fear and Trembling* that stresses its structural formality. I am relying on these hints to suggest a more comprehensive interpretation of the notion of religious regulativity than I sketched at the end of the previous section.

In the following passage, Perkins connects the religious normativity of *Fear and Trembling* with a Kantian, regulative approach to duties: "Kant, in the *Foundations* and in the second *Critique*, did not suggest any specific duties, and Kierkegaard, like Kant, is concerned with the logic of duty, in this case, theological or theonomous duty. *Fear and Trembling* supplies no content for the concept of theonomous duty; it is an effort to map the boundaries."[39] Hannay seems to share this view when he claims that the story of the *Akedah* symbolizes the "formal features" of the "compound attitude" of faith. However, when he tries to unpack the normativity present in *Fear and Trembling*, he provides an explanation that remains in the realm of ethics rather than supplying *content* related to theonomous duties. Hannay focuses on the apparent contradiction that Abraham is convinced that he is really going to kill Isaac even though he also believes that he will eventually get Isaac back. According to Hannay, the belief that Isaac must be sacrificed means that "nothing in the world has value simply because one values it," whereas Abraham's belief that he will get Isaac back means both that "things have their value nonetheless" and that their value exists "on their own account and from God."[40] Mooney, who broadly supports Hannay's view, takes this to mean that "however important to us our cares may be, anything that possesses *real* value will possess it regardless of our attitudes toward it."[41] As Lippitt elegantly puts it, "The recognition that the value of something is ultimately not a function of the fact that I value it . . . neither is what I value dependent upon 'the universal' (in the Hegelian sense)."[42] However, Lippitt proposes a different (and in my view more convincing) solution, namely that a "part of *Fear and Trembling*'s message is that any approach to dilemmas that supposes a definitive 'right' answer can be given is untrue to the nature of such dilemmas"[43] (more on this shortly).

At this point, one could object that however interesting this debate is, it is still situated within the realm of ethics. In contrast, what I have been suggesting is that the *Akedah* can be considered as a model for *religious* rather than *moral* behavior—that is, as providing regulativity for those situations in which the ethical is teleologically suspended. One possible way of avoiding this problem is to argue (as Mooney does, for example) that the teleological suspension of the ethical is not *really* a suspension. It just *appears* to be so to those who embrace an (essentially Hegelian) morality "that absolutizes the claims of community, communication and reason."[44] Mooney thinks that *Fear and Trembling* offers a deeper sort of ethics according to which what matters is the agent rather than the act. I agree with Mooney that the problem is essentially a matter of perspective, but my interpretation of the teleological suspension of the ethical differs from Mooney's insofar as I think that there is a sense in which ethics really *is* suspended in *Fear and Trembling*. This happens when sin enters the equation. In this vein, a fundamental claim that has attracted a lot of attention from Kierkegaard scholars is made by Johannes in the third *Problem*: "An ethics that ignores sin is an altogether futile discipline, but if it asserts sin, then it is for that very reason beyond itself" (FT, 86).[45] Significantly, this claim plays an important role in the fourth level of meaning suggested by Green.

To make sense of this passage, it is useful to appeal once again to the distinction between *first ethics* and *second ethics* drawn in the Introduction to *The Concept of Anxiety*. There it is said that the first ethics is "shipwrecked on the sinfulness of the single individual."[46] First ethics (an ethics that ignores sin, in Johannes's words) concerns itself with *rightness* and *wrongness* and with the (Kantian) idea that it is always possible to determine what is right.

However, first ethics turns out to be inadequate. Several commentators agree that the reason for the inadequacy of first ethics is that "it is defined by a commitment to living up to a set of standards that are in fact impossible to live up to."[47] Significantly, to clarify this point, two of these commentators (Quinn and Evans) make the same reference to what John E. Hare calls the "moral gap": that is, "the gap between the moral demand on us and our natural capacities to live by it."[48] Interpreted in this light, the claim that the first ethics is "shipwrecked" on sin "looks like a claim to the effect that the necessity of universality of sin undermines the validity of the ethical standpoint."[49] In other words, Kierkegaard's conception of sinfulness, with its commitment to the Lutheran doctrine of Total Depravity, means that we can never "get it right"—hence the claim, "Before God, we are always in the wrong."[50] On one hand, once sin enters in, the very idea of ethical perfection is (as Mulhall stresses) "utterly lost."[51] On the other hand, to accept sin means also to accept the possibility of salvation through the agency of divine grace. In fact, we can be forgiven *precisely* because we are sinner and because we have now realized that we cannot be ethically perfect. From this angle, the *Akedah* might be said to effectively symbolize and exemplify the "double movement of faith" (FT, 29, 105). In my interpretation, the first movement is the acknowledgment of our unavoidable condition of sinners, and the second movement the belief that we can be forgiven by God.[52]

However, even if we leave first ethics behind and embrace the second (Christian) ethics[53] (and the conception of sin that comes with it), we do not find ourselves in a haven of rest. Pace Johannes, the religious is not opposed to the ethical, but rather represents (as suggested by Evans) a higher type of ethics, or a "morality in a new key."[54] Second ethics inevitably implies an entire different set of duties: theonomous duties, or duties toward God. These duties may potentially conflict with straightforward ethical duties. Such conflicts generate dilemmas—not pure ethical dilemmas, but rather *tragic dilemmas*. Here I rely on the definition provided by Lippitt: "Tragic dilemmas present situations in which whatever action one takes, one's life will be marred."[55]

Let us take a step back. What is the normativity of theonomous duties? Of course, this cannot be the traditional normativity that demands right and wrong answers. However, it also cannot be a divine-command ethics, because such an ethics would retain the possibility of providing *right* answers to dilemmas.[56] Hegel, who shares Kierkegaard's criticism of Kant's absolutism, relies on recognition; hence the notion of *Sittlichkeit*. However, according to Johannes (and Kierkegaard), this notion cannot be applied to the realm of religion. For theonomous duties, we require something else: a regulativity that is specifically religious.

I suggest that sinfulness as it is presented in *Fear and Trembling* means that some (tragic) dilemmas are insoluble for us because sinfulness is, first and foremost, "our absolute difference from Absolute Goodness."[57] Faith, by making us confront our theonomous duties, potentially puts us in situations in which we no longer have access to that haven of rest that is represented by first ethics (we have lost the illusion that we can be ethically perfect). Nonetheless, we still need to decide what to do.[58] This is why, in the realm of theonomous duties, we require regulative ideas.

This approach can be labeled *regulative contextualism*,[59] the idea that different forms of regulative normativity and corresponding different forms of duties are appropriate in different contexts. For Kant, ethical duties should be conceived of as if they were theonomous duties; the real religious duties are also ethical duties. Even if one considered Green's thesis that some of Kant's reflection on religion in general and on Abraham in particular may have provided the stimulus for *Fear and Trembling* as an exaggeration, Kierkegaard's awareness of the Kantian regulative approach to religious notions and narratives would be still more than plausible, especially because a regulative understanding of religion had already been developed by Schelling and other post-Kantians.[60] Kierkegaard retains the regulative structures that are implied in the Kantian conception but separates theonomous duties from ethical duties. Ethical duties based on social recognition are appropriate in the context of first ethics (thereby constituting something analogous to the Hegelian notion of *Sittlichkeit*). Theonomous duties based on exemplars are appropriate in the religious context. In other words, theonomous duties can only be guided by religious exemplars whose main characteristic is that they are independent of customs. Abraham, in his willingness to sacrifice his son Isaac, is a perfect exemplar of a faith effectively independent of customs, and his circumstances are paradigmatic of those tragic dilemmas in which ethical duties and theonomous duties exist in opposition. Because he is beyond ethics, Abraham cannot explain the reasons for his actions, but his behavior can serve as a regulative model for our own religious behavior.

Clearly, it is not groundbreaking to suggest that, for Kierkegaard, Abraham is meant to be an exemplar of faith (rather than ethical action); this interpretation has already been advanced by other commentators.[61] However, in claiming that Abraham is an exemplar of faith, I do not mean simply that his story presents a metaphor or a symbol (in a weak sense) that serves to illustrate some (religious) content. Indeed, I think that its use should not be regarded in the way that the use of religious notions and narratives in Kant is often *mistakenly* interpreted as suggesting. We noted that for Kant religious *Darstellungen* are transitional forms that must be used to apply the pure principles of practical reason to experience and that these forms play a regulative role in the application of moral ideas to the world. Kierkegaard, once he has claimed autonomy for theonomous duties, has found himself in a predicament analogous to the "special difficulties" mentioned by Kant in relation to the application of the moral law: he must find regulative forms that can make *religious* ideas applicable to the world. Interpreted in this way, Abraham is not merely a metaphor or a symbol in a weak sense but is instead one of those regulative exemplars that are an essential component of Kierkegaard's philosophy.

From this angle, *Fear and Trembling* might be regarded as an introductory work, in which a fictional author (Johannes) struggles with the fascination and the appalling generated by dealing with Abraham as an exemplar of faith. It should not be forgotten that according to an ancient and well-established tradition, Abraham is considered a *figura Christi*, a figure of Christ. In this respect, the reference to the Virgin Mary in *Fear and Trembling* (FT, 57) might represent a hint pointing in that direction. In fact, the inclusion of Mary as one of the exemplars of religious life changes the way in which the function of sacrifice is talked about in *Fear and Trembling*. In a few paragraphs, Johannes emphasizes Mary's willingness to self-sacrifice. This short digression might be taken as an anticipation of the indication (which is explicit in other pseudonymous and non-pseudonymous works) of Christ as the exemplar on which Christians should model their religious *and* ethical behavior (in the context of *second* ethics).

If regulative exemplars are acknowledged as an essential component of Kierkegaard's philosophy, then Kierkegaard can be regarded as a philosopher who certainly goes beyond and, to some extent, against Kant (he is skeptical regarding Kantian moral absolutism, and he thinks that the realm of faith should be conceived more autonomously than Kant concedes), but he does so in a way that is nevertheless true to the spirit of Kant's original critical philosophy because he applies the idea of regulativity to the realm of faith.[62] In fact, what appears clear from *Fear and Trembling* is that religion is not a set of dogmatic truths but should instead be approached as a way of life. This is definitely a very Kantian approach.[63] However, for Kierkegaard, a religious way of life cannot merely adopt ethical normativity. Rather, it needs its own regulativity.

Viewing Abraham's willingness to sacrifice Isaac as a regulative exemplar solves the *reality of sacrifice* problem: his act should not be read literally or metaphorically but should be considered regulatively. When Johannes devotes himself to describing the knight of faith whom it would be possible to encounter today, he invokes the image of a taxman whose behavior is (externally) very ordinary. None of his actions is as extreme as that of preparing to sacrifice one's own son. As Mooney puts it, "If the knight can be Abraham or a serving maid or a shopman, then we are forced away from reading the story as advocating sacrifice on demand."[64] On this basis, Mooney concludes that "to be a knight of faith is to have had one's soul tempered through ordeals."[65] My conclusion is that *Fear and Trembling* asks us to consider some examples, such as the *Akedah*, as regulative ideas on which to model our theonomous duties.

One question still needs to be examined. We have said that Abraham's willingness to sacrifice Isaac and any other violent and unethical action of that sort is not a necessary requirement for faith. These actions serve mostly as regulative ideas. However, in certain extreme cases in which the theonomous duty is not simply *not dependent* on ethical duties but in fact actually runs contrary to ethics (as in the *actual* case of Abraham), should a knight of faith *actually* be ready to sacrifice his or her own son? It seems that Johannes, Kierkegaard's fictional author (and indeed a character in his own piece), thinks so.[66] Interpreted in this way, the picture presented in *Fear and Trembling* would ultimately be incompatible with both Kant's and Hegel's philosophy. However, one should not forget that the text's epilogue tells a story in which some Dutch merchants dump a few loads at sea "in order to drive up the price" of spices during a time when the price is slack (FT, 107). Perhaps this is what Kierkegaard (via Johannes) is doing in *Fear and Trembling*: using an extreme story (Abraham's) to *force up* the price of faith. He emphasizes the necessity of regulative ideas regarding theonomous duties by "artificially raising the price of faith."[67] As I anticipated in the second section, I think that *Fear and Trembling* plays a preliminary and yet pivotal role in Kierkegaard's overall strategy, namely, in the pursuit of the philosophical goals that Kierkegaard wants to achieve. From the perspective of Johannes de Silentio (someone who is "outside faith"), sacrifice serves as an entry point to that "paradoxical religiousness" that represents the essence of Christianity—the position of the knight of faith. In *Fear and Trembling*, the "price of faith" is deliberately exaggerated, with the aim of reacting against the "veritable clearance sale" (FT, 3) in which faith is sold at a too cheap price. This is the reason why Johannes draws a strong distinction, and often contrasts, *ethical* behavior and *religious* behavior.

If the inner meaning of *Fear and Trembling* is religious regulativity (exemplified, in turn, by sacrifice), then the text can be regarded as developing the Kantian problems of formality and religion in an alternative direction to that of Hegel's absolute idealism. This solution offers three interrelated advantages and one significant drawback.

First, Kierkegaard's approach has the advantage of dealing with religious faith by trying to understand what it actually *is* rather than speculating on what it *should* be. As Agacinski puts it, "Kant's "pure rational faith' may well be genuinely pure; but in that case it can no longer be faith."[68] When forging his idea of religion, Kant inevitably makes it too abstract (something of which Hegel is also critical). Although Kant maintains that we need religious symbols to apply the principles of morality to experience, so that they can serve as models for our behavior, and he goes as far as presenting Christ as the prototype of a pure moral disposition, his approach to *religious* regulative ideals remains consistent with his philosophical agenda—the advancement of a "pure rational faith." As remarked in the context of our discussion of Kant's treatment of sacrifice, for him the idea of an omnipotent being sacrificing his absoluteness and divinity was absurd. Conversely, as it will be clear from an analysis of *Works of Love*, Christ's willingness to sacrifice himself in a kenotic fashion is precisely what Christians should imitate.

Second, and in line with this phenomenological approach, Kierkegaard's work in general and *Fear and Trembling* in particular have the advantage of claiming autonomy for the realm of religion. Kierkegaard wants faith to be more autonomous from ethics than Hegel typically concedes (or is usually *regarded* as conceding). If my interpretation of *Fear and Trembling* is correct, the core of Kierkegaard's message is precisely a notion of regulativity that can be applied to the religious realm (what I have called regulative contextualism).

Third, against Kant *and* Hegel, Kierkegaard affirms the need to emphasize the *personal* dimension of faith. Kierkegaard's claim in favor of the autonomy of the religious realm is intrinsically connected with the idea that faith is really meaningful only if it is conceived as a relationship of trust and love with a personal God. Although the concept of belief in a personal God as one of "trust" is not completely absent from Kant's philosophy,[69] Kant and (even more) Hegel tend to present God as an idea, and Christ as a symbol. And clearly, we can *rely* on an idea or a symbol, but we cannot *trust* them in the way we *trust* a person. *Fear and Trembling* emphasizes the need to think of the relationship to God as a personal relationship of trust. As Westphal puts it, "We are reminded that what is essential to love (and faith) is an element of passion that is neither reducible to nor deducible from any form of learning, the theoretical learning of the learned or the practical learning of the socialized."[70]

Because theonomous duties express a personal and unique relationship with God, we cannot expect Kierkegaard to provide a detailed description of what the knight of faith is *expected to do*. To use Abraham's willingness to sacrifice Isaac in a regulative manner is to adapt this notion to a particular situation or need and abandon the norms that result when they no longer fit the situation. It is this conception of regulativity that underlies Kierkegaard's preference for *exempla*. The knight of faith cannot be described in terms of action but can only be portrayed through exempla, as Nietzsche's overman. This comparison is not, I think, out of place. Both Kierkegaard's knight of faith *and* Nietzsche's overman refuse to depend on specific norms, and they adopt regulative principles (including the notion of sacrifice) that are not applied in the name of (ethical) values or according to customs or habits. They are guided by superior principles—a personal relationship with God for Kierkegaard and a responsibility toward the species for Nietzsche. This makes clear, however, the problematic aspect of Kierkegaard's solution.

Kierkegaard tries to answer the problem that Kant's philosophy was meant to address: namely, the need for some way to make moral and religious concepts applicable to the world. Hegel's solution to this problem lies in the dynamic of recognition and the notion of *Sittlichkeit*. However, Kierkegaard regards this solution as too reductive, and supports the idea of *faith* as a personal and absolute relationship to God. This faith is not irrational and is in fact governed by a regularity that makes use of exemplars, which in turn serve as models for religious behavior. If faith is a personal relationship, then this regularity must be *subjective* (and Kierkegaard's emphasis on subjectivity need not be stressed). However, it is precisely this subjectivity that constitutes the main problematic aspect of Kierkegaard's solution. Obviously, no issue exists if the *Akedah* is used only as a way to force up the price of faith, as previously suggested. But when we have excluded the recourse to recognition, subjectivity can definitely have dangerous consequences. Kierkegaard thinks that this is a worthwhile price to pay, but Hegel would certainly disagree. Kierkegaard is not concerned with the political implications of his use of the notion of sacrifice, but it could be argued that he should be. Accepting the idea of a *personal* and *subjective* regularity effectively means to exclude human actions from the control of reason (both the "pure" Kantian reason and the "social" Hegelian reason), and to legitimate (at least potentially) any action done in the name of a personal relationship with God. However, Kierkegaard's approach and his emphasis on the symbolic and regulative meaning of religious notions can be regarded as a useful corrective to Hegel's recognition approach. As it is presented in *Fear and Trembling*, the story of Abraham shows how sacrifice can be used as a regulative notion when dealing with *theonomous* duties. The notion of sacrifice cannot be exhaustively explained on ethical grounds, as it features an irreducible *religious* content. However, the adaptation of this notion to specific situations requires trust in God and in the divine grace; and Johannes cannot be explicit on this, as he does not have faith.

Therefore, the view of sacrifice presented in *Fear and Trembling* is not exhaustively representative of Kierkegaard's view as a whole. Although humble self-denial is alluded to in *Fear and Trembling* with respect to Abraham's disposition in reply to God's command as well as in the brief discussion of sin, the *kenotic* aspect of sacrifice, which is prominent in other works such as *Works of Love*, does not come across explicitly in Johannes's analysis of the *Akedah*. This is, after all, consistent with the premises: Johannes does not have faith, and therefore he is not able to grasp the importance of this aspect. From this angle, *Fear and Trembling* should be regarded as a preliminary work that clears the way for a more comprehensive treatment of sacrifice as a regulative notion. But this treatment would not be possible without the reestablishment of religion as based upon trust and grace.

Kierkegaard's Kenotic Sacrifice

Kierkegaard's emphasis on sacrifice and kenotic love can be regarded as his peculiar attempt to respond to the Kantian paradox (as diagnosed by Pinkard). In order to contextualize Kierkegaard's response, however, let us take a step back to consider the possible solutions to the Kantian paradox as well as Kierkegaard's response to it.

The Kantian paradox paves the way for four possible developments. First, the subject is regarded as the source, in itself, of norms—playing, so to speak, the role of God (e.g., as happens with Fichte and left Hegelians such as Feuerbach). Second, the very idea of norms is put into question, as the discovery that norms are human or culturally dependent leads to the relativistic and skeptic conclusion that 'all is permitted' (as happens with Nietzsche). The third solution is represented by Hegel's absolute idealism, according to which norms "are afforded a type of necessity" that "is part of the status they have *as* norms."[71] The fourth strategy is, obviously, the return to the idea of God as the source of norms: man is not the author of moral laws—God is.

Kierkegaard embraces the fourth strategy. There is no doubt that for him God is the ultimate source of morality. This has often led to Kierkegaard being regarded as a supporter of a divine-command ethics. This traditional view is now often rejected (or at least presented in a nontraditional way) in regard to *Fear and Trembling*; but in *Fear and Trembling* "first ethics" is at issue, whereas second, or "Christian" ethics (the ethics which turns particularly on the consciousness of sin) is fully developed in *Works of Love*. It is generally taken as indisputable that the divine command plays a role in Christian, ethics. However, some specifications are necessary. The divine command for Kierkegaard is not an ethical rule to be applied to traditional ethical problems;[72] rather, it is limited to the core of Christian ethics—that is, the *duty to love*. Kierkegaard defends the claim that "to love is a duty" despite the fact that he himself admits that the claim is "contradictory" (WL, 24). Here Kierkegaard is probably referring to Kant's argument that there cannot be a duty to love, because this would be a contradiction.[73] Kant considers love as a feeling (which therefore cannot be commanded), whereas Kierkegaard's love is a different kind of love—the love of one's neighbor that is required of a Christian. Indeed, Christian love is a "commanded love" (WL, 19) because the love of one's neighbor that is required of Christians is unnatural for humans and thus needs to be made into a duty.[74] As Quinn remarks, "For Kierkegaard, as for Kant, the moral life is at its best a progress from bad to better":[75] because the love of one's neighbor is unnatural, we need the divine command to initially perform works of love. However, this does not make Kierkegaard's second ethics a "divine-command theory" in the traditional sense. The duty to love is *formal* in a Kantian sense, in the same way the categorical imperative is formal: it does not tell us *what* we must do (that is, it does not *command* a specific choice in an ethical situation), but *how* we must do what we do (that is, it *commands* us to act only in accordance with this principle).

Further evidence that the conceptual framework adopted by Kierkegaard here is, structurally at least, a Kantian one, is provided by the fact that Kierkegaard inevitably deals with the same struggle that Kant faced as a consequence of the formality of his ethics—that is, the need for some way of making moral concepts applicable to the world. Most notably, the answers provided by the two philosophers are very similar. For Kant, moral laws need to be symbolized: religious symbols, therefore, must be used to apply the principles of practical reason to experience, so that they can serve as models for our behavior and play a regulative role in the application of moral ideas to the world (RGV, 6:65/107). The religious symbol *par excellence* is identified by Kant in the figure of Christ, "the Master of the Gospels." Christ represents the *prototype* of a pure moral disposition, one willing to undergo the greatest sacrifice (sacrifice until death) to be morally perfect.

That Kierkegaard thinks that Christian ethics is actually possible only if one takes Christ as his model to be followed in concrete, everyday life, is evident from a wide range of passages. In the years following the writing of *Works of Love* (1847), Kierkegaard increasingly emphasizes the necessity for a Christian to take seriously Christ as his or her concrete model. In *Practice in Christianity*, published in 1850, Kierkegaard's pseudonymous author

Anti-Climacus says that "Christ's life here on earth is the paradigm; I and every Christian are to strive to model our lives in likeness to it."[76] And later on he remarks that Christ came into the world with the purpose "of being the *prototype*, of leaving footprints for the person who wanted to join him, who then might become an imitator."[77]

This emphasis is not in itself surprising—after all, the "imitation of Christ" represents an ancient and important tradition in Christian ethics. What is particularly notable, however, is that Christ is recommended as a model—indeed, as the *prototype*—of that kenotic attitude of sacrifice to which every Christian is called. "Christ freely willed to be the lowly one," Anti-Climacus says, "and although his purpose was to save mankind, yet he also wanted to express what the truth would have to suffer and what the truth must suffer in every generation."[78] As Quinn comments, this means that "anyone who becomes a contemporary of Christ . . . will have to come to grips with Christ in his lowliness and abasement."[79] And some entries in the *Journal* show that Kierkegaard agrees with his pseudonymous author. Christ is "the prototype" precisely because "he was a human being like everybody else"; he also "constitutes the eternal strenuousness in what it means to be a human being."[80] In short, Kierkegaard sees Christ as a tangible model for our earthly behavior,[81] and as the exemplar in performing the kenotic sacrifice that is required of a Christian. This is consistent with *Works of Love*, where Christ's self-sacrifice is indicated as the most important content of imitation: "He sought his own *by giving himself* for all *so that they might be like him* in what was his own, in sacrificial giving of himself" (WL, 264; emphasis added). In other words, the core of Christian ethics consists in the duty to imitate Christ and give ourselves up in sacrifice. This claim is obviously still vague, as by the word *sacrifice* a variety of actions and behaviors might be signified. And in fact, a significant portion of *Works of Love* is devoted to answer this question—namely, what is the sacrifice to which a Christian is called?

In the next section, I will analyze the notion of sacrifice that emerges from *Works of Love*, identifying its characteristic features. This analysis aims to determine if the sacrificial, or kenotic ethics advanced by Kierkegaard is effectively livable. It also serves to pave the way for a comparison with Hegel's notion of sacrifice in the following section.

Features of Kenotic Sacrifice

Works of Love can be considered in its entirety as a progressive clarification *via negationis* of the real kenotic sacrifice. In other words, Kierkegaard keeps introducing newer and newer distinctions and specifications and, by stressing what the true sacrifice *is not*, provides the reader with a "distillation" of the kenotic sacrifice, or (considering the difficulties implied in the conceptual presentation of such a dynamic) a good approximation of it.

The first and most basic distinction is that between the alleged "sacrifices" implied in relationships of erotic love and friendship, and the real kenotic sacrifice that is required of a Christian. The former "sacrifices" are only inappropriately or improperly called this way, as in reality they derive from a union or "alliance" in selfishness. Kierkegaard writes:

> What the world honors and loves under the name of love is an alliance in self-love. The alliance also requires sacrifice and devotion on the part of the one it will call loving; it requires that he sacrifice a portion of his own self-love in order to hold together in the united self-love, and it requires that he sacrifice the God-relationship in order to hold together in a worldly way with the alliance that excludes God or at most takes him along for the sake of appearance. By love, however, God understands self-sacrificing love in the divine sense, the self-sacrificing love that sacrifices everything in order to make room for God, even if the heavy sacrifice became even heavier because no one understood it, something that in another sense belongs to true sacrifice, inasmuch as the sacrifice that people understand has its reward, after all, in popular approval and to that extent is not true sacrifice, which must unconditionally be without reward. (WL, 119–120)

In this passage, some fundamental features of kenotic sacrifice appear clearly. Love, as God understands it, is a love that, Kierkegaard says, is willing to sacrifice everything *without reward*. Additionally, the specification that people *understand* the "improper" sacrifice seems to suggest that, conversely, nobody will understand those who perform the "authentic" kenotic sacrifice. The sacrifices implied in the relationship of erotic love and friendship seem to maintain a reasonableness that is absent in the context of kenotic sacrifice. The reasonableness is first of all represented by the presence of a *limit*. "Erotic love and friendship," Kierkegaard writes, "have a limit; they can give up all things for the other's distinctiveness but not themselves, love and friendship, for the other's distinctiveness" (WL, 273). Conversely, the sacrificing love is willing to make every sacrifice, for "it does not seek its own" (WL, 265–278).

So far we have been told that the real kenotic sacrifice implies a willingness to sacrifice everything without getting anything in exchange. However, the definition of sacrifice is still vague. What does Kierkegaard mean by "everything"? How radical is this sacrifice supposed to be? Should it be the sacrifice of one's life? Or an everlasting sacrifice of one's identity, in the form of self-denial? What does kenotic sacrifice mean, *in concreto*?

In order to answer this question, it is useful to refer to the taxonomy of kenotic sacrifice provided by Coakley[82] and amended by Groenhout,[83] and already used, in the context of Kierkegaard studies, by Lippitt.[84] Lippitt broadly agrees with Groenhout's analysis, and seems to consider both self-giving and self-emptying as authentic forms of kenosis of the kind recommended by Kierkegaard in *Works of Love*—although self-emptying is clearly indicated as the highest form of kenosis.[85]

Let us assume both Groenhout's sliding scale, and Lippitt's identification of self-emptying (as described by Groenhout) as the highest form of kenosis. So far, we also know that Christ's kenotic love is the model of the sacrifice to which a Christian is called. On the basis of *Works of Love*, what are the main characteristics of this kenotic sacrifice?

The first characteristic is, no doubt, *gratuitousness*—that is, the absence of any reward. Kierkegaard says that explicitly: "The inwardness of love must be self-sacrificing and therefore without the requirement of any reward" (WL, 130). This obviously distinguishes proper sacrifice from all those inauthentic sacrifices that are, in fact, only masked investments, as they hide expectations for rewards of some kind.

Second, the object of sacrifice must be something essential to the subject—that is, something that *constitutes* the subject—as happens with Christ's renunciation of his divinity in the incarnation. This is the feature grasped by Groenhout with her account of self-giving.

The third characteristic of kenotic sacrifice represents the closest point of connection with sacrifice as it is presented in *Fear and Trembling*: it is the *non-communicability* of the act. Here the difference between the one who makes sacrifices for the sake of erotic love or friendship and who performs an authentic kenotic sacrifice of love is similar to the difference between the knight of infinite resignation and the knight of faith. Kierkegaard writes: "One is willing to sacrifice this or that and everything, but one still hopes to be understood and thereby to remain in a connectedness of meaning with people, who must acknowledge one's sacrifices and rejoice in them. One is willing to forsake everything, but one still does not expect as a result to become forsaken by language and people's understanding" (WL, 131). Being an unnatural act, and the result of the fellowship of Christ's model, kenotic sacrifice is not expressible or explainable via rational thought or words:

those who perform a sacrifice of love cannot hope to be understood. The kenotic sacrifice is even more radical than Abraham's sacrifice, as Johannes de Silentio thinks that Abraham believed that he will eventually get Isaac back, whereas in *Works of Love* the absence of *any* reward is, as we have seen, the most fundamental characteristic of an authentic sacrifice. It is precisely this gratuitousness that makes the kenotic sacrifice not understandable, and which leads the performer to be considered as foolish. Kierkegaard writes: "the merely human idea of self-denial is this: give up your self-loving desires, cravings, and plans—then you will be esteemed and honored and loved as righteous and wise," whereas "the Christian idea of self-denial is: give up your self-loving desires and cravings, give up your self-seeking plans and purposes so that you truly work unselfishly *for the good*—and then, for that very reason, put up with being abominated almost as a criminal, insulted and ridiculed" (WL, 194; emphasis added).[86] This passage also provides another important specification: it clarifies that—to use Lippitt's words—"proper self-sacrifice is not self-sacrifice for its own sake, but rather needs to be *oriented towards the good*."[87] That is to say, the absolute gratuitousness of kenotic sacrifice does not mean the absence of any teleological orientation. Quite the opposite—kenotic sacrifice must be done "for the good." I will come back to this important issue later on.

The fourth characteristic of kenotic sacrifice is *the absence of any consciousness and recognition* of giving up and sacrificing—in Kierkegaard's words, one must be able to "make himself anonymous, must magnanimously will to annihilate himself" (WL, 276). This self-annihilation does not mean a destruction of the self; it means that the giver must somehow be unconscious of the greatness of his act—otherwise, the greatness might become the main motive for the act itself, which conversely must be gratuitous and made only *for the good*.

In short, for a sacrifice to be a real kenotic sacrifice, it must be a *gratuitous* (that is, implying no reward), *incommunicable*, and even *unconscious* surrender of something essential to the giver. The model of this sacrifice is Christ: "By love," Kierkegaard writes, "God understands self-sacrificing love in the divine sense, the self-sacrificing love that sacrifices everything in order to make room for God" (WL, 119–120).

These characteristics are *regulative* features of the kenotic sacrifice (once again, they do not tell us *what* sacrifice we must do, but *how* we must do the sacrifice that we do). Therefore, Kierkegaard provides the reader with an account of the kenotic sacrifice through two metaphors.

The first metaphor is that of an "infinite debt." The main idea here is that we are always in debt to others. Therefore, the sacrifice that we do, not only must not imply the expectation of any reward, but must also be conceived as something *due* to others. Unfortunately, rather than being just explanatory, this metaphor exposes the notion of kenotic sacrifice to a notable objection. In fact, if our debt to others is virtually "infinite," does this mean that we should not stop anywhere, up to complete self-annihilation? Is Kierkegaard invoking sacrifice without limits? As Ferreira remarks,[88] this is a version of what Outka calls the "blank-check objection," namely, the question of whether there is "any way to differentiate between attention to another's needs and submission to his exploitation."[89] This is a real risk. However, both Ferreira's and Lippitt's analyses have showed that Kierkegaard is very aware of this risk, and that in fact he sets, if not limits, at least *restrictions* or *borders* for the kenotic sacrifice. The first restriction, grasped by both Ferreira and Lippitt, is the recognition of the value of the self. God commands you to love another person as yourself, not *more* than yourself. Second, "[s]acrifice and self-denial are not a goal in themselves but the substance of forgetting one's own in loving the other."[90] Third, and most importantly for our purposes, although Kierkegaard preserves the regulative structure of Kant's practical philosophy, he nevertheless distances himself from Kant by not putting his "imperative" in an abstract, impersonal way. Consider the second formulation of Kant's categorical imperative: "Act in such a way that you treat humanity, whether in your own person or in the person of any other, always at the same time as an end and never merely as a means to an end." This is valid for *me*, for *you*, and for *everybody*. In a hypothetical Kantian community, if I feel that you are not treating me as an end, I might invoke the categorical imperative—you *must* treat me as an end, as I treat you as an end. Conversely, for Kierkegaard I can only say that *I* must sacrifice *myself* for you, but I cannot *demand* the same from you, because sacrifice must be a voluntary, gratuitous act—otherwise, it is not real sacrifice.

As already outlined in the previous section, the distance between Kant and Kierkegaard here concerns the *source of norms*. For Kant, the human being is the source of moral laws; natural inclinations can be counteracted only by human reason and will. Kierkegaard thinks that this is not enough to reach the required kenotic sacrifice: the Christian, Kierkegaard says, needs God as "the middle term" to effectively love the neighbor (WL, 57–58). In other words, we need divine grace to bridge what Hare calls the "moral gap."

The second metaphor that Kierkegaard employs to provide an account of the kenotic sacrifice is peculiarly connected with the fourth characteristic identified above, namely, the absence of any consciousness and recognition of one's sacrifice. The metaphor is a bizarre, but brilliant one: the dash (—). The example Kierkegaard uses is the following: "This person is standing by himself—through my help" (WL, 275). This sentence is effectively the negation, Kierkegaard says, of an authentic sacrifice. In fact, what follows the dash shows a self-awareness, or self-recognition, of one's sacrifice. However, in kenotic sacrifice the main concern must be the other; this specification effectively nullifies the sacrifice. The real kenotic sacrifice is that which is expressed by the first half of the sentence alone. In Kierkegaard's words: "He is standing by himself—that is the highest; he is standing by himself—more you do not see" (WL, 275). This metaphor is particularly relevant for our purpose, as it represents—as I am going to show—at the same time the closest and the farthest point of connection between Kierkegaard and Hegel.

Kierkegaard, Hegel, and Sacrifice

In the chapter on Hegel, some features of the Hegelian notion of sacrifice have been identified. Sacrifice, as it is presented in the *Phenomenology of Spirit*, has three fundamental features. First, it has to be performed *consciously*. Second, it needs to be considered as a selfless sacrifice that *does not expect anything in return*. Third, its genuineness (its being a real and actual sacrifice) depends on its capacity to be effective (to reach its proposed goal) and unselfish (to not *really* expect anything in return, beyond any possible self-deception). We can speak of a genuine sacrifice only when the object of sacrifice is something *essential* to the subject, that is, something that constitutes the subject, as happens with Christ's renunciation of his divine absoluteness.

Now, consider the "forgiveness and reconciliation" episode in the *Phenomenology of Spirit* (PG, 665–671/403–409). What the judgmental consciousness has to give up in the act of mutual concession and forgiveness is the immediate identification with the absoluteness of God's law. Here one can appreciate the distance between Kant and Hegel: while Kant invited the moral agent to listen to moral commands *as if* they were spoken by the voice of God (which is Kant's way to respond to the paradox diagnosed by Pinkard), and thus invoked the identification with the absoluteness of God's law, Hegel goes in the opposite direction. This is even more evident when one considers Hegel's emphasis on the figure of Christ: God *recognizes* humanity by renouncing his own absoluteness and accepting his continuity with humanity, and he does so through the incarnation of Christ. What is peculiar to the sacrifice of Christ is the fact that the *subject* sacrifices something *essential* to himself—that is, something that *constitutes* the subject.

Now, compare Hegel and Kierkegaard on sacrifice. In the previous section, we identified four characteristics of sacrifice as it is described in *Works of Love*. The first is gratuitousness—sacrifice must not imply any reward. As it is clear from the brief outline above, Kierkegaard and Hegel are in agreement on this point. This in itself might not be particularly surprising: after all, the agent should not expect any return (otherwise, its act would not be a sacrifice at all, but rather an *investment*). However, there is another important similarity between the two conceptions. A real kenotic sacrifice, Kierkegaard says, must be the surrender of something *essential* to the giver (it is the second characteristic identified in the previous section). Again, Kierkegaard and Hegel are in perfect agreement: even for Hegel, in fact, we can speak of a genuine sacrifice only when that which is sacrificed is something *essential* to the subject. And significantly, even for Hegel the prototype of a genuine sacrifice is Christ's renunciation of his divine absoluteness.

The fourth characteristic previously identified for Kierkegaard's notion of kenotic sacrifice—non-communicability—is definitely more problematic than the first two. On one hand, Hegel would probably subscribe a certain difficulty of communication of a real kenotic sacrifice, but just because a real kenotic sacrifice is such, for Hegel, only *from the point of view of the Spirit*. Only a more developed form of consciousness might be able to grasp a kenotic sacrifice: in this sense, we might say that the consciousness in a specific phenomenological moment cannot properly "communicate" its sacrifice. On the other hand, however, Kierkegaard's emphasis on the non-communicability of sacrifice is strictly connected with the presence of God as the middle term of sacrificial love: kenotic sacrifice cannot be, strictly speaking, "understood," because it is, like faith, the product of a direct, "immediate" relationship between God and the subject. For Hegel, the middle term is rather represented by the necessity of recognition: the breaking of the judge's hard heart represents the necessity of giving up one's absoluteness in front of the right to recognition through forgiveness (represented by the beautiful soul). What makes the sacrifice of the hard-hearted judge a particularly genuine and effective form of sacrifice is, for Hegel, the fact that, unlike what happens in other phenomenological stages, this sacrifice is a *conscious* giving up. This obviously leads to the discussion of the fourth characteristic identified for Kierkegaard's kenotic sacrifice in the previous section—namely, *the absence of any consciousness and recognition* of giving up and sacrificing. Here we can really appreciate the distance that separates Kierkegaard from Hegel.

Hegel explicitly says that love is "a *self-conscious* activity, the supreme surrender [of oneself] in the other" (Rel, 27)—in other words, it is a full acceptance of otherness. On a superficial reading, it might be easy to set Kierkegaard's emphasis on *love* against Hegel's emphasis on *reason*. But this would be a mistake. As it is evident from the passage mentioned above, Hegel does not underestimate the relevance of love in intersubjective relationships. He maintains, however, that the more conscious sacrificial love is, the more effective it is. Hegel wants love *and* reason; it could not be otherwise, because in his view reason is the only medium that humans can use. Conversely, Kierkegaard wants love *alone*, because any rational interference, or "conceptual mediation," might contaminate the purity of the immediate relationship with God. This effectively marks the difference between Hegel's and Kierkegaard's conceptions of sacrifice: while for Kierkegaard one has to empty oneself to make room for God—and, through God, make room for others—, for Hegel one has to develop the self in such a way that the kenotic withdrawal eventually appears as the most adequate strategy to further develop one's consciousness. As a consequence, our disposition towards kenotic sacrifice is for Hegel a matter of *responsibility*, whereas for Kierkegaard it is a matter of *divine grace*.

The distance that separates Hegel and Kierkegaard also marks, paradoxically, a similarity in their rejection of Kant's practical philosophy. In fact, they both reject the Kantian identification of the "voice of morality" with God's law, but they do so for very different reasons. Kierkegaard opposes the Kantian approach because the identification of something "human," such as the "voice of morality," with God sounds like a blasphemy. On the contrary, Hegel opposes the Kantian approach because the identification with the divine absoluteness—the God's-eye view—is precisely what has to be given up to promote forgiveness and reconciliation—in a word, *recognition*.

The topic of recognition represents another important factor in the comparison between Hegel and Kierkegaard on sacrifice. It has been said that both Hegel and Kierkegaard agree that sacrifice must be gratuitous—that is, it must not imply any reward. For Hegel, however, *from the point of view of the (absolute) spirit*, the real and genuine sacrifice ultimately leads to a gain from giving up one's absoluteness: it *displays* the process of recognition (but, once more, this gain can appear in all its clarity only *retrospectively*).

Hence, the following questions arise: Is Kierkegaard's ethic an ethic of sacrifice for its own sake? And if it is not, what is the sacrifice's ultimate goal?

Kierkegaard's Sacrifice: An Alternative to Hegel?

An in-depth reading of *Works of Love* is sufficient to adequately show that Kierkegaard's ethic is *not* an ethic of sacrifice for its own sake. Kierkegaard's kenotic sacrifice is *neither* the sacrifice suggested by Solger (that sacrifice which is, in itself, the "highest token of our superior destination"), *nor* the sacrifice advanced by Georges Bataille—namely, sacrifice as pure expenditure (*dépense*). Kierkegaard is explicit on this point. He writes that "the Christian idea of self-denial is: give up your self-loving desires and cravings, give up your self-seeking plans and purposes so that you truly work unselfishly *for the good*" (WL, 194; emphasis added). Thus, sacrifice *has* a purpose. The important question is: *what is "the good"*? Kierkegaard does not provide an explicit answer to this question. Is it love, maybe? Clearly, it is not erotic love or friendship we are talking about. Erotic love and friendship are *not* true love, Kierkegaard argues, but only "preference": I *isolate* a specific individual from the rest of humanity, and I make him or her the target of *my* desires, cravings, passions, etc. Therefore, this individual becomes "the *other self,* the *other I*" (WL, 53). In this kind of relationship, I do not really *recognize* another person as such, but I just *relate to myself* through another person.

Ferreira is right when he states that "Kierkegaard's ethic is not an ethic of sacrifice for its own sake but of the necessary sacrifice that is asked of us as we seek to promote forgiveness and reconciliation and as we seek to build up love in others."[91] The emphasis Kierkegaard puts on these topics in the second series of deliberations (especially 2:V, "Love Hides a Multitude of Sins," and 2:VI, "Love Abides") seems to confirm that forgiveness and reconciliation are central aspects of "the good." In fact, in order to "forgive" the other and be "reconciled" with him (something that clearly presupposes that some offence or hurting have been done), I need to recognize him as a genuine "other," and not as a mere reflection of myself. The one who forgives and the one who is forgiven are *distinct* but *equal* at the same time: *distinct*, because they mutually recognize each other as persons; and *equal*, because the one who forgives acknowledges the fact that nobody is exempt from the need of forgiveness, because—to quote *Either Or*—"Before God, we are always in the wrong."[92] God is, once again, the "middle term" that allows one to recognize the other as an authentic "other" and, at the same time, to recognize himself and the other as "equal."[93] According to Kierkegaard, this recognition is not possible without *faith in God*, because God is the ultimate *source* of this love.

As a conclusion of our survey on Kierkegaard's notion of sacrifice, it is fruitful to come back to the "Kantian paradox." For Kant, human reason is the source of norms, but in order to avoid the paradox of being bound by laws of which one is also the author, the moral agent is invited to listen to moral commands *as if* they were spoken by the voice of God. For Hegel too, human reason is the source of norms—not *individual* reason (the "moral law within me," according to Kant's famous expression), but *social* reason. The moral agent is always historically and geographically located: as such, he cannot secure any "bindingness" for the moral law, and therefore needs the *recognition* of another agent of it.[94] However, recognition always implies (as it is shown in the "forgiveness and reconciliation" episode) kenotic sacrifice, insofar as it implies the renunciation of one's absoluteness to "make room" for the other.

For Kierkegaard, the ultimate source of norms is God. Forgiveness, reconciliation and—most importantly—real sacrifice (in a word, the "recognitive structure" of *Works of Love*) are not possible without the Christian willingness to obey God's command.[95] Therefore, *faith*, and not *reason*, is the faculty that should guide us in our life. Without God we are completely powerless. In fact, Garff has formulated the phrase "will to powerlessness" to describe Kierkegaard's drive in *Works of Love*.[96] This definition is particularly appropriate in the context of a discussion of Kierkegaard's philosophy of sacrifice as a way to respond to the Kantian paradox. In front of Hegel's strategy of relying on *social* reason, Kierkegaard reacted by stressing human impotence and the Christian will to rely on God alone. However, the phrase "will to powerlessness" immediately recalls another phrase: Nietzsche's "will to power." Nietzsche's account of sacrifice will be considered in the next chapter. For now, it is important to remark that for Nietzsche there is no other source of norms than man himself; more specifically, not human reason, but human *will*: the will to power. Kierkegaard and Nietzsche definitely have something in common: the distrust of reason. They do not think that reason—neither Kant's universal reason, nor Hegel's social reason—can be effective in grounding norms. Therefore, they place the source of norms in something external to reason: Kierkegaard in God, and Nietzsche in human will.

From this angle, it is not difficult to see Kant's shadow behind them both. Kant invited the human being, who is the author of the moral law, to listen to moral commands *as if* they were spoken by the voice of God. Kierkegaard emphasizes the second part of Kant's claim (to the detriment of the first part of the claim), by maintaining that it is *really* the voice of God that gives us the most important commands—namely, the commands of love and sacrifice. Conversely, Nietzsche develops the first part of Kant's claim by stressing that man is the sole author of the moral law, and he completely dismisses the second part of the claim. Consistently, Kierkegaard relies on faith, whereas Nietzsche relies on human will. However, it is already possible to notice a possible weak point in Nietzsche's strategy. As Lippitt writes, "if, as Nietzsche claims, our tests are 'taken before ourselves and before no other judge' (JGB, 241) how, if I am my own examiner, can I be sure that I won't let myself cheat?."[97]

By making God the source of the law of love and sacrifice, Kierkegaard apparently builds his strategy on more solid grounds; and yet, God's voice always needs to be interpreted and applied. Kierkegaard claims that loving is "in love of the truth and of humanity to will to make every sacrifice in order to proclaim the truth, and, on the other hand, to will not to sacrifice the least bit of truth" (WL, 366). The point is that, as Løgstrup comments, this reference to the truth is not particularly helpful in explaining what we should do.[98] It might be argued that, for Kierkegaard, Christian truth does not need to be *understood*, but *lived*; and for this purpose, Kierkegaard suggests to use the actual relationships and experiences of Christ and his disciples as tangible models for behavior. This strategy is, after all, not inherently different from Nietzsche's strategy—the overman is not *described* by Nietzsche but only *portrayed* through exempla.[99] Apparently, Kierkegaard and Nietzsche are not able to provide a more developed answer to the problem that Kant's philosophy was meant to answer: that is, the need for some way of making moral concepts applicable to the world. Eventually, their strategy remains within the lines traced by Kant's *regulative* use of (aesthetic or religious) symbols to apply the pure principles of practical reason to experience, so that they can serve as models for human behavior.

Unsurprisingly, Hegel remains the most powerful alternative to Kierkegaard. As shown through this brief analysis, their respective accounts of kenotic sacrifice have more in common than expected, and they present striking similarities. Hegel and Kierkegaard both realize the importance of kenotic sacrifice (the withdrawal, the "giving up" of oneself to "make room" for the other) for forgiveness, reconciliation, and mutual recognition. They differ in the choice of the faculty on which we should rely: (social) reason for Hegel; faith for Kierkegaard.

On the one hand, Kierkegaard certainly has the merit of having called attention to the role of (sacrificial) love in the definition of the self—the self is constituted in the authentic recognition with the other *as other*, and this is possible only through a withdrawal of the self (WL, 264). He also has the merit of having explicitly emphasized the concreteness of this sacrifice and, through examples, its presence and relevance in everyday life. On the other hand, by stressing the necessity of relying on faith, he has restricted the access to kenotic sacrifice to Christians alone. Furthermore, as already mentioned, laws (even the law of God) always need to be interpreted; and once one has rejected the judging role of (social) reason, every interpretation becomes (in principle, at least) legitimate.

5

Nietzsche

The Sacrifice of the Overman

Three Meanings of Sacrifice

It is possible to identify three meanings of the notion of sacrifice in Nietzsche's thought. Since sacrifice is a human practice, its meaning depends on the moral system within which it is performed. In other words, once Nietzsche's genealogical method is applied to morality, the notion of sacrifice assumes different meanings for each system, that of master morality and slave morality, but also for the breakdown of all moral systems under nihilism.

A clear overview of this threefold account can be found in *Beyond Good and Evil*:

> There is a great ladder of religious cruelty with many rungs; but three of them are the most important. *At one time* one sacrificed human beings to one's god, perhaps precisely those human beings one loved best—the sacrifice of the firstborn present in all prehistoric religions belongs here, as does the sacrifice of the Emperor Tiberius in the Mithras grotto on the isle of Capri, that most horrible of all Roman anachronisms. *Then*, in the moral epoch of mankind, one sacrificed to one's god the strongest instincts one possessed, one's "nature"; the joy of *this* festival glitters in the cruel glance of the ascetic, the inspired "anti-naturalist." *Finally*: What was left to be sacrificed? Did one not finally have to sacrifice everything comforting, holy, healing, all hope, all faith in a concealed harmony, in a future bliss and justice? Did one not have to sacrifice God himself and out of cruelty against oneself worship stone, stupidity, gravity, fate, nothingness? To sacrifice God for nothingness—this paradoxical mystery of the ultimate

act of cruelty was reserved for the generation which is even now arising: we all know something of it already. (JGB, 55; my italics)[1]

Therefore, it is appropriate to analyze the meaning of the notion of sacrifice in master morality, slave morality, and in the age of nihilism. Let us start with sacrifice in master morality.

In the *Second Essay* of *On the Genealogy of Morality*, Nietzsche offers a detailed analysis of the genesis of the practice of sacrifice in primeval times. The practice derives from the "conviction that the species [*Geschlecht*] exists only because of the sacrifices [*Opfer*] and deeds of the forefathers" (GM, II 19).[2] Thus, Nietzsche continues, the forefathers "have to be *paid back* with the sacrifices and deeds: people recognize an *indebtedness* [*Schuld*], which continually increases because these ancestors continue to exist as mighty spirits, giving the community new advantages and lending it some of their power." In these primordial times, sacrifices include "food in the crudest sense, [. . .] feasts, chapels, tributes, above all, obedience" and, from time to time, "a payment on a grand scale," like the "sacrifice of the first-born, for example, blood, human blood in any case." In the long run, the ancestors of the most powerful communities are eventually transfigured into gods. Nietzsche underlines how this primeval meaning of sacrifice remains the same during "the middle period in which the *noble* stocks [*die vornehmen Geschlechter*] developed."[3] "The middle period in which the noble stocks developed" is the age dominated by master morality.

The notion of sacrifice that stems from this morality system is twofold. From the primeval "barbarian" times, it inherits the idea of sacrifice as a tribute paid to the ancestors (now transfigured into gods), that is, the sacrifice of the "best-loved." As Nietzsche explains, "a payment on a grand scale" is felt as necessary from time to time. The more loved the "object" is, the more valuable (and appreciated by gods) the sacrifice will be (JGB, 55). In addition, through the self-generated idea of "good," nobles develop the sacrifice of the weak ones, that is, the sacrifice of the slaves. According to Nietzsche, the noble accepts the fact of his egoism without question (JGB, 265): "the essential thing" in a healthy nobility is that it "accepts with a good conscience the sacrifice [*Opfer*] of innumerable men who *for its sake* have to be suppressed and reduced to imperfect men, to slaves and instruments" (JGB, 258). Whereas the sacrifice of the best-loved is an intentional *action*, the sacrifice of the slaves is a *consequence* of the general noble activity. The well-being of slaves and even their lives are sacrificed by the masters. The harm caused to the slaves is mere consequence of actions, since they are not perceived as proper sacrifices by the masters. A slave is anyone who is perceived by masters as "lowly, low-minded, common and plebeian," that is, as opposite to what is noble. Nobles are simply indifferent to their destiny.[4] However, these actions, obviously harmful to the slaves, are indeed seen as sacrifices by those who are sacrificed—namely, slaves themselves.[5] And their picture of sacrifice results from the reversal of values, which leads to slave morality.

The two forms of sacrifice within master morality have the same origin. They arose from spontaneity, from the affirmation of the self and from the aspiration for ruling. In *The Will to Power*, Nietzsche writes:

> It is richness in personality, abundance in oneself, overflowing and bestowing, instinctive good health and affirmation of oneself, that produce great sacrifice and great love: it is strong and godlike selfhood from which these affects grow, just as surely as do the desire to become master, encroachment, the inner certainty of having a right to everything. What according to common ideas are opposite dispositions are rather *one* disposition. (WM, 388; cf. 10[128] 12.530)[6]

Both the forms of sacrifice within master morality originate from "instinctive good health." As Nietzsche writes: "In the foreground stands the feeling of plenitude, of power which seeks to overflow, the happiness of high tension" (JGB, 260).[7] Hence, there is no wickedness in the attitude of the masters, but only the innocence with which "large birds of prey" carry off little lambs. They have no *ressentiment* in them. This incapacity to hate others is a distinctive feature of the master type and originates from his "abundance in himself" (GM, I 10).

Therefore, in master morality sacrifice means both the sacrifice of the best-loved as well as the sacrifice of the weak ones. And since for Nietzsche the masters represent "the whole love of the earthly and of dominion over the earth" (JGB, 62 5.82), this implies that the sacrifices they perform come under the sign of affirmation.

If this was the "original" notion of sacrifice, "How," Nietzsche wonders, "was one able so to transform these instincts that man thought valuable that which was directed against his self? When he sacrificed his self to another self" (WM, 388; cf. 10[128] 12.530).

Nietzsche's answer is that master morality originally includes not only the ethics of warriors, but also that of the priests. The warrior is reflected in the virtues of body, the priest—in the virtues of spirit. "The priestly method of valuation," Nietzsche points out, "splits off from the chivalric-aristocratic method" and develops further into its opposite. This is *the slaves' revolt in morality* (GM, I 7).

The slaves' revolt in morality originates in *bad conscience*. Bad conscience is "a sickness" (GM, II 19) developed by the slaves as a consequence of their submissive condition. Oppressed by the masters, they can no longer express their instincts, so they turn their violence toward themselves. Hence, they develop an inner life and bad conscience (GM, II 17). The priests used their bad conscience to carry out their revenge against the warriors. In fact, the priests inevitably feel *ressentiment* against the warriors and, being unable to control the warriors in the battlefield, they develop a different *table of values*.

Within slave morality, everything is falsified and corrupted: death is interpreted as punishment, eternal life as a reward. The old noble notion of sacrifice originated from instinctive good health, from the "love of the earthly and of dominion over the earth." It was what led the master to bestow the best-loved and to have no pity toward the weak ones. But this old notion of sacrifice as sacrifice of others is no longer acceptable within slave morality. Thus, if the egoistic sacrifice of others is not regarded as "moral" anymore, another form of sacrifice (the *unegoistic* sacrifice) becomes possible due to the newly developed bad conscience. The slave turns the violence toward himself: he cannot sacrifice others anymore, but he can still sacrifice *himself*. Referring to the notions of *selflessness* (*Selbstlosigkeit*), *self-denial* (*Selbstverleugnung*) and *self-sacrifice* (*Selbstopferung*), Nietzsche writes:

> I do not doubt that we know one thing—what kind of pleasure it is which, from the start, the selfless, the self-denying, the self-sacrificing feel: this pleasure belongs to cruelty.—So much, for the time being, on the descent of the 'unegoistic' as a moral value and on the delineation of the ground on which this value has grown; only bad conscience, only the will to self-violation provides the precondition for the *value* of the unegoistic. (GM, II 18)

Bad conscience produces *ressentiment*, which is the driving force of slave morality, and *ressentiment* turns the original notion of sacrifice (of others) into self-sacrifice. A fundamental feature of self-sacrifice is the cruelty that emerges from *ressentiment*, a feeling completely foreign to master morality, which was substantially driven by spontaneity and by love for life. Conversely, slave morality is "hostile to life" (GM, III 11). All the violence that is not directed toward others is directed toward oneself and particularly against the healthy instincts once celebrated by master morality: victory, vigor, pleasure, fortune, beauty, abundance, improvement of selfhood, self-celebration, and sacrifice as *affirmation*. Within slave morality "an attempt is made to use power to block the sources of the power"; therefore "satisfaction is *looked for* and found in failure, decay, pain, misfortune, ugliness, voluntary deprivation, destruction of selfhood, self-flagellation and self-sacrifice" (GM, III 11).

Christianity is notoriously considered by Nietzsche as a powerful expression of slave morality. "Christianity's stroke of genius" is "God sacrificing himself for man's guilt [*Schuld*]" (GM, II 21).[8] And sacrifice is one of the main polemical targets of Nietzsche's violent criticism of Christianity. Nietzsche writes: "The Christian faith is from the beginning sacrifice: sacrifice of all freedom, all pride, all self-confidence of the spirit, at the same time enslavement and self-mockery, self-mutilation" (JGB, 45). For Nietzsche, Christian sacrifice is a masochistic self-sacrifice. It is an aberration of the original notion of sacrifice. Christianity preaches renunciation and humility and affirms the pointlessness of every sacrifice that is not this masochistic and degenerate self-sacrifice, which is the absolute negation of the original, regenerating and necessary sacrifice. It invites man to deny his own essence, because it arises from a denial of life. Nietzsche writes:

> Through Christianity, the individual was made so important, so absolute, that he could no longer be sacrificed: but the species endures only through human sacrifice [. . .] This universal love of men is in practice the preference for the suffering, underprivileged, degenerate: it has in fact lowered and weakened the strength, the responsibility, the lofty duty to sacrifice men. All that remains, according to the Christian scheme of values, is to sacrifice oneself: but this residue of human sacrifice that Christianity concedes and even advises has, from the standpoint of general breeding, no meaning at all. The prosperity of the species is unaffected by the self-sacrifice of this or that individual [. . .] Genuine charity demands sacrifice for the good of the species—it is hard, it is full of self-overcoming, because it needs human sacrifice. And this pseudo humaneness called Christianity wants it established that no one should be sacrificed. (WM, 246; cf. 15[110] 13.470–471)

The transformation of the sacrifice of the weak ones into self-sacrifice is regarded by Nietzsche as a very serious aspect in the reversal of values. In fact, the sacrifice of the weak ones contributed to the health of mankind, whereas slave morality worships the opposite values and, in doing so, jeopardizes the health of mankind.⁹ This is the reason why "[t]he feelings of devotion, self-sacrifice for one's neighbour, the entire morality of self-renunciation must be taken mercilessly to task and brought to court" (JGB, 33).

Therefore, in slave morality sacrifice is essentially self-sacrifice: sacrifice of one's own instincts and natural dispositions, that is, sacrifice of everything that is love of the earthy, of health and life. Slaves can be convinced that they make self-sacrifice into a form of "altruism," but in fact they sacrifice themselves just because of their profound hatred of the earth and the earthly. Without this hatred, there would not be any "slave morality."

Nietzsche concludes the *Second Essay* of *On the Genealogy of Morality* with the statement that slave morality (and equally the values that it yields, such as the notion of sacrifice as self-sacrifice) is not the "last word" in the history of mankind. "A reverse experiment" is, "in principle," possible: bad conscience, which in slave morality sacrifices and contrasts natural instincts, can be turned against what opposes these instincts. However, "for that purpose, we would need another sort of spirit," "the redeeming man of great love and contempt, the creative spirit." This "man of the future," Nietzsche adds, "will redeem us, not just from the ideal held up till now, but also from those things which had to arise from it, from the great nausea, the will to nothingness, from nihilism" (GM, II 24). The reference to Zarathustra in the concluding paragraph of the *Second Essay* leaves no doubt that Nietzsche is talking about the overman (GM, II 25).

The final chapter of *Beyond Good and Evil* presents an account of the noble type in the age of nihilism and distinguishes him from the slave type. The noble type conceivable today is not the master described in *On the Genealogy of Morality*. As previously stressed, the main features of the master type are spontaneity and irresponsibility. There is no self-reflection involved in the sacrifice of the best-loved and in the sacrifice of the weak ones. Self-reflection is, in fact, characteristic of the slave type, marked by bad conscience and inner life. Indeed, as Gemes stresses following John Richardson, Nietzsche "admires the slaves for the formative power that issues from their repression of desire for immediate gratification."¹⁰ Inner life cannot be simply dismissed in order to grasp archaic forms of instinctive life once again. In a *Nachlass* note of 1888, Nietzsche asks once again "*What is noble?*" and answers: "That one instinctively seeks heavy responsibilities" (WM, 944; cf. 15[115] 13.475). Responsibility *toward the species* constitutes a feature of the noble type (JGB, 61), which is therefore different from the ancient master type.

In *Beyond Good and Evil* Nietzsche affirms that the noble type is

> he who has really gazed with an Asiatic and more than Asiatic eye down into the most world-denying of all possible modes of thought—beyond good and evil and no longer, like Buddha and Schopenhauer, under the spell and illusion of morality [. . .] may have had his eyes opened to the opposite ideal: to the ideal of the most exuberant, most living and most world-affirming man, who has not only learned to get on and treat with all that was and is but who wants to have it again <u>as it was and is</u> to all eternity, insatiably calling out <u>da capo</u> not only to himself but to the whole piece and play. (JGB, 56)

This "opposite ideal" recalls the "man of the future" of *On the Genealogy of Morality*, whose enterprise is the redemption both from the old values and "from the will to nothingness, from nihilism" (GM, II 24). In *The Will to Power* Nietzsche distinguishes between two kinds of nihilism: "A. Nihilism as a sign of increased power of the spirit: as active nihilism. B. Nihilism as decline and recession of the spirit: as passive nihilism" (WM, 22; cf. 9[35] 12.350–351). Later on, Nietzsche explains that the latter is

> the weary nihilism that no longer attacks; its most famous form, Buddhism; a passive nihilism, a sign of weakness. The strength of the spirit may be worn out, exhausted, so that previous goals and values have become incommensurate and no longer are believed.

The form of nihilism Nietzsche is referring to in *On the Genealogy of Morality* mirrors this description. Conversely, Nietzsche explains that active nihilism

> can be a sign of strength: the spirit may have grown so strong that previous goals ('convictions,' 'articles of faith') have become incommensurate [. . .]. It reaches its maximum of relative strength as a violent force of destruction—as active nihilism. (WM, 23; cf. 9[35] 12.350–351)[11]

Active nihilism as destruction of all metaphysical values, particularly those attached to the Platonic-Christian idea of a "true" world, is essential to make room for the transvaluation [*Umwertung*] of all values, which is the task of the overman. Of course the slave type cannot play any role in the generation of such a figure. Therefore, the noble type—he who has "his eyes opened" to this "ideal"—is the prefiguration of the overman.[12]

As explained above, self-sacrifice derives from bad conscience and *ressentiment* and is justified by a reference to the "true world." The condemnation of this kind of sacrifice is implied in the words Nietzsche uses regarding the Christian sacrifice (WM, 246; cf. 15[110] 13.469f). However, for the noble type—and all the more for the overman—sacrifice does not mean the return to the meaning of sacrifice characteristic of master morality, namely, the sacrifice of the "best-loved" and of the weak ones. When Nietzsche considers the option of a reverse experiment, he does not support the idea of a return to instinctive life, but wishes "an intertwining of bad conscience with perverse inclinations, all those other-worldly aspirations" (GM, II 24). In other words, the overman is called upon to integrate inner life (which implies responsibility) with the transvaluation of values. "Faced with the inevitability of conflicting drives he does not suppress, or seek to extirpate any drive, this being the typical genesis of *ressentiment*, but rather he achieves a redirection of various drives."[13] Instincts *plus* responsibility constitute one of the main features of the overman.

As a consequence of these two dimensions, the notion of sacrifice acquires a new meaning. The indifference toward the weak ones within master morality was unwittingly consistent with the universal principle that "the species endures only through human sacrifice" (WM, 246; cf. 15[110] 13.470). Slave morality affirms the opposite of this principle in demanding that "no one should be sacrificed" (WM, 246; cf. 15[110] 13.471). The overman, attuned to the danger posed by nihilism to the human species, is aware of the necessity of human sacrifice and consciously follows this principle. Nietzsche is very clear about this point: "The fundamental phenomenon: innumerable individuals sacrificed for the sake of a few, in order to make the few possible" (WM, 679; cf. 7[9] 12.296).

As we have seen, the ancient master type acted spontaneously, even when he sacrificed other people. For the overman, this is no longer possible. The reversal [*Umkehrung*] of values has introduced consciousness, and consciousness implies responsibility. The overman never sacrifices people thoughtlessly. He is perfectly aware of the great responsibility that this kind of action implies, and does not refuse this responsibility, but comes to terms with it. He is the one who is able to "bear the greatest responsibility and not collapse under it" (WM, 975; 1[56] 12.24). Nietzsche gives the example of Napoleon, whose enterprises are compared to a "disinterested" work on marble, "whatever be the number of men that are sacrificed in the process"

(WM, 975; 1[56] 12.24).¹⁴ Napoleon is still a figure of transition. Nietzsche calls him "this synthesis of *Unmensch* [brute] and *Übermensch* [overman]" (GM, I 16).¹⁵ "The highest man," says Nietzsche, is "he who determines values and directs the will of millennia by giving direction to the highest natures" (WM, 999; cf. 25[355] 11.106). If the will to power is "the basic character trait of those who rule" (WM, 55; cf. 5[71] 12.214), then sacrifice is an expression of the will to power. Therefore, the new meaning of sacrifice inherits the necessity of sacrificing others from master morality, but this necessity is combined with consciousness and responsibility inherited from slave morality. The key difference is that the new form of responsibility is oriented toward the species (JGB, 61). What is more, the new meaning of sacrifice inherits the self-sacrificial dimension from slave morality, but this dimension is corrected by the complete absence of resentment inherited from master morality.

In fact, it would be a serious misunderstanding to think that the overman is free of sacrifice. On the contrary, he is destined for sacrifice more than any other man. The sacrifice of the best-loved characteristic of master morality is now revaluated here as self-sacrifice. The noble-type, which constitutes the prefiguration of the overman, is described as the "initiated" and as the "almost sacrificed" (JGB, 270) because he rebels against the confinement within the herd. The sacrifice of the overman is even higher, because he has to carry the weight of the responsibility of sacrificing others. The overman represents the best lamb of the herd, whose destiny is to sacrifice himself precisely because it is the best one. It is a very peculiar kind of *kenotic* sacrifice, but it is clearly *kenotic* in essence: the overman must give his plenitude. He is gifted with a "superabundance of power," and he is thus called to give it through his own sacrifice. To rule implies self-sacrifice.

The difference between the self-sacrifice of the overman and the Christian self-sacrifice is that the overman does not sacrifice himself in the herd's stead, but in order to emerge from it. Or, better, he sacrifices himself *by emerging from it*, for the overman, if he really is an overman, cannot avoid his own sacrifice. This "emergence" is what constitutes the authentic sacrifice, as it involves a superhuman effort and a complete acceptance of the death of God. Christian sacrifice is renunciation: one renounces something in this world in order to obtain something else in the true world, of which our world is only a pale copy. The overman's self-sacrifice, conversely, is affirmation: one does not renounce anything, but suppresses something so as to affirm something else, firmly remaining in the immanent world. And he does so not from resentment, but rather from his own plenitude, fulfilling the duty embodied in the will to power, with the clear awareness that pain has no redemptive value. The profound difference between the one who presents the sacrificial offering to Dionysus, and the one who offers it to Christ consists in the way in which the pain is lived. Christians, when accepting pain, look for redemption and salvation. Christian sacrifice, as Nietzsche reads it, remains confined within the dualism of metaphysics, and persistently attempts to find meaning and redemption for the weakness of the finite in the transcendent and eternal. The overman's sacrifice, on the contrary, is generated by the will to power. He does not try to resist pain, but accepts the fact that this pain is senseless.

Therefore, the overman's sacrifice is both the conscious sacrifice of others for the prosperity of the species, and self-sacrifice, conceived as the endurance of the responsibility of sacrificing others. In both cases, sacrifice is conceived as *affirmation*: the overman makes sacrifices for "genuine charity" (WM, 246; cf. 15[110] 13.471) and for the love of the earthly, and thus his sacrifice is an expression of the will to power.

Political Implications of Sacrifice

Perhaps surprisingly, Nietzsche's tripartite account of sacrifice can be used to consider the implications of the various meanings of sacrifice—including political implications. In fact, now that we are almost at the end of our journey through the post-Kantian tradition, it is time to wonder what impact the notion of sacrifice can have on the sociopolitical realm.

First, consider the implications of sacrifice in master morality. In master morality the meaning of sacrifice is twofold: sacrifice of the best-loved and sacrifice of the weak ones. The sacrifice of the best-loved, as a tribute paid to the ancestors, has no significant social and political consequences. On the other hand, the sacrifice of the weak ones has political implications, as it is functional to the organization of ancient society. Ancient Greek society and politics can be considered as an expression of master morality.

In *The Greek State* (1872) Nietzsche affirms that for the Greeks "work is a disgrace" ["*die Arbeit eine Schmach sei*"].[16] "Slavery belongs to the essence of a culture": the enormous majority must be slavishly subjected to the struggles of life in the service of a minority. "Power [*Gewalt*] gives the first *right*, and there is no right that is not fundamentally presumption, usurpation and violence."[17] This is the origin of the state: as Nietzsche underlines in *On the Genealogy of Morality*, "the oldest 'state' emerged as a terrible tyranny, as a repressive and ruthless machinery." In this way, the "conqueror and master race" sacrifices the well-being and the lives of slaves.

This is not a conscious sacrifice from the point of view of the "involuntary" and "unconscious" masters. They are simply indifferent to the slaves. "They do not know what guilt, responsibility, consideration are [. . .]; they are ruled by that terrible inner artist's egoism which has a brazen countenance and sees itself justified to all eternity by the 'work,' like the mother in her child" (GM, II 17).

The work Nietzsche is referring to is the *state*. The Greeks are considered by Nietzsche as "political men *par excellence*"; and actually history "knows of no other example of such an awesome release of the political urge, of such a complete sacrifice [*Hinopferung*] of all other interests in the service of this instinct towards the state."[18] However, the state is not the ultimate goal. The state is just functional to the creation of society. Nietzsche recognizes the barbarism of this kind of political organization, but he thinks that it can be justified by the final outcome, namely, Greek society.

There is no *ressentiment* implied in the ancient battles. The Greek prince recognized in the Trojan prince a peer. They fought because of "a certain need to have enemies (as conduit systems, as it were, for the emotions of envy, quarrelsomeness, arrogance—fundamentally so as to be able to be a good *friend*)" (JGB, 260). This picture, which represents the master type as the one who rules and the slave type as the one who succumbs, is the image of the ancient world, and even Nietzsche himself seems to believe that it is neither possible nor desirable to reconstruct that world.[19]

Master morality is jeopardized by bad conscience. For bad conscience causes *ressentiment*, and *ressentiment* is exploited by the priests. Thus, the slaves' revolt in morality marks the end of the ancient organization of society. Accordingly, the idea of the state will change in order to be consistent with the new morality, that is, slave morality.

Now, consider the implications of sacrifice in slave morality. With the French Revolution, "the last political nobility in Europe [. . .] collapsed under the *ressentiment*-instincts of the rabble" (GM, I 16). Nietzsche notes that the Enlightenment is deeply indebted to Christianity, and that the French Revolution is the "daughter and continuation of Christianity" (WM, 184; cf. 14[223] 13.396). It seems that, according to Nietzsche, modern democracy is just another phase in the exacerbation of passive nihilism. Nietzsche writes:

> *Morality is in Europe today herd-animal morality* [. . .]—indeed, with the aid of a religion which has gratified and flattered the sublimest herd-animal desires [. . .]: the democratic movement inherits the Christian [. . .]. Europe seems threatened with a new Buddhism; at one in their faith in the morality of mutual pity

[. . .]—at one, one and all, in their faith in the community as the saviour, that is to say in the herd, in 'themselves.' . . . (JGB, 202)

The democratic system theorized by the Enlightenment is also the heir to Christianity in regard to the notion of sacrifice. If all citizens are equal, nobody can be sacrificed. Such a system, even conceding that it makes society "better," always makes it *sicker*. Requiring that nobody is sacrificed means, in the last resort, sacrificing mankind, sacrificing man as a whole.

It is important to clarify that sacrifice of individuals, often demanded by nationalist ideologies,[20] does not fit with the necessity of sacrifices stressed by Nietzsche. In fact, when Nietzsche focuses on contemporary Europe, he ascribes slave morality to the mass movements of nationalism. Nationalism, which is described by Nietzsche as "a lapse and regression into old loves and narrowness" (JGB, 241), refuses the distinction between aristocrats and plebeians (similarly to the priests of the origin) and prefers a "nationalistic" distinction, which opposes aristocrats and plebeians of one nation, with aristocrats and plebeians of another nation. In this sense, nationalism is "vulgar" by definition. It cancels the distinctions between aristocrats and plebs in the name of a superior unity—the *national* unity. Thus, nationalism implies the denial of aristocracy altogether.

However, this unity—this "lunacy of nationality," as Nietzsche describes it (JGB, 256)—is a pretense, just like the transcendent world in the name of which the priests invite slaves to revolt against masters.[21] "The vehemence with which our most intelligent contemporaries lose themselves in wretched nooks and crannies, for example into nationalism [*Vaterländerei*],"[22] Nietzsche writes, "always manifests above all the *need* for a faith, a support, backbone, something to fall back on."[23] And in a *Nachlass* he is, if possible, even clearer: "What is the meaning of our nationalism? The metamorphosis of the cross."[24] From a Nietzschian perspective, the demand for self-sacrifice in the name of 'the nation' is not different from the demand for self-sacrifice in the name of God or the salvation of the soul.

Nietzsche's approach here is not historical. He focuses on the characteristics of the slave type. He criticizes any morality generated by any mass movement. From this point of view, modern nationalism is a mass movement like any other. The passage from medieval theocracy to modern nationalism is an internal change within a morality that remains a slave morality. With the disintegration of Christianity, religious values are not believed in anymore. The loss of the faith in God coincides with a decline and a regression of the power of spirit, that is, with the aggravation of (passive) nihilism. Pessimistic contemplation in the absence of meaning drives men to pursue meaning in something absolutely absurd, that is, in a nonexistent national identity that has nothing to do with the nobility of spirit. And this aggravation continues through the rise of modern democracy, as "a principle of dissolution and decay" (JGB, 259).

This claim can already be recognized in *Human, All Too Human* where Nietzsche writes that "modern democracy is the historical form of the *decline of the state*."[25] Nietzsche adds that this decay is not unfortunate, as the belief in the existence of the state is of religious origin. Further on, Nietzsche returns to this point, affirming that "democracy tries to create and guarantee independence for as many as possible in their opinion, way of life, and occupation."[26] Thus, the problem does not seem to be the goal of democracy, but rather its means—the right of universal suffrage, for instance. Nietzsche's worry regarding current democracy (which is different from democracy as "a thing to come," as Nietzsche himself stresses) is, above all, the assignment of power on the basis of quantity, power that is consequently in the hands of the "vulgar mediocrity."[27] Mob at the top and mob below, is Nietzsche's description of Europe (WM, 752; cf. cf. 26[282] 11.224).

In slave morality, as we have seen, sacrifice is essentially self-sacrifice. "Bad conscience" dictates that self-sacrifices are made in the name of "altruism." In his reading of the French Revolution as "the continuation of Christianity" (WM, 184; 14[223] 13.396), Nietzsche considers the democratic notion of "equality" as the political equivalent of the religious-moral notion of altruism: "its instincts are against caste, against the noble, against the last privileges" (WM, 164; cf. 11[360] 13.158). For Nietzsche the lack of sacrifice in democracy presents a threat to—a potential sacrifice of—"the good of the species."

Most importantly, since ruling always implies sacrifice, especially self-sacrifice, leaders should be "great men." But today's leaders are just those "petty politicians" that Nietzsche criticizes. They are not able to accept the responsibility implied in sacrifice. Therefore, they exercise power "with a kind of inner remorse."[28] To justify their bad conscience, they present themselves as the executors of orders emanating from the "general will." They claim to be the first servants of their country. The reality is that they have lost the *art of giving commands*.[29]

The majority of the electorate is composed of mediocre persons. They are the petty ones, "those who think only of narrow utility" (JGB, 260). In *The Will to Power*, Nietzsche writes that the self-deception of the masses in every democracy "is extremely valuable: making men smaller and more governable is desired as 'progress'!" (WM, 129; cf. 36[48] 11.570). Since leaders draw their power from the consent of the masses, they flatter them.[30] In that manner, leaders become "servants of the other servants." Subsequently, the leaders are imitated by the majority, and the process of "mediocritisation" continues. Nietzsche writes: "'Be like them! Become mediocre!' is henceforth the only morality that has any meaning left, that still finds ears to hear it" (JGB, 262). This is a vicious circle, where people become more and more mediocre.[31]

In that manner, the refusal to sacrifice others and the invitation to self-sacrifice (always made in the name of a "superior world," whether it is the religious ideal of the Christian heaven or the secular ideal of the nation), which are features of slave morality, constitute important elements of modern democracy. The master's instinct of command is replaced by the herd instinct of obedience. Democracy comes with the risk of a continuously increasing mediocratization. It is against this process that the overman stands.

In order to gauge the political implications of nihilism, it is useful to distinguish between modernist and postmodernist interpretations of the will to power.[32] Postmodernist approaches tend to interpret the will to power as a primordial impetus or impulse, as a principle of the eternal struggle of forces. Conversely, modernist approaches tend to interpret the will to power as a historical and anthropological principle. Of course, there are many possible versions within each of these approaches, and many of these versions have contemporary advocates. For the purpose of this book, I will refer to the interpretation provided by Pierre Klossowski[33] as an instance of the former, and for the latter I will mainly focus on the post-Kantian interpretation of Nietzsche developed by Will Dudley.[34]

According to Klossowski, the will to power is totally assimilated by Nietzsche to a primordial impulse (*impulsion*) deprived of any anthropocentric support, a merely psychological intensive state of the soul in constant fluctuation.[35] Klossowski links the will to power to the eternal recurrence and considers the will to power in terms of the conflict between the Apollonian and Dionysian. Klossowski emphasizes that Nietzsche thinks of the Apollonian and Dionysian not as fixed *forms*, but rather as dynamic *forces*. In his early works like *The Birth of Tragedy*, Nietzsche presents the Apollonian and the Dionysian—reason and life—as intrinsically permeating each other. From the *Zarathustra* onward, the Dionysian is not simply presented as the other and complementary side of the Apollonian, but as the manifestation of the will to power. Klossowski underlines that for Nietzsche all forms of enthusiasm and ecstasy are Dionysian, as in such states man gives up his individuality. The Dionysian, Klossowski argues, becomes more and more powerful in the age of active nihilism, that is, after the declaration of the death of God. As Daniel W. Smith explains: "One of Klossowski's most persistent themes is that the death of God implies the loss of both the identity of the Self and the coherence of the World."[36] As the eternal recurrence is the ultimate goal of the overman,[37] it follows that the will to power ultimately disappears, or exists only as a will to the dissolution of the self in the recurring circle.

It seems that the ultimate sacrifice of the overman, in the postmodern interpretations of Nietzsche (at least as it appears in Klossowski's interpretation), is the abandonment of consciousness, the loss of individual identity. The overman is the man who does not define himself anymore on the basis of his own eternal identity (principle of individuation), but on the basis of the eternal becoming of the self (principle of Eternal Recurrence).[38] But if we opt for this interpretative possibility, if we accept the idea of the will to power as the victory of the Dionysian over the Apollonian, how could Zarathustra still talk? How would it still be possible to communicate? With the break of the principle of individuation, not only do the notions of "truth" and "lie" cease to make sense, but language itself would be excluded from the Dionysian universe where the will to power rules. It is a dangerous option, because the outcome is a "dead end," a real linguistic and rational aphasia. This is the direction pursued by some other postmodern interpreters of Nietzsche such as Georges Bataille. Interestingly enough, Bataille founded a secret society, *Acéphale*, conceived as a social and political experiment centered precisely on the notion of sacrifice. The meetings of the society were even supposed to include a real human sacrifice—a very real dissolution of the self. As Roger Caillois states, Bataille and the other members of *Acéphale* each agreed to be the sacrificial victim as part of the inauguration of the society; none of them agreed to be the executioner.[39] This impossibility marked the failure of the experiment. This episode might be taken as evidence that certain "excesses" appear as just impracticable and nonsensical once one tries to make them real—and, from this point of view, they do not even deserve a moral condemnation.

It is thus clear that if the postmodern interpretation of the will to power is applied, the notion of sacrifice has no social or political consequences. In this case, the possibility of using language and the capacity of cooperation and communication are seriously compromised.

If, on the other hand, the will to power is considered as a historical and anthropological principle, typical of modernist interpretations of Nietzsche, the social and political implications are markedly different. Woodward identifies the crucial point of what she calls "the modernist interpretation of Nietzsche" in "the possibility of overcoming nihilism, the conviction that there shall come a time in history when nihilism shall be left behind." In the age of *complete* nihilism, marked by the abandonment of metaphysical values, "it is possible to leave nihilism behind and actively create new categories of valuation that will be wholly affirmative and free from nihilism."[40]

This modernist approach to the will to power as manifested by creation of values allows a large and diverse range of interpretations of the political implications of the age of nihilism (or post-nihilism). Some modernist interpreters such as Wilfried Van der Will consider post-nihilism as a post-democratic age in which "'a new caste' of the strong should dominate the weak globally in order to push culture to new heights of risk, of tragedy, excellence and genius."[41] Others such as Nicola M. De Feo identify the post-nihilistic and post-democratic age as the realization of communism.[42] Of course there are other possible versions within the modernist interpretation that lie between these extremes. For our purposes, it is sufficient to show that, even if the will to power is considered as a historical and anthropological principle, sacrifice again poses a challenge to the compatibility of Nietzsche's thought with democracy.

The sacrifice of the overman means the sacrifice of others for the sake of the species. Leaders must bear this heavy responsibility, and to do so they must be "great men." In *On the Genealogy of Morality* Nietzsche writes: "The amount of 'progress' can actually be *measured* according to how much has had to be sacrificed to it; man's sacrifice *en bloc* to the prosperity of one single stronger species of man—that *would be* progress . . ." (GM, II 12). And in *The Will to Power* he expresses the same idea in even clearer terms:

> My ideas do not revolve around the degree of freedom that is granted to the one or to the other or to all, but around the degree of power that the one or the other should exercise over others or over all, and to what extent a sacrifice of freedom, even enslavement, provides the basis for the emergence of a higher type. Put in the crudest form: how could one sacrifice the development of mankind to help a higher species than man to come into existence? (WM, 859; 7[6] 12.280–281)

In response to such passages, some commentators have argued that Nietzsche develops an aristocratic political perspective, based on the firm belief that leaders must be intrinsically superior to others. That is to say, they must be overmen.[43] The overman is the one who thinks (and acts) differently from the herd, who takes into account neither private nor national interests.[44] He is the one who knows that something is a hundred times more important than the question of whether we feel well or not: basic instinct of all strong natures—and consequently also whether others feel well or not. In sum, that we have a goal for which one does not hesitate to offer human sacrifices, to risk every danger, to take upon oneself whatever is bad and worst: *great passion*. (WM, 26; cf. 9[107] 12.398)

Clearly the notion of sacrifice is central to this picture. Political decisions can be hard and unpopular, and they could also lead to the sacrifice of men.

At first glance, these comments seem unacceptable. One could say that Nietzsche is inviting us to build a world where the slave type is destined to succumb to the master type, whose rules entail the power to judge who should be sacrificed. However, a post-Kantian reading of Nietzsche along the lines proposed by Will Dudley offers an alternative and challenges the critique claiming that Nietzsche is anti-democratic across the board. Central to such an interpretation is the claim that active nihilism is not simply the capacity to create new values. The key element is that this capacity is reflective and guided by regulative principles. Kant introduced regulative ideas as general guidelines that do not consist of specific rules. That is, they are not heteronomous and are not connected with laws or entities whose content is predetermined. Hegel built on Kant's philosophy by moving from impersonal reason to a form of *reflective social* practice (spirit). What if we read Nietzsche's philosophy as suggesting that the overman must be committed to a reflective capacity to autonomously create new values (conceived as regulative ideas) that are independent of customs, that is, independent of the social aspect that characterized Hegel's spirit?

The hypothesis that the creation of new values is reflective and guided by regulative principles can appear as highly disputable in the face of much Nietzschean rhetoric. In fact, Nietzsche is really ambiguous on the issue of creation of new values. However, if it cannot be maintained that Nietzsche is totally committed to a reflective and regulatively guided creation of new values, it is at least possible, and indeed fruitful, to give consideration to this interpretation, among the several possible directions that Nietzsche's philosophical thought can take.

Following this train of thought, Will Dudley has provided an interpretation of freedom as a Nietzschian regulative idea.[45] Dudley considers both Hegel and Nietzsche as critics of Kant's formalism of morality. Kant's freedom is understood through his concept of the moral will, which is empty and formal. Nietzsche, on the other hand, links freedom with the will to power and thus grants freedom its independence from morality. Dudley's account can be read as the progressive history of liberation of the notion of freedom from metaphysical constraints. Dudley analyses the notion of freedom in noble morality, slave morality, passive nihilism, and active nihilism, arguing that humans fail to be free in the first three cases:

a) *Master morality* is guided by an independent will and affirmation of life. "Its fundamental features [. . .] are its selfishness, its ability to be indifferent to the suffering of others, and its hardness, its willingness to reduce others to expendable slaves for the sake of its own affirmations."[46]

b) *Slave* or *herd morality* is guided by reaction and *ressentiment*. Hence its claims, which form the "metaphysics of weakness," are basically negative and empty.

Both these moralities, Dudley maintains, are forms of heteronomy. This is quite obvious regarding slave morality, as the latter basically consists in reaction to preexisting values. But even master morality is heteronomous, because it excludes what is alien to its standards. That is, insofar as values are shared, communal, and dependent on customs and habits, they are also herd-like. This dependence is a form of heteronomy.

c) The third form of "unfreedom" is represented by "the peculiarly modern sickness arising after shedding the constraints of tradition and being open to everything, of being unable to forge an independent will, and thus being turned over to one's instincts."[47]

d) The only real freedom is the "tragic freedom" of the overman, who overcomes the self-affirming will in a new *unsittliche* will, that is, a will that is independent of customs. "Those capable of the repeated self-overcoming necessary to freedom go by many names and descriptions in Nietzsche's texts. One thing they certainly are is *unsittlich*, unethical in the sense of not being firmly attached to any given set of customs. This is in contrast not only to the *Sittlichkeit* of herd morality, but also to that of nobility."[48]

The result, Dudley argues, is "a spiritual nomadism"[49] and experimentalism, in which "the free spirit adopts a particular set of convictions and virtues because they are well-suited to the self she has created, and she eventually abandons them because no set of convictions and virtues can permanently contain or measure that self."[50] This "nomadism" is not compatible with the tendency to assimilate that is characteristic to the will to power. Thus, according to Dudley, real freedom in a complete nihilistic society implies the overcoming/sublimation of the will to power.

Not dependent on specific customs and norms, tragic freedom is not heteronomous and does not connect to any metaphysical principle or entity. Nevertheless, tragic freedom guides toward the ongoing creation of a normativity that would approach compatibility with the created self. This compatibility is not constitutive and merely serves as direction for the independent freedom. Tragic freedom is thus a regulative principle, in the Kantian sense explicated above.

Since sacrifice is an expression of the will to power and since the will to power is intimately linked with freedom, the different conceptions of freedom are associated with respectively different conceptions of sacrifice. In the political realm, sacrifice is thus related to the type of freedom that characterizes the political leaders.

The current unwillingness of petty politicians to sacrifice is clearly connected to the passively nihilistic unfreedom (option c above). The return to the noble attitude to the sacrifice of others and the noble indifference to the suffering of others (option a) is neither possible anymore, nor desirable. Slave morality (option b) implies sacrifices for the sake of metaphysical values and realities.

Dudley's account of freedom in the post-nihilistic age, that is, tragic freedom (option d), is a regulative principle that should be therefore associated with a regulative notion of sacrifice. That is to say, if the overman as a political leader has the tragic freedom to choose values, sacrifice cannot be an activity that results from a fixed value or principle. Typically of a regulative principle, the sacrifice of the overman refuses heteronomy, whether it is the one implied in master morality (according to which are sacrificed those who are alien to its standards) or the one that is implied in slave morality (according to which the self is sacrificed for the sake of metaphysical values). Sacrifice is nevertheless necessary and serves as a general guideline to the overman.

The overman as a ruler, in sacrificing others, is guided only by that "faithfulness to earth," which is expressed by his responsibility towards the species (JGB, 61). In other words, sacrifice is regulative insofar as it is practiced not in the name of metaphysical values or according to customs or habits, and insofar as it is guided by responsibility for the future of the species. Furthermore, since its purpose is the future of the species, sacrifice as a principle does not explicitly state who or what has to be sacrificed. In master morality sacrifice is necessarily that of the slaves as a class, and in slave morality sacrifice is necessarily of the self. The overman, conversely, determines what is sacrificed only by his independent and *unsittliche* will, which only the overman is able to forge, and which is guided exclusively by the responsibility for the good of the species.

The perspective of sacrifice as a regulative principle has several implications in the political realm. First, since sacrifices are not made for the sake of metaphysical values or entities, this perspective can help avoid the risk of a democracy in which a common belief in ideals degenerates into fanaticism, as often happens in the case of nationalism. This perspective is also compatible with the claim repeated by Nietzsche in late notebooks that "there are no facts, only interpretations."[51] That is to say that nobody can legitimately claim to hold an unquestionable truth. This does not mean that every mystification is possible but that every position can be questioned.

Second, as explained earlier, the main risk that Nietzsche sees in democracy is the ongoing process of mediocratization. Political decisions in democracy are often based on the consent leaders expect to receive.[52] However, in some cases, rulers should be able to take unpopular decisions such as sacrifice. According to Nietzsche, only the rulers who have the capacity to forge an independent will are able to do so. This perspective resists mediocratization because rulers are not conditioned by the "mediocre majority"; on the contrary, their decisions (including sacrifices) can help human excellence to emerge. This perspective is evidently more aristocratic than democratic, because it implies the exercise of the power by those who have the capacity for an independent will—and they are, from this point of view, "better" than the mediocre majority. However, this perspective can be seen as an "aristocratic tool" within democracy, as it is helpful in avoiding the risk of the degeneration of democracy into a "dictatorship of mediocrity," which merely follows the emotional consent of the majority.

Third, the regulative meaning of sacrifice can help avoid the risk of a politics that is unable to commit itself to the future. The grounding of political decisions in the consent of the majority also entails a lack of attention toward future generations. As Nietzsche stresses, the supporters of metaphysical values, together with those passive nihilists whose "openness to everything" is ultimately a commitment to nothing, "sacrifice" [*kreuzigen*][53] the future to *themselves*—they sacrifice all man's future, where "man's future" is the *higher man*.[54] Once again, the refusal to make sacrifices signifies the sacrifice of humankind as a whole. Conversely, the acceptance of the responsibility of sacrifice and self-sacrifice also entails the acceptance of the responsibility towards future generations. Those who accept that responsibility are to be the "*guarantors* of the future" (GM, III 14).

These arguments are not meant to constitute a detailed account of the political implications of the regulative meaning of the notion of sacrifice. For such an account would include specific and explicit norms and thereby conflict with the philosophical perspective which gives rise to it. To use the notion of sacrifice in a regulative manner means to adapt this notion to a particular situation or need, and to abandon altogether the norms that resulted from that adaptation when they no longer fit the situation. Similarly, an artist adopts a criterion of beauty that can be realized in a particular work of art, but that cannot be applied as a rule in order to create another work of art. It is this aesthetic conception of politics that stands behind Nietzsche's reluctance to indulge in detailed descriptions and his preference for *exempla*. Similarly to Kierkegaard's knight of faith, the overman is not described by Nietzsche but only portrayed through exempla.[55]

Even if Nietzsche's philosophy can be reconciled with democracy when interpreted as a critique made from within democracy, the compatibility of Nietzsche with democratic commitments should not be taken too far. Some scholars have overemphasized in this connection Nietzsche's affirmation that the juxtaposition between noble and slave moralities can happen "even within the same man, within *one* soul" (JGB, 260). This, they claim, means that Nietzsche does not speak about specific rulers but rather calls for a process of *leveling up* instead of a process of *leveling down* to the most common denominator. In that manner, these scholars present a Nietzsche who refuses *plebeianism* because he wants a genuine *democracy*.[56] This interpretation may be tempting, but Nietzsche is critical of any kind of leveling.

Nietzsche is quite ambiguous on the question of democracy. He continually oscillates among different options, sometimes affirming that aristocracy must eventually replace democracy, and sometimes wishing an aristocratic reform of democracy.[57] And yet, as shown above, Nietzsche's remarks on sacrifice have political consequences that imply a critical examination of the weaknesses of contemporary forms of democracy.[58] In other words, Nietzsche's picture of sacrifice can *inspire* a political theory that has an aristocratic flavor, but that can contribute to the development of democracy. One can find inspiration in his warnings and reflections, even if what he *really* meant may remain obscure.

In his 1998 book *Nietzsche contra Democracy*, Appel considered the compatibility of equal rights with human excellence as one of the major challenges of our times, and regretted that most contemporary thinkers were not responding to this challenge because of fear that such problems "invariably introduce metaphysical or religious values that may not be to everyone's liking in modern pluralistic society."[59] More than a decade has passed since the publication of Appel's book, and there has been little progress to date on this issue. Nietzsche's reflections on the notion of sacrifice are closely connected to the risk of mediocratization and to the broad problem of the compatibility of equal rights with human excellence. His reflections can inspire the electorate to notice those politicians who do not only seek consent, but seem to exercise an independent will. Nietzsche's reflections could also encourage politicians to explain and convince the electorate of the necessity to sometimes make unpopular decisions, which in some cases involve sacrifice. The outcome could (hopefully) be the opposite of a process of mediocratization, namely, a process of *elevation*. This elevation is of the people as a political whole that includes the rulers and the electorate, and is thus essentially different to the leveling up of the simple sum of individuals. I believe that a post-Kantian interpretation of Nietzsche—that is, an interpretation that considers post-metaphysical nihilism not as an absolute relativity of values or as the end of the human *à la* Klossowski, but as a process of reevaluation of values in their *regulative* significance—can provide instruments to give a contribution to an analysis propaedeutic to this process. As Robert Pippin states:

> The unresolved tensions in Nietzsche's account, or the position of his Zarathustra, homeless both when in isolation and noble indifference and when wandering among the mankind he finds himself inextricably attached to, would represent the still unresolved problems of the resolutely self-critical modern age itself, rather than evidence of any revolutionary turn. Nietzsche is not bidding modernity farewell; he is the first, finally and uncompromisingly, to understand its implications and to confront its legacy.[60]

With Nietzsche, the very idea of norms is put into question; in fact, if norms are culturally dependent, the only possible answer to the Kantian paradox is a relativistic and skeptical one. We no longer have norms, but only regulative notions created by the will to power. Consistently, sacrifice becomes a regulative notion dependent on the will to power. However, Nietzsche's solution introduces new problems, both for sacrifice (sometimes conceived as sacrifice of others, sometimes as self-giving, and sometimes as self-annihilation, thus generating an unresolved ambiguity), and more broadly for regulativity, which is now disconnected from the judging role of social reason. These problems are inevitably part of Nietzsche's legacy in twentieth-century European philosophy, and one might wonder whether it is possible to find a solution to them without reconsidering the trajectory of Western thought on regulativity and sacrifice from Kant onwards—something that we have tried to do in the previous chapters. Therefore, it is now time to provide a recapitulation of our survey, to take positions about the relative importance and merits of the different thinkers we have considered, and to extend the analysis with brief treatments of some twentieth-century figures.

6

Conclusion

The Long Way of Sacrifice

Sacrifice from Kant to Nietzsche . . .

We are at the end of our survey of the notion of sacrifice in nineteenth-century post-Kantian philosophy. Obviously, the history of the notion of sacrifice does not end with Nietzsche; however, while standard accounts tend to consider the philosophical question of sacrifice as arising in the hermeneutic/postmodern tradition of the twentieth century (which will be the subject of a brief excursus in the next section), the analysis carried on in the previous chapters shows that the origins of the question, as well as possible strategies to deal with it, are to be found in the mainstream post-Kantian tradition of the nineteenth century. This conclusive chapter is therefore devoted to appreciating how the various approaches to the notion of sacrifice from Kant to Nietzsche have laid out an array of interrelated philosophical questions from which philosophers in the twentieth century have drawn, and to suggest an answer to the ultimate question: on the background of the post-Kantian tradition, what theory of sacrifice is the most reliable and the most appropriate to face contemporary challenges? Before that, however, it is useful to recap the fundamental steps of our journey, in order to stress lines of continuity and appreciate the legacy of this tradition.

While "sacrifice" is usually regarded as meaning the suppression or the destruction of something for the sake of something else, the focus of our analysis has been an alternative meaning of sacrifice: *kenotic* sacrifice. Assuming the taxonomy of kenotic sacrifice provided by Coakley,[1] and amended by Groenhout,[2] we have seen that kenotic sacrifice, as it features in the philosophies under scrutiny, effectively oscillates between the three different forms of kenosis identified by Groenhout—namely self-limitation, self-giving, and self-emptying.

There are two other lines of continuity that have found confirmation through our analysis of kenotic sacrifice. The first is my suggested extension of Pinkard's reading of the history of German Idealism as a history of attempts at responding to the question of the source of norms (the Kantian paradox)—that is, that the problems generated by this paradox are addressed by post-Kantian idealists *and* by philosophers who are usually regarded as *extraneous* to post-Kantian idealism. The second line of continuity that has found confirmation through our analysis of sacrifice is Redding's interpretation of the history of the post-Kantian tradition as the history of perspectivism. Perspectivism can be defined as the philosophical view that all ideations take place from particular perspectives, implying that there are many possible conceptual schemes in which judgment of truth or value can be made. It is Nietzsche who is most well-known for alluding to the significance of this account for the cognitive relation, but as we have seen all the philosophers taken into consideration here can be regarded as attempting to think through the same account.

A question that is now worthy of being asked is: is there any relation linking the "sliding scale" of kenotic sacrifice, the different solutions offered to the problem of the source of norms, and the increasing perspectivism of nineteenth-century post-Kantian philosophy?

My answer to this question is positive. My thesis is that as the source of norms weakens, the corresponding perspectivism becomes increasingly radical—and more we ascend in the sliding scale of kenosis. In the remaining part of this section I will offer some arguments in support of this thesis for each of the philosophers considered in the previous chapters.

With the transcendental turn, Kant broke with traditional metaphysics, moved away from the traditional ideal of the God's-eye view, and proposed a modest cognitive ideal, a universal subjectivity that is deeply affected by spatio-temporal and causal constraints. This is not a proper form of perspectivism, because objectivity remains Kant's philosophical ideal—although Kant's objectivity is merely a universal subjectivity. The source of norms for Kant is human reason; this position generates the paradox that one has to be bound by laws of which one is also the author. As we have repeated innumerable times through the volume, this in turn generates Kant's attempted response to the paradox, that is, the suggestion for the moral agent to listen to moral commands as if they were spoken by the voice of God. As a result, sacrifice—a regulative symbol—does not go for Kant beyond the first degree of the sliding scale, that is, self-limitation.

Solger's position is not an easy one to address in this context. It might be said that Solger attempts to unify theoretical and practical philosophy once again in order to solve the Kantian paradox at its roots. If the theoretical and practical categories are unified, it is clear that there is no need to resort to transitional forms (symbols) to apply the principles of practical reason to experience. Strangely enough, symbols are maintained by Solger (especially aesthetic symbols) as representations of the metaphysical structure of reality. In addition, the unification between the theoretical and the practical is not accomplished through a logical coincidence between theoretical and practical categories (as it happens with Hegel), but through a re-thinking of the relationship between the finite (human being) and the infinite (God). This relationship is intrinsically perspectival, as there is no "objective" way to describe it. Thus, the Infinite (God) and the finite (human being) are both real, but one is real as the nothingness of the other, and vice versa. This is a peculiar kind of perspectivism, concerned with only two (but very relevant) perspectives: the divine perspective and the human perspective. Although limited to two perspectives, this perspectivism is extremely radical, at the point of negating one's own reality—which is conversely maintained from the other perspective. Having proclaimed the failure of reason when it establishes a connection with reality, no other source of norms is left than the metaphysical (and irrational) structure of the world in itself, whose drive is precisely (kenotic) sacrifice. A sacrifice so radical that can be easily identified with the other extreme of the spectrum, namely, self-annihilation. Solger's response to the Kantian paradox strongly relies on a sacrificial dynamic, which effectively constitutes the relationship between the finite (human being) and the infinite (God); but the notion of sacrifice is employed within a larger strategy of a valorization of irrationality which, as we will briefly see in the next section, will provide the model for some twentieth-century solutions.

Hegel's absolute idealism represents a point of equilibrium between Kant and Solger. In the chapter devoted to Hegel, I have extensively argued for Hegel's perspectivism. For Hegel, there are different perspectives upon reality. When thought posits a category, it effectively embraces a perspective on truth. Then the category collapses because it generates a contradictory negation, and thus a more complex perspective grows out to make sense of that contradiction. Not only humans are affected by such a partiality in perspective; God himself, insofar as he accepts becoming human, is affected by the same partiality. Because of this partiality in perspective, the moral agent cannot secure any "bindingness" for the moral law, which can be established only through a process of mutual recognition. As we know this is, according to Pinkard, Hegel's response to the "Kantian paradox." Hegel's theory of sacrifice might not be extremely evident prima facie, but in light of a deeper analysis kenotic sacrifice is effectively what makes possible both Hegel's perspectivism and the recognition process.

Phenomenologically, sacrifice can take place as self-limitation, self-giving, or self-emptying; however, from the point of view of the absolute spirit, it is the form of self-giving that best describes the real and actual sacrifice. In fact, a real sacrifice requires a giving up of something that constitutes the subject; a self-limitation would not be enough, and a self-annihilation would be too much (as for Hegel the identity of the subject needs to be preserved). Therefore sacrifice becomes, for Hegel, the *Darstellung* of recognition, thus preserving its symbolic and regulative value.

Kierkegaard's peculiar form of perspectivism can be deduced by a close reading of the two works that have been specifically put under scrutiny in this volume (namely, *Fear and Trembling* and *Works of Love*), but it is more explicitly thermalized in the *Concluding Unscientific Postscript to Philosophical Fragments*. Here Johannes Climacus, Kierkegaad's pseudonymous author, claims that "subjectivity is truth."[3] This means, Johannes explains, that insofar as each individual has his/her own past, present, and future, these experiences are unique, and this implies a different and unique point of view on the world for each existing individual. Significantly, Kierkegaard himself—via Johannes—establishes a connection between perspectivism and the question of the source of norms. The problem of subjectivity, Johannes claims, is to decide how to choose. What is right? What is the ultimate source of norms? According to Kierkegaard, philosophy cannot answer this question; only faith can, relying on Christ's command to love and sacrifice everything to your neighbor. On this point, Johannes Climacus, the (pseudonymous) author of the *Postscript*, and Kierkegaard (the author of *Works of Love*) are in perfect agreement: to be truly an individual, one has to establish an authentic relationship with the other, recognizing her *as other* (that is, as distinct from oneself); and this is possible only through a withdrawal of the self. Like Hegel, Kierkegaard places his kenotic sacrifice in the middle of the sliding scale—self-giving. These are important philosophical achievements. However, I have already stressed the problematic implications of Kierkegaard's view. With Kierkegaard's reintroduction of God as the source of norms, sacrifice maintains a strong symbolic and regulative value; but once one has rejected the judging role of social reason, every application of sacrifice, commanded by God and exemplified by Christ, becomes legitimate.

Nietzsche takes perspectivism to its extreme consequences. For him, the discovery that norms are human and culturally dependent leads to relativistic and skeptical conclusions. As stressed by Redding,[4] a meaningful example of

Nietzsche's perspectivism is represented by the dialogue between Zarathustra and the "Spirit of gravity" in *Thus Spoke Zarathustra*. The two are conversing about the nature of time. The Spirit of gravity claims that "All truth is crooked, time itself is a circle." This is a claim that Zarathustra should support; after all, he himself has made several claims that seemed to lead to the affirmation of the circular nature of time. Nevertheless, Zarathustra's reaction is impressively negative: "Spirit of Gravity!" he says in return, "Do not treat this too lightly!"[5] Why does Nietzsche make Zarathustra react in such a way? Clearly, it is not the *content* of the claim that Zarathustra objects to, but rather, the fact that it is put forward as a general claim made outside of any particular perspective point. What Nietzsche criticizes is the ideal of aperspectival knowledge of the world. Zarathustra's reaction is an acknowledgment of the time-bound position of any act of thinking. "There are no facts, there are only interpretations," Nietzsche famously claims: all forms of knowing the world are made from some particular perspective.[6] Nietzsche undermines the coherence of any notion of thought that is not "merely" one perspective on the world among many. Consistently, the meaning of sacrifice depends on the moral system within which it is performed: suppressive sacrifice of others in master morality, self-annihilation in slave morality, and self-giving in the breakdown of all moral systems under nihilism. The latter form of sacrifice is linked with the will to power, and therefore its meaning depends, as we have seen, on the way the will to power is interpreted. If it is interpreted as a primordial impetus or impulse, then some postmodernist interpreters of Nietzsche are correct in identifying in the annihilation of the self the final outcome of nihilism. Conversely, if the will to power is interpreted as a historical and anthropological principle, sacrifice is the giving up of the overman for the sake of "genuine charity" and for the "faithfulness to earth." Most importantly, it is the acceptance of a new form of responsibility—that is, responsibility toward future generations and the prosperity of the species. As such, sacrifice is a regulative notion linked with the will to power, which thus grants freedom its independence from morality and aims at generating a more concrete form of regulativity. Nevertheless, this move introduces new problems. First, it is interesting to note that, in a philosophy that is grounded on the absence of any source of norms (apart from human will), the sacrifice of others (as opposed to kenotic sacrifice, which is always *self*-sacrifice) is reintroduced. Second, even *kenotic* sacrifice constantly oscillates between self-giving (for the sake of the prosperity of the species) and self-annihilation. Lastly, Nietzsche's solution falls into the same problem already mentioned for Kierkegaard: once one has rejected the judging role of social reason, every application of sacrifice becomes, in principle, legitimate. Thus Nietzsche reestablishes a position with elements of Kantian regulativity, but without the resolution found in Hegel.

. . . And Beyond

What happens after Nietzsche? Clearly, the philosophical history of sacrifice does not stop at the end of the nineteenth century. Obviously it is beyond the purpose of this book to analyze the history of the notion of sacrifice in the twentieth century; another book would be necessary—or better, multiple books. However, I think it is interesting to briefly take into consideration some of the twentieth-century accounts of sacrifice by focusing on their connections with the philosophical positions examined in the previous chapters and showing which aspects of the array of post-Kantian alternatives are taken up, and which rejected.[7]

It is possible to identify three major trends in the twentieth-century "Continental" philosophy with respect to the notion of sacrifice.

The first trend is represented by an anthropological reading of God as a mere projection of human desires. Early instances of this trend are already present in nineteenth-century philosophy, and specifically in the philosophies of the so-called left Hegelians. Feuerbach's philosophy can be considered the prototype of this approach. The reading of God as a human "creation" represents a serious regression into pre-Kantian metaphysical realism—in fact, if God is, for Feuerbach, a "mere" projection, the "human being" is regarded as a metaphysical entity that is there "anyway," independently from any act of human recognition. Despite a superficial resemblance, this position is obviously distinct from Nietzsche's approach, as for Nietzsche nothing is there "anyway" (hence, Nietzsche's famous claim that the "true world" *becomes a fable*). The anthropological reading and the regression into pre-Kantian metaphysics are features that can be found in several philosophical approaches in the twentieth century, so many and so different from each other that a list would inevitably be incomplete and confusing. For our purposes, it is important to remark the implications that this approach has for the notion of sacrifice. With the reintroduction of the distinction between what is "real" and what is a "projection," sacrifice is considered either as an *ethical* category (when its meaning is not simply exhausted in other ethical categories), or as a *religious* category that belongs to the realm of myths and, therefore, cannot have a serious philosophical value.

The second trend is a valorization of irrationality. Kierkegaard and Nietzsche are usually considered responsible for this; but when irrationality is criticized in contemporary Continental philosophy, the real target to be hit is often an *implication* of irrationality, namely—to use Levinas' words in his famous attack against Kierkegaard—"the relegation of ethical phenomena to secondary status and the contempt of the ethical foundation of being which has led, through Nietzsche, to the amoralism of recent philosophies."[8] The valorization of irrationality is a feature that can be already found, in a peculiar exemplary way, in Solger's philosophy. Re-introduced in the history of philosophy by Kojève, this valorization of irrationality, often expressed by an exaltation of paradox, has been influential through various trends in the Continental tradition, such as French Existentialism and contemporary French Phenomenology. Grounding this conception of the paradox is the idea that in order to speak truly about the transcendent, namely, the unspeakable by definition, it is necessary to show not only the relativity of concepts, but, most of all, to show the failure of reason—its *wreck*, to use Solger's word—exactly when it establishes a connection with reality. In Solger's estimation of failure there is something more radical than in Kierkegaard's position—as Camus noted about Kierkegaard, "Reconciliation through scandal is still reconciliation."[9] For Solger, philosophy should not renounce reason, but accompany reason toward its failure. Thus sacrifice becomes, as we have seen, the most powerful symbol of this valorization of irrationality. We find something similar in Nietzsche's late reflections. Nietzsche is sometimes tempted to consider the dissolution of the principle of individuation as the most desirable outcome of the human adventure: the ultimate sacrifice is represented by human reason destroying its own foundation (the principle of individuation). This is the direction effectively pursued by some postmodern followers of Nietzsche. Once again, it is a paradoxical option, because the outcome is—as already stressed in the chapter on Nietzsche—a "dead end," a real linguistic and rational aphasia; and sacrifice is often indicated as the most powerful symbol of this process.

The third trend is a valorization of the *symbolic* over the *regulative*. These two notions have their origins in Kant's philosophy and are, as we know, strictly interconnected. Kant introduced "symbols" as transitional forms to be used to apply moral laws to experiences. In this way, symbols also play a *regulative* role in the application of moral ideas to the world. Symbols are meaningful because they symbolize a moral law that is regarded by Kant as certain and immutable: therefore, they are *intrinsically* regulative. However, once the idea of one certain and immutable moral law is put under attack (because it is considered as too abstract, and/or because it is objected that it does not take into consideration the historical and geographical context), the regulative dimension of symbols becomes the first victim. Nevertheless, this attack leaves a void that needs to be filled in one way or another. In fact, a whole range of "ideas" had found a place in Kant's philosophy as symbols—most notably, religious and aesthetic ideas. What are symbols once they are deprived of their regulative dimension? *Either* they are reduced to the rank of fictional projections of human impulses or, at best, mere metaphors aimed at expressing vague ethical indications (a strategy typical of that "anthropological reading" mentioned above), *or* they are enhanced as standing by themselves. The second solution effectively is a variation of a *third* solution that I have not mentioned yet—namely, Hegel's idealism. To say that metaphysical objects have an ideal rather than a naturalistic existence implies a rejection of the anthropological reading (which conversely represents a regression into pre-Kantian metaphysics) and an extension of the regulative dimension to all the objects of metaphysics. The Hegelian regularity, however, is not connected to an abstract moral law, but it is grounded on recognition. Nevertheless, Continental philosophy after Nietzsche has not followed Hegel; conversely, some of the most influential philosophical traditions of twentieth-century continental Europe, such as Phenomenology and Existentialism, have their origins in a reaction *against* idealism. And yet, they preserve a quasi-idealistic take towards symbols—a form of idealism that, however, is closer to the classic Platonic idealism than to Hegel's *post-Kantian* idealism. This is particularly evident, I think, in some forms of Hermeneutics. In the thought of Paul Ricoeur, for example, symbols are signs able to transmit a meaning and, as such, they are relevant in themselves. Ricoeur maintains that the main feature of a symbol is *opacity*: an opacity that can be penetrated, but never solved in perfect transparency. The rationalization of the sacred and of the question of evil, which is always indissolubly bounded to religion, ended up dissolving the symbolic and regulative meaning of religious experience itself. Hence, Ricoeur's conclusion that it is necessary to "undo the concept," to pass through the defeat of knowledge to find meaning in the symbols of religious experience. I will briefly come back to Ricoeur in the final section. For now, I just want to stress that the main risk of this approach is that once symbols have been deprived of their regulative status, they maintain a merely *descriptive* value.

The case of sacrifice is emblematic of this process. For the anthropological reading, as I have already stressed, sacrifice is a mere metaphor or a vague ethical indication. Alternatively, most of the debates on sacrifice

Conclusion 149

in twentieth-century European philosophy do not consider the regulative aspect of sacrifice, and tend to overemphasize its symbolic aspect. As such, the notion of sacrifice loses the normative status that, as I argued, has been fundamental in the development of Kantian and post-Kantian philosophy.

It is not worth focusing on the first trend—the anthropological reading—because, as we have seen, its consequences for the notion of sacrifice are quite trivial. Conversely, I want to briefly focus on two specific philosophers, who exemplify the second and third trend respectively: namely, Bataille and Derrida. To these two philosophical viewpoints I will then add Girard's mimetic theory, as it represents an unavoidable milestone for an account of sacrifice in the twentieth century. Finally, I will devote some conclusive remarks to the role of sacrifice in contemporary philosophical hermeneutics.

Bataille

No doubt, Georges Bataille has provided one of the most influential theories of sacrifice in the twentieth century. Bataille's account of sacrifice as pure expenditure (*dépense*) turned out to be seminal for further developments in postmodern approaches. What is more, Bataille presented his theory of sacrifice as deriving from (and partially reacting against) Hegel's account of sacrifice (and, more broadly, Hegel's conception of the negative). Bataille's essay "Hegel, la Mort et le Sacrifice,"[10] provoked by Kojève's influential lectures on Hegel,[11] ended up establishing an interpretation of Hegel's notion of sacrifice that has subsequently been assumed without questioning its premises.[12] Unfortunately, this reading of Hegel is a misleading one—or at least it is a reading that expresses Bataille's own take more than Hegel's.

In addition to a range of interpretative errors, Bataille does not grasp the *kenotic* component of Hegel's theory of sacrifice. It is useful to briefly address the interpretation provided by Bataille in his essay to show the interpretative mistakes of such an approach and to appreciate which aspects of the array of post-Kantian alternatives are taken up in Bataille's theory of sacrifice (and which are rejected).

For Bataille, who strongly relies on Kojève's reading of the *Phenomenology of Spirit*, the master-slave dialectic is the key element to understand Hegel's philosophy. Here, the work of the slave is taken to represent human action and understanding: it is that struggle for dialectic transformation that gives man his own consciousness, which is first of all consciousness of his own death. Consciousness separates man from nature, and this separation is regarded by Bataille as negativity. The main question for Bataille is how to deal with this consciousness of one's death. The answer is *sacrifice*: in fact, the sacrificer can experience death through identification with his victim. According to Bataille, Hegel understood that sacrifice could effectively express the "power of negativity." but he was only partially successful, because (Bataille claims) he ended up "domesticating" the negative, by turning sacrifice into a kind of "fiction." In other words, sacrifice is indeed the only path to the negative, but it is also a representation, or even a "spectacle": it is as if the sacrificer died, while retaining consciousness of his own death. In Bataille's view, Hegel has the merit of having identified in the sacrificial dialectic the fundamental strategy to dealing with the negative. However, Hegel has forgotten that the death or annihilation that happens in sacrifice is a *representation*—it is not *my* death. By doing so, Bataille claims, Hegel made that death somehow 'livable' and integrated it into a system whose ultimate goal is wisdom—but in doing so, he has removed its power.

Bataille's criticism is particularly evident in relation to the figure of the "sage." According to Kojève, the core of Hegel's philosophy is represented by the story of the working slave who builds his world by making his Lord's consumption more "rationally productive." However, according to Bataille, the struggle between master and slave and its outcome still have a goal—the goal being the struggle for recognition. The master can die; but if he does not die, he has reached his goal, that is, he has been recognized as the lord by his slave. In opposition to this (Hegelian) notion of lordship, Bataille sets his own notion of sovereignty (*souveraineté*). What distinguishes sovereignty from lordship is that in the former no project or goal is involved. To keep his lordship, Bataille argues, the Hegelian lord must become the slave of his slave: he must put in place a set of ruling techniques that involve work, goals, projects, etc. Conversely, Bataille's sovereignty is pure expenditure (*dépense*), that is, an unfruitful negativity that does not wait for anything—or, better, is a waiting for *nothing*.

What is wrong with this picture? In general terms, there are a number of problematic issues regarding Bataille's approach to Hegel's philosophy. First, Bataille follows Kojève in his use and overemphasis of the master and slave episode, which is considered as the key to Hegel's entire philosophy rather than as a specific dialectical moment. Second, Bataille identifies negativity with (the consciousness of) death, probably influenced by his Heideggerian readings—but for Hegel, negativity is not primarily the consciousness of one's own death. Third, and more broadly, Bataille's interpretation is marked by his idea that consciousness and understanding represent *the* fundamental rupture with nature (which is the negative), and it is therefore necessary to "reconnect" human being with nature. This idea, however, is far from consistent with Hegel's philosophy, which is concerned with the progressive elevation of humans into more and more culturally complex beings.[13]

More specifically, Bataille's account does not do justice to the complexity of Hegel's notion of sacrifice. Bataille insists that Hegel correctly regards sacrifice as the suppression or destruction of something, but he objects that in Hegel's philosophy sacrifice remains at the level of representation. In light of a deeper analysis, this conclusion simultaneously gives "too much" and "too little" importance to the notion of sacrifice. It gives sacrifice too much importance because when Hegel considers sacrifice as the mere destruction or suppression of something, he does not consider it an important strategy aimed at dealing with the negative. Sacrifice as suppression has other functions, the basic function being the establishment of a connection with the transcendent through reciprocal recognition, and the subsequent recognition of common values and beliefs. As we have seen, this use of sacrifice is particularly clear in the analysis of the cult that Hegel pursues in the *Phenomenology* (PG, 718/434).

Furthermore, Bataille's account gives Hegel's notion of sacrifice too little importance because he sees sacrifice *merely* as destruction or suppression. However, as we know, this is only *half* of the story; and the kenotic aspect of sacrifice remains, in Bataille's account, totally unexplored. This is consistent with our formula that links the weakening of norms, perspectivism, and kenosis, insofar as to a substantial absence of norms corresponds, in Bataille's thought, a substantial absence of kenosis; also, despite the Nietzschean legacy, Bataille's thought does not appear marked with perspectivism, as sacrifice is rather conceived as an attempt to reestablish a connection with objects, and with other human beings, beyond any possible "reflective" and perspectival position.

Bataille's thought is exemplary of that valorization of irrationality that, reintroduced by Kojève, has found its *raison d'être* in the exaltation of paradox. Bataille deals with Hegelian themes (most notably, negativity), but the focus of his thought is very far from Hegel's philosophical goals. Obviously Nietzsche plays a major role in informing Bataille's approach—or rather, an *interpretation* of Nietzsche that overemphasizes the idea of the will to power as a primordial "impetus" or "impulse" at the expense of everything else. As we have seen, the main consequence of this reading is the consideration of the dissolution of the principle of individuation as the most desirable outcome for humans. From *this version* of Nietzsche, Bataille borrows the idea of sacrifice as the symbol of the failure of reason when it connects to reality—the same dynamic that is at work in Solger's dual dialectic. Solger, however, still believed in the possibility of a paradoxical connection between the finite (human being) and the infinite (God). This option is not contemplated by Bataille; and thus the paradox inevitably turns into a "dead end." In fact, if the goal is the dissolution of one's identity, every act of consciousness should be discouraged, insofar as it inevitably is an affirmation of one's identity. What is more, Bataille's proposed goal is affected by a serious internal contradiction—namely, that the dissolution in a hypothetical pre-rational organic nature (that which Bataille calls "totality") is possible if and only if there is something *different from that totality*. In other words, a conscious human being, in order to get rid of his own consciousness (the loss of individuation that should happen in the act of sacrifice, for example), must inevitably perform a *conscious* act. Bataille was aware of these problems, which probably lead him to choose, in his further writings, a narrative style (in the form of novels or short stories) to replace a more traditional philosophical style (in the form of papers and essays).

Derrida

In *The Gift of Death*, Jacques Derrida offered an account of sacrifice, based on the *Akedah* and on Kierkegaard's *Fear and Trembling*, which has attracted considerable attention in the last decades. His basic idea is that *sacrifice* is what we do each time we embrace responsibility toward a *specific* "other" and, in doing so, we put the interest of that specific "other" above the competing interests of other "others": "I cannot respond to the call, the request, the obligation, or even the love of another"—Derrida writes—"without sacrificing the other other, the other others."[14]

I am not interested in challenging Derrida's view here, or in wondering if his account can effectively represent a suitable interpretation of Kierkegaard's *Fear and Trembling*[15]—but, once again, I am interested in understanding how his account of sacrifice is related to the "standard" accounts of sacrifice that we have identified in nineteenth-century post-Kantian philosophy. First, we can note that Derrida's account is effectively related to an aspect of Kierkegaard's thought, namely his critique of Kantian ethics. Rightly or wrongly, Kierkegaard identified the main flaw of Kant's ethics in his *moral perfectionism*—that is, in the idea that there is *one* moral law, that it is certain, and that if we follow it we can be "in the right." Kierkegaard was very critical of this (alleged) conceitedness: not only because over against God we are not "in the right," but always in the wrong, but also because ethics is not the answer to the divine command to love one's neighbor. As we have seen in our survey of *Works of Love*, Kierkegaard thought that human ethics was simply insufficient to satisfy the *divine* law—which is the reason why we need God's command to love our neighbors. From this angle, Derrida's view is a development of this idea: the insufficiency of ethics, and sacrifice as the symbol of this insufficiency. What is lacking in Derrida's story is the *positive* side, which is conversely prominent in Kierkegaard. For Kierkegaard, sacrifice is not just the symbol of the insufficiency of morality. Sacrifice is the self-emptying of oneself to make room for others. This is not enough to grant us salvation, of course—according to Kierkegaard, we need the divine grace for that. But still, this is our duty. Our *theonomous* duty, as we have remarked several times: we are completely *outside* ethics here.

Derrida does not follow Kierkegaard in suggesting that we should "simply" follow God's command. The Kantian, immutable moral law has been discharged, and the regulativity of symbols has been dismissed with it. Kierkegaard's solution—his peculiar love-centered divine command theory—implies a fideistic turn, and Derrida is not willing to go that way. However, Derrida cannot take the other extreme either—the other extreme being the consideration of symbols as *mere* metaphors (the anthropological reading can make such a claim, but the consideration of symbols as metaphors implies a metaphysical structure of reality to which symbols are referred *as metaphors*—and this is precisely the structure that Derrida wants to deconstruct). The only other possible solution, therefore, is considering symbols as standing by themselves. This idea, however, can have two main possible philosophical developments. The first is Hegel's idealism: if all objects of reason have an ideal (and not a naturalistic) existence, it follows that they also have a normative dimension. In other words, Kant's move is turned upside down. For Kant, *first* we have the moral law, *then* we have symbols (transitional forms) to apply moral laws to experiences, and *consequently* symbols should be considered as regulative. Conversely, for Hegel, *first* we have objects of reason; objects of reason have an ideal existence, that is, they are based on recognition; insofar as they are based on recognition, some of those symbols are granted a regulative role—and this *finally* constitutes morality.

Even Hegel's solution sounds too "metaphysical" to Derrida. To an extreme weakening of the idea of norms—basically, to their complete dissolution—corresponds a perspectivism as much as extreme. Consistently, Derrida's conception of sacrifice is also taken to an extreme point: in principle, every ethical behavior towards someone becomes a suppressive sacrifice (in the form of an exclusion) toward everybody else; and the kenotic ideal—withdrawing and giving up something of oneself to make room for others—becomes unattainable, even a paradox. As already stressed, the *Akedah* has lost any regulative value, and the sacrificial-kenotic symbol stands by itself. There is something *romantic* in Derrida's use of the *Akedah*; and in fact, the way symbols stand by themselves for Derrida could be connected to a return to Nietzsche's romanticism. Although this topic cannot be dealt with in great depth here, I find it remarkable that Derrida rarely provides an extensive account of symbols. In *Of Grammatology*, for example, he seems to consider symbols only the natural signs (say, a lion as a symbol of royalty or bravery), just to point out that these symbols escape semiology—but without providing an argument (at least not in a strict sense) for this exclusion.[16]

Is the *Akedah*, in Derrida's terms, a symbol? Let us assume so. In that case, it is a symbol that stands by itself (its legitimacy is grounded neither on the moral law, nor on recognition, nor on the divine authority of a text, nor on anything else). Additionally, it does not have any regulative value—the events happened on the Mount Moriah merely *symbolize* our impotence (as well as the insufficiency of ethics). This use of symbols is close to that of Nietzsche. For Nietzsche, strictly speaking, symbols can bear different meanings, but ultimately they express cultural attitudes to the will to power.[17] More broadly, symbols are used by Nietzsche to convey his ideas—they have, in other words, an *aesthetic* value. From this point of view, Derrida's approach might be regarded as a return to Nietzsche's romanticism: similarly to *Thus Spoke Zarathustra*, most of Derrida's works take the form of artworks, with the central messages presented in the form of deconstructed myths. As already stressed, the main consequence of this approach is that symbols end up by either maintaining a merely descriptive value or turning into an aesthetic component. This aesthetic drift has been remarked by several scholars, most notably, within studies on sacrifice, by René Girard, who wrote that "deconstruction seems content with [. . .] pure literary effect; it risk degenerating into pure verbalism."[18] In fact, as we are going to see, Girard is developing the Kantian and post-Kantian legacy in a completely different direction.

Girard

The account of sacrifice elaborated by René Girard does not fit with any of the three major trends in twentieth-century Continental philosophy that we have previously identified. This might be due to the fact that Girard is not, strictly speaking, a philosopher. His account of sacrifice has its roots in literary criticism and anthropology rather than in philosophy. Maybe because of this, Girard has been able to formulate a fresh approach to sacrifice, with a major emphasis on the more concrete aspects of this notion.

Prima facie, Girard's so-called "mimetic theory" does not seem to be connected in any way to the Kantian and post-Kantian tradition. Conversely, a deeper analysis shows that Girard's account of sacrifice is indebted to Kantian and post-Kantian perspectivism. One of the most striking evidences of this legacy is represented by the notion of "the sacred" as it is described and addressed in Girard's work. "The sacred," in Girardian terms, is the sacrificial violence. Just as mimetic desires can come to bear on the same objects, so the mimetic violence can arbitrarily converge on a particular person (a scapegoat), one who catches the attention of the others by some peculiarity of appearance or who has a defect that renders him or her vulnerable (a disabled person, a stranger, etc.). The scapegoat then becomes the object of sacrificial violence and is killed. Thus the community finds itself united. This violence is subsequently perpetuated in the narratives of the original event. The point of view of those mythical narratives is that of the persecutors: the victim is obviously presented as guilty. Furthermore, this point of view must be absolute: in fact, only if it is absolute, that is, universally shared, it guarantees that unanimity which is a fundamental element for the efficiency of the scapegoating mechanism. Therefore, the event is presented from a "detached" or "objective" perspective—that is, from the God's-eye point of view. However, Girard claims, the myth of the detachment is "the greatest myth of all."[19] The truth of the victim is *eo ipso* perspectival. It is perspectival first because it contrasts the "absolute" point of view of the persecutors with an "alternative" point of view—a discordant voice. Second, and most importantly, the truth of the victim is intrinsically perspectival. In fact, while according to the "truth" of the persecutors the victim is guilty without appeal, the demystification shows that every victim is guilty and innocent *at the same time*—guilty insofar as it is responsible for mimetic violence like everyone else; but innocent of the crimes that are ascribed to it (the case of Oedipus is meaningful in this respect). On the other hand, while according to the story of the persecutors the victim is evil, the demystifying perspective shows us that it is inappropriate to think of the persecutors as evil: they just look for the peace "as the world can give it": literally, "they know not what they do."

The reference to Christ's words is important here because, according to Girard, if we now have the possibility to contrast the point of view of the persecutors with another point of view, and—even more fundamentally—if we are able to talk about "points of view" rather than acritically considering the sacrificial narrative, it is because we are benefiting from the demystification of the Gospels, which according to Girard have taught us to consider different perspectives.

At the core of Girard's mimetic theory there is a strong, although partially hidden, endorsement of perspectivism. Perspectivism, however, is *not* relativism—a feature that according to Girard belongs to Deconstruction, and against which Girard is very critical. In fact, Deconstruction feigns a detachment that, Girard claims, "perpetuates the status quo, prolongs the occulting of the scapegoat, and makes us effective accomplices of the persecutors."[20] "The true science of man," Girard continues, "is not indifferent."[21]

Girard seems to suggest that to face up to violence, disorder, and rivalry, our culture should develop a progressive sharing of perspectivism, a perspectivism strong enough to abandon not only the myth of "detachment," but also that last (even more dangerous) sacral vestige represented by the myth of the disenchantment—without at the same time requiring the commitment to a specific perspective considered as "absolutely true." In fact, apart from the evangelical demystification concerning the only truly innocent victim of the history of mankind (Christ), every human version of the "truth of the victim" is exposed to the risk to be reversed in its opposite and become a lie. There are plenty of examples of victims who reverse the roles and turn themselves into persecutors, while still presenting themselves as victims.

To clarify this important but rarely explored issue in Girard's thought, one might turn to the distinction between *truth* and *truthfulness* (*Wahrhaftigkeit*), introduced by Kant in his essay "Concerning the Possibility of a Theodicy and the Failure of All Previous Philosophical Attempts in the Field."[22] In commenting the Book of Job, Kant writes:

> Hence only sincerity of heart and not distinction of insight; honesty in openly admitting one's doubts; repugnance to pretending conviction where one feels none, especially before God (where this trick is pointless enough)—these are the attributes which, in the person of Job, have decided the preeminence of the honest man over the flatterer.[23]

The knowledge to which one should aspire does not depend on the subtlety of the arguments, but on the faith in the truthfulness of one's claim. Kant states:

> One cannot always stand by the *truth* of what one says to oneself or to another (for one can be mistaken); however, one can and must stand by the *truthfulness* of one's declaration or confession, because one has immediate consciousness of this.[24]

From this angle, Girard's mimetic theory represents an original development of Kant's philosophy. The reader might recall that the thesis that has oriented our discussion in this chapter is that as the source of norms weakens, the corresponding perspectivism becomes increasingly radical—and the more we ascend in the sliding scale of kenosis. Girard provides a *dualist* solution to the question of the source of norms. A similar solution was offered by Kierkegaard: there is an (insufficient) source of norms in human reason, governing the world of ethics, and there is an (adequate but difficult to follow) source of norms in the divine command to love. Similarly, and even more radically, Girard seems to suggest that there is a (human) source of norms in the logic governing the mimetic victimage, and a (divine) source of norms in the command to renounce the sacrificial violence. As in the case of Kierkegaard, to a strong source of norms corresponds a modest form of perspectivism. But whereas Kierkegaard had developed, as we have seen, a profound theory of kenotic sacrifice, this dynamic seems to be completely absent from Girard's account. Self-sacrifice is indeed considered by Girard, but—at least in his main works—it does not differ from any other form of violent sacrifice, and it is basically represented as a masochistic "self-immolation." Where is kenotic sacrifice? Isn't it possible, in Girard's terms, an act of gratuitous love, a "withdrawal," a "making room" for others?

The problem, here, is terminological. Girard does recognize the love implied in the conscious and nonviolent acceptance of the sacrificial suffering, of which the passion of Christ is considered the prototype; what he does not seem willing to accept is the *necessity* of Christ's sacrifice for the human salvation. In other words, the death of Christ means the "abandonment of the direct and easy way, which would be for all to accept the principles of conduct that he has stated" and the turning "to the indirect way, the one that has to by-pass the consent of all mankind and instead pass through the Crucifixion and the Apocalypse."[25]

More recently, Girard has acknowledged the intentional and active use of sacrificial symbols both in the Old and in the New Testament, even (commendably) disavowing his previous expulsion of the *Letter to the Jews* (previously judged too "sacrificial") from his own personal "canon." Now Girard claims that the crucifixion of Christ has to be defined in terms of self-sacrifice, actively made out of love for the mankind; and yet, he does not clarify reasons and consequences of these changes. Significantly, when Girard makes such claims, he suddenly feels the need to distance his thought from that of Gianni Vattimo, the Italian philosopher who in the last few years has repeatedly claimed his proximity to Girard's interpretation of sacrifice. Whereas the distance between them is quite evident in relation to the notion of truth (for Vattimo the trajectory of contemporary philosophy is "a passage from *veritas* to *caritas*," from truth to charity, whereas Girard is not willing to get rid of the notion of truth, "because in Christianity truth and love coincide and are one and the same"[26]), the distance between them on the notion of sacrifice is not made clear by Girard.

Girard's account of sacrifice has a peerless *descriptive* value because it provides a meaningful description of what *suppressive* sacrifice is. However, it is defective in that it does not provide a *normative* account of sacrifice—which is consistent with the premises of his thought, because in the Girardian world one *either* sacrifices someone else (by scapegoating him), *or* is subjected to sacrifice (by passively accepting his role as scapegoat, like most of the victims do, or by actively denouncing his innocence, like Job or Christ do); but the absence of a positive and active sacrifice (such as the kenotic sacrifice) makes a hypothetical normativity of sacrifice completely superfluous, and even inconsistent with Girard's premises. Conversely, once the possibility of the kenotic sacrifice is endorsed, it seems to be logically coherent to develop sacrifice in the direction broadly suggested by Vattimo. However, as we are going to see, this implies a strengthening of perspectivism; something that apparently Girard is not ready to accept. Thus, both perspectivism and kenotic sacrifice remain underdeveloped in Girard's mimetic theory.

Vattimo

Gianni Vattimo, a student of the Italian seminal philosopher Luigi Pareyson[27] (one of the three great "fathers" of contemporary philosophical hermeneutics together with Gadamer and Ricoeur, albeit the less known in the Anglophone world), is famous for a philosophical approach named *"pensiero debole"* (weak thought). "Weak thought" is basically concerned with arguing for philosophical anti-foundationalism: drawing on the philosophy of Nietzsche, Heidegger, and Gadamer, Vattimo advocates the rejection of metaphysics and a reinterpretation of truth as the opening of horizons. In the last fifteen years, Vattimo has engaged with Girard an intermittent dialogue about the notion of secularization, the end of metaphysics, and—most significantly for our purposes—sacrifice interpreted in a kenotic fashion. It is not possible here to adequately address the notion of kenosis in Vattimo's thought (a task that would imply an analysis of the relationship of his thought to Pareyson's philosophy). However, some brief remarks might shed light on both the insufficiency of Girard's thought, and on the way in which the notion of kenotic sacrifice has been received in one of the most prominent trends of twentieth-century Continental philosophy—namely, philosophical hermeneutics.

Vattimo's thought has its roots in Nietzsche and Heidegger. From Nietzsche, Vattimo borrows (and endorses) the claim that "there are no facts, only interpretations."[28] That is to say that nobody can legitimately claim to hold an unquestionable truth. From Heidegger, Vattimo takes the idea that Being cannot be identified with objective presence, and he builds on this to develop the idea of a "post-metaphysical philosophy" able to think the event of Being "in terms of an indefinite type of ongoing subtraction, a weakening, a taking-leave, or long farewell."[29] Vattimo claims that the weakening of Being is "an analogon" of Girard's dissolution of the violence of the sacred, and comments: "Kénosis is probably the word best suited to connect these two discourses, which are apparently so different."[30] For Vattimo, the kenotic moment resides, for both Girard and Heidegger, in the self-consumption of (religious and metaphysical) violence. What seems lacking in Girard's account, according to Vattimo, is the notion of grace, "the salvation that is inherently related to the incarnation of Jesus Christ." In other words, Vattimo's account is different from Girard's insofar as for Vattimo salvation is not primarily a matter of consciousness (the choice between sacrificial violence and love), but a progressive (kenotic) reduction of the violence of the sacred.

Vattimo's thoughts on this issue remain, at least partially, underdeveloped. And yet, the idea that the abandonment of metaphysics implies a kenotic attitude surfaces in several of his discussions on the topic. As a hermeneutic thinker, Vattimo is the heir of a long tradition that—as his mentor Pareyson has brilliantly shown—has its roots in German Idealism. His emphasis on kenosis, therefore, seems to be a direct consequence of the fundamental perspectival feature of that tradition. One might object that Vattimo has been often charged with being a relativist rather than a perspectivist—and sometimes he has also proudly accepted this charge. However, one might respond to this objection by claiming that Vattimo's alleged relativism might be considered more apparent than real. It is interesting to note that in the context of a brief polemic against Vattimo,[31] Girard remarks that Nietzsche's slogan "There are only interpretations" is often practically disregarded by Vattimo himself, insofar as in front of a choice between the "truth of the victim" and "the lies of the persecutors" (to use Girard's terminology), Vattimo would not claim that all interpretations are equally valid, but would stand firmly for the truth of the victim. Hermeneutical perspectivism, for Vattimo, prior to having a cognitive/epistemological value, has an ethical significance: it means that I should put my point of view in perspective to take into consideration the perspectives of others. If nobody has access to the truth, then I have to "listen to others": "We don't reach agreement when we have discovered the truth, we say we have discovered the truth when we reach agreement. In other words, charity takes the place of truth."[32] For Vattimo, the only source of norms is charity, which is based on mutual recognition, and which has to be chosen in name of the primacy of ethics.

On the ground of this brief survey of the relevance of kenosis in Vattimo's thought, two implications can be drawn. First, postmodern approaches to sacrifice in twentieth-century Continental thought have often overemphasized its symbolic aspect, while neglecting at the same time its regulative meaning. This happened because, as we have seen, the weakening (or even the absence) of the source of norms has deprived the symbol of sacrifice of its regulative aspect. It is this that is behind the pervasive miscomprehension of sacrifice in modern and contemporary culture: it is difficult to deal with a symbol that does not seem to be meant for anything else apart from *being a symbol*. Vattimo touches a raw nerve, when he claims that a "postmetaphysical philosophy" should be able to rethink the notion of Being not in objective terms, but in terms of an ongoing "taking-leave." As far as sacrifice is concerned, this links to the possibility of a type of thinking in which sacrifice can be thought of philosophically, without turning it into an abstract or fictional reconstruction. How can this be done?

A return to the post-Kantian tradition of the nineteenth century might effectively help in providing an answer to this question. After all, the normativity of symbols after the weakening of the source of norms that followed Kant's critical philosophy is a theme that is found in different ways in most of the post-Kantians, such as Hegel, Kierkegaard, and Nietzsche. Most notably, the integration of Christian symbols in Hegel's metaphysics is connected with Hegel's opposition to the skepticism that is associated with the discovery that the norms to which we hold are finite—as Redding has noted, "[b]ecause even God is affected by such finitude [. . .], Christian mythology gives expression to a stance which undermines the normative assumptions upon which scepticism makes sense."[33] This emphasis on perspectivism might lead to considering Hegel as a "hermeneutic theorist" *ante litteram*.[34] Moreover, and most interestingly for our purposes, this might provide a hint that indicates the path that should be followed to develop a theory of sacrifice both philosophically valid and suited to face contemporary challenges.

What Theory of Sacrifice?

At the end of our journey, it is now time to evaluate the contribution of nineteenth-century post-Kantian philosophy to the development of a theory of sacrifice, and appreciate to what extent this tradition still represents a valuable resource to re-think sacrifice today. Obviously these final remarks will not be oriented toward the identification of the "best" theory of sacrifice among those previously taken into consideration. That would be naïve, and not only for the obvious reason that there would be something superficial in "ranking" first-class philosophers. There are at least two more profound reasons suggesting a different approach.

First, an adequate treatment of the notion of sacrifice necessarily implicates epistemological, ethical, and religious considerations. In the previous chapters we have seen that it is impossible to deal with the notion of sacrifice within a specific philosophical account without bringing into play the most fundamental features of that account; in fact, we have been often led to analyze the broad philosophical framework of the philosopher in question in order to understand the role and significance of the notion of sacrifice. This is one of the reasons why sacrifice is actually so important: it is one of those privileged hermeneutic keys that highlight the connections between the theoretical, the practical, and the religious realms within a given philosophical thought.

Second, all the post-Kantian philosophers considered here have dealt with the same array of problems arising from Kant. The solutions that have been offered are diverse, and sometimes, in solving those problems, they created several other problems (as it often happens in philosophy). Therefore, rather than identifying one single philosophical account among those that have been considered, we should consider the contribution that this tradition, considered as a whole, has given to the understanding of the notion of sacrifice. The idea here is that the different, and sometimes opposed, philosophical perspectives of the post-Kantian thinkers on the notion of sacrifice need to be considered all together in order to compose a strategy that allows the notion of sacrifice to be dealt with in a way that avoids the problems implied in other approaches.

If we analyze these philosophical perspectives all together, we first note that the notion of kenotic sacrifice always plays an important role. Clearly, they are not employing the notion of kenosis in the same way, and there are important differences, as we have often noticed through our survey. And yet, it is possible to identify some common issues.

The first issue is a strict interrelation between the kenotic conception of sacrifice and the establishment of a perspectival account of knowledge, which is connected with Kant's transcendental move and which is one of the most important features of the post-Kantian tradition. This is important, because it effectively represents a shift in the understanding of the kind of knowledge that is aspired to in philosophy. Modern philosophy, and specifically British empiricism, had introduced an idea of epistemology as the study of the conditions and limits of knowledge of the world—what is there "anyway." This was a *naturalistic* epistemology, and as such, it did not pose epistemological questions concerning *metaphysical* (rather than empirical) inquiry. One of the significant features of Kant's breakthrough was to pose those questions. Kant introduced a clear distinction between the realm of empirical, everyday knowledge (including natural sciences, which are an extension of this), and the realm of metaphysical knowledge. From this angle, the primary task of philosophy becomes the reflection on the nature of our claims about the world, rather than trying to figure out something about the basic structure of the world that is not available to natural sciences. Kant's main concern, which effectively oriented all the further inquiries of the post-Kantians, was an investigation of what allows metaphysics to be a human enterprise. Kant's answer was to re-think metaphysics in *practical* terms, as that "realm of reason" endowed with a normative structure—a turn that effectively paved the way for the German idealists.

Kant's breakthrough is relevant in terms of our account of sacrifice for two reasons. On one hand, the Kantian turn allows a better understanding of sacrifice, as well as a better understanding of all similar notions and dynamics that cannot be explained in purely naturalistic terms or in terms of everyday empirical knowledge. On the other hand, this shift in epistemology implies renouncing the idea of the possibility of claiming something about the basic structure of the world as it is "anyway"—in other words, it implies renouncing the God's-eye view as the goal aspired to in philosophy. This renunciation is effectively a kenotic sacrifice; thus, sacrifice is the prerequisite, or condition, of this epistemological shift, which in turns allows an understanding of kenotic sacrifice—that is, the movement that has made it possible. From this angle, the post-Kantian tradition can even be considered the philosophical expression of kenotic sacrifice, that is, an attempt to make explicit what it means to recognize other points of view.

The second issue that emerges if we consider all the post-Kantian accounts of sacrifice in terms of a unified approach is that, although in different ways, they all consider sacrifice both in its symbolic *and* regulative meaning—that is, as a symbol that has a *normative* value. From Kant onwards, all the philosophers considered in this book regarded symbols as (needed) representational forms of a content that could also be expressed in conceptual form. Even Kierkegaard, whose attitude toward abstract thought was certainly not one of overconfidence, considered desirable the employment of a conceptual translation of symbols (the whole structure of the *Concluding*

Scientific Postscript can be read in this way). It is the permanence of this connection of the symbol with its conceptual counterpart (the symbolized concept, as it were) that allows the symbol to maintain a normative (and not just a descriptive) value.

Conversely, as stressed in the previous section, most accounts of sacrifice developed in the context of twentieth-century Continental thought tend to consider sacrifice as a symbol deprived of a specific regulative or normative value—in other words, the connection between the symbol and the symbolized concept is lost, with the symbol standing by itself. As already mentioned, according to Ricoeur, who was definitely one of the most brilliant theorists of symbol in the last century, symbols are signs able to transmit a meaning and, as such, they are relevant in themselves: they are descriptive, but not normative. A symbol is richer than a concept because of its opacity, which makes it inexhaustible. And its opacity can be penetrated because a symbol refers to a complex system of signs, references and other symbols as well. This system is what we name "culture." Hence, a symbol is completely meaningful only within a particular culture. Now, the most relevant problem in this approach is the impossibility to re-translate symbols into conceptual form, thereby recovering their regulative status. Our times characterized by a loss of shared values and by the confrontation (if not conflict) between different cultures, seem to issue to philosophy the challenge of working on shared and "usable" symbols. And this is indeed possible only if symbols are, so to say, "translatable." An "untranslatable" symbol—a symbol standing by itself—loses the greatest part of its richness and sometimes even its utility when our main urge is to find a common cultural language that may be accepted and shared, even among different cultures.

The third issue emerging from a consideration of all the post-Kantian accounts of sacrifice considered in this book in terms of a unified approach, is the way in which the kenotic sacrifice is always developed and employed as to exclude the identification of kenotic sacrifice with the self-annihilation, or the sacrifice "without reserve." As we have seen, both Hegel and Kierkegaard are explicit in excluding this idea of sacrifice. Sacrifice as self-annihilation is present in Nietzsche as a sort of "temptation," which is usually resisted. However, relying on *this* aspect of Nietzsche's account of sacrifice, some twentieth-century postmodern philosophers, such as Bataille, Derrida, and Žižek,[35] have often offered an account of sacrifice as self-annihilation. This "radicalization" of sacrifice might be regarded as an attempt to make the symbolic aspect of sacrifice "stronger" and more meaningful, in an effort to compensate for the lack of regulative meaning derived from the absence of any connection to the conceptual counterpart. However, it has already been stressed that if sacrifice becomes self-annihilation, it is no longer a proper *kenotic* sacrifice. A sacrifice conceived as self-annihilation obviously cannot have any regulative value, because, at least in its radical form, can be performed only *once*—if I annihilate myself, I cannot do that again because I no longer exist. Conversely, an authentic kenotic sacrifice does not imply the "dissolution" of the self, but rather a "renegotiation" of one's own identity as a result of one's withdrawal. However, one more question arises: Why should one "renegotiate" one's identity? Why should one take the notion of sacrifice seriously in its normative aspect, and embrace it? In short, what is the ultimate goal of (kenotic) sacrifice?

First, the answer to this question leads back to the issue of the relation between the epistemological and the ethical value of sacrifice. As previously stressed, a kenotic attitude is the condition for the establishment of a perspectival account of knowledge, insofar as it implies the renunciation of the God's-eye view and the willingness to make room for other points of view. The idea here is simply that knowledge is perspectival—if it is not perspectival, it is not real knowledge at all. Here we are talking about metaphysical, and not empirical knowledge. In the context of everyday, empirical, and scientific knowledge, perspective does not matter, or matters in a very limited way. But Kant has suggested that when it comes to metaphysical objects (objects of reason), we are in a different realm. Kant has indeed tried to save the idea of objectivity, by employing fixed transcendental structures. However, this was perceived as a problem by all the post-Kantians; and with Hegel we have another important breakthrough—the idea that our conceptual forms are not fixed and universal, but (at least to some extent) historically and socially determined; that is, necessarily perspectival. However, as we have already stressed several times, this epistemological move is not possible without a kenotic attitude.

Second, kenotic sacrifice has an *ethical* value. I withdraw and I put my point of view in perspective to take into consideration the perspectives of others. This is also one of the conditions of the idea of modernity, insofar as modern freedom is based on the rejection of any dogmatic truth. As we have seen, kenotic attitude and perspectivism are two aspects of contemporary philosophical hermeneutics, and this may well be considered a legacy of nineteenth-century post-Kantian thought.

Finally, if one values love in itself (and engaging in a philosophical justification of love would be going too far here), forgetting one's own in loving the other—which is effectively the substance of kenotic sacrifice—seems to be essential for the definition of true love.

These are the common elements that we can trace in the post-Kantian discussion on sacrifice. Although this philosophical strategy emerges from a broad consideration of the philosophers considered here, Hegel's theory of sacrifice seems to hold all the mentioned elements in a very structured form, with the addition of some qualifications that might be used to distinguish a real kenotic sacrifice. As we have seen, for Hegel kenotic sacrifice has to be performed consciously; it is a selfless sacrifice that does not expect anything in return (even beyond any possible self-deception); and it has to be sacrifice of something that really belongs to the subject at the point of being something *essential* to him. And as already emphasized, Kierkegaard fundamentally subscribes to this theory. Actually, while they present other problems that do not make their respective accounts more convincing than Hegel's, both Kierkegaard's and Nietzsche's thought can be considered valuable additions and, in some case, corrections to Hegel's theory of sacrifice. Kierkegaard had the merit of having called attention to the role of sacrifice in the definition of the self, and of having emphasized the concreteness of sacrifice and its relevance in everyday life. Nietzsche has clarified how the notion of sacrifice can be specifically employed regulatively—that is, adapting it to a particular situation, and abandoning the norms that resulted from that adaptation when they do not fit the situation anymore.

As mentioned in the Introduction, a Vedic hymn says that sacrifice is "the navel of the world." meaning that all that exists is made to share in sacrifice. I will not go so far as suggesting this as the concluding motto of this book. However, I think that the thinkers examined here have effectively identified something important about the role that (kenotic) sacrifice plays in our epistemological and ethical attitudes, that is, two of the main questions affecting human existence. If the ultimate goal of philosophy is to question the meaning of human existence (and I believe it is), then we should reserve to the notion of sacrifice a place of honor in the gallery of the most relevant philosophical questions.

Notes

Introduction

1. A notable exception is represented by a recent book by Douglas Hedley, *Sacrifice Imagined: Violence, Atonement, and the Sacred* (London: Continuum, 2011). This excellent book challenges influential theories of sacrifice as violence, such as those of René Girard and Walter Burkert, and presents a theory of sacrifice as renunciation of the will, drawing from the thought of Joseph de Maistre and of the Cambridge Platonists. My approach to sacrifice has some elements in common with Hedley's approach, but also differs from it in many respects. Considering the proximity of the topic, a close engagement with Hedley's work would lead to a long series of comparative remarks through the various chapters of this book—remarks which might sound pedantic to the reader. Therefore, I will rather let my theory of sacrifice speak for itself, and the reader familiar with Hedley's work will have no difficulty in grasping points of agreement as well as differences in approach.

2. From the Greek verb κενόω, which literally means "to empty." In an extended sense, it means "to make ineffective."

3. Literally, "retraction." *Tsimtsum* is a term used in the Kabbalistic teaching of Isaac Luria, a Jewish mystic of the sixteenth century. It is the first act of God; it is the retraction of his light from a certain space, so as to reduce its intensity and allow created beings to exist.

4. German theologian Jürgen Moltmann, explaining the kenotic view of creation, writes that "God 'withdraws himself from himself to himself' to make creation possible. His creative activity outwards is preceded by this humble divine self-restriction. In this sense God's self-humiliation does not begin merely with creation, inasmuch as God commits himself to this world: it begins beforehand, and is the presupposition that makes creation possible. God's creative love is grounded in his humble, self-humiliating love. This self-restricting love is the beginning of that self-emptying of God that Philippians 2 sees as the divine mystery of the Messiah. Even to create heaven and earth, God emptied himself of all his all-plenishing omnipotence, and as Creator took upon himself the form of a servant." Jürgen Moltmann, *God in Creation: A New Theology of Creation and the Spirit of God*, trans. M. Kohl (San Francisco: Harper & Row, 1985). For an introduction to the employment of the notion of kenosis in connection with God's creation, see John Polkinghorne, ed.,

The Work of Love: Creation as Kenosis (Grand Rapids: Eerdmans, 2001).

5. "In Eckhart is found a profound mystical understanding of this twofold kenosis: the one occurs in the *bullitio*, the 'boiling over,' of the Trinity from the nothingness of the desert and in which the Father pours the totality of his divinity into the Son; the other occurs in the *ebullitio*, 'flowing out,' of the Trinity towards creation, and the Son's self-emptying of his divinity for the sake of the world." Beverly J. Lanzetta, "Three Categories of Nothingness in Eckhart." *The Journal of Religion*, 72:2 (1992), 260.

6. It is "through him," Hegel claims, "that philosophy of a distinctive character first emerged in Germany." G. W. F. Hegel, *Lectures on the History of Philosophy 1825–1826*, Vol. III: Medieval and Modern Philosophy, trans. Robert F. Brown (Oxford: Oxford University Press, 2009), 20:80/120. Cf. also Andrew Weeks, *Boehme: An Intellectual Biography of the Seventeenth-Century Philosopher and Mystic* (New York: State University of New York Press, 1991), 2–3.

7. Weeks, *Boehme*, 2–3.

8. See, for instance, Kant's use of *Aufgeopfert* and *Verlassen* in Immanuel Kant, *The Metaphysics of Morals*, trans. Mary J. Gregor (Cambridge: Cambridge University Press, 1991), 127. Cf. Chapter 1.

9. Johann Gottlieb Fichte, *The Science of Rights*, trans. A. E. Kroeger (London: Routledge & Kegan Paul, 1970), 147.

10. Robert Williams, *Hegel's Ethics of Recognition* (Berkeley: University of California Press, 1997), 69. Hansson comments: "Perhaps the mature adult relationship which parents and their children can experience together would serve as an illustration. To let people go and still preserve the relationship." Mats G. Hansson, *The Private Sphere: An Emotional Territory and Its Agent* (New York: Springer, 2008), 81.

11. Sarah Coakley, *Powers and Submissions: Spirituality, Philosophy and Gender* (Oxford: Blackwell, 2006), 30.

12. Sarah Coakley, "Kenosis: Theological Meanings and Gender Connotations," in J. Polkinghorne (ed.), *The Work of Love: Creation as Kenosis* (Grand Rapids: Eerdmans, 2001), 192–210.

13. Ruth Groenhout, "Kenosis and Feminist Theory," in C. S. Evans (ed.), *Exploring Kenotic Christology* (Oxford: Oxford University Press, 2006), 291–312.

14. Coakley, "Kenosis." Coakley refers here to the theory of kenosis elaborated by John C. Polkinghorne, "Kenotic Creation and Divine Action," in Polkinghorne, *The Work of Love*, 96.

15. See George Ellis, "Kenosis as a Unifying theme for Life and Cosmology," in Polkinghorne, *The Work of Love*, 123.

16. Jürgen Moltmann, "God's Kenosis in the Creation and Consummation of the World," in Polkinghorne, *The Work of Love*, 149.

17. Groenhout, "Kenosis and Feminist Theory," 297.

18. Ibid.

19. Ibid.

20. This methodology might also be considered as "hermeneutic history of philosophy." Cf. Adriaan Theodoor Peperzak, *System and History in Philosophy* (Albany:

State of New York Press, 1986), 69ff. For an overview of key issues surrounding the debate between analytic and contextual history of philosophy, see Tom Sorell and G. A. J. Rogers (eds.), *Analytic Philosophy and History of Philosophy* (Oxford: Oxford University Press, 2005).

21. Sebastian Gardner, *Kant and the "Critique of Pure Reason"* (London: Routledge, 1999), 22, 30–33.

22. Paul Redding, *Continental Idealism. Leibniz to Nietzsche* (London and New York: Routledge, 2009), 2, 47, 62.

23. Terry Pinkard, *German Philosophy 1760–1860: The Legacy of Idealism* (Cambridge: Cambridge University Press), 227.

24. Klaus Hartmann, "Hegel: A Non-Metaphysical View," in Alasdair MacIntyre (ed.), *Hegel: A Collection of Critical Essays* (New York: Anchor Books, 1972).

25. Robert B. Pippin, *Hegel's Idealism: The Satisfactions of Self-Consciousness* (Cambridge: Cambridge University Press, 1989).

26. Robert R. Williams, *Recognition: Fichte and Hegel on the Other* (Albany: State University of New York Press, 1992); *Hegel's Ethics of Recognition* (Berkeley: University of California Press, 1997).

27. Ludwig Siep, *Anerkennung als Prinzip der praktischen Philosophie* (München: Alber, 1979).

28. Andreas Wildt, *Autonomie und Anerkennung. Hegels Moralitätskritik im Lichte seiner Fichte-Rezeption* (Stuttgart: Klett-Cotta, 1982).

29. "Hegel's resolution of the Kantian paradox was to see it in social terms. Since the agent cannot secure any bindingness for the principle simply on his own, he requires the recognition of another agent of it as binding on both of them." Robert B. Pippin, "Hegel's Practical Philosophy: The Realization of Freedom," in Kar Ameriks (ed.), *The Cambridge Companion to German Idealism* (Cambridge: Cambridge University Press, 2002), 185.

30. Immanuel Kant, *Critique of Practical Reason*, trans. Werner S. Pluhar (Indianapolis, IN: Hackett Publishing, 2002).

31. A world that "is there *anyway*" is one of the central images essential to realism. Cf. Peter G. Railton and Gideon Rosen, "Realism," in J. Kim and E. Sosa (Eds.), *A Companion to Metaphysics* (Oxford: Blackwell, 1995), 433.

32. Most philosophical puzzlements consist of making sense of a preexisting "practical know-how." For instance, we all, in some sense, know what time is, but we cannot say what it is, which is why we keep reading Augustine's reflections on the nature of time. We all know what it is to know something, and yet there is a discipline called "epistemology." The list could go on.

Chapter 1

1. Some examples are: Keith Ward, "Kant's Teleological Ethics," *The Philosophical Quarterly* 21 (1971): 337–351; Donald Mackenzie MacKinnon, "Kant's Philosophy of Religion," *Philosophy* 50 (1975): 131–144.

2. John Millbank, *Being Reconciled. Ontology and Pardon* (London and New York: Routledge, 2003).

3. Thomas E. Hill, "Kantian Constructivism in Ethics," *Ethics* 99:4 (1989): 752–770.

4. David Cummiskey, "Kantian Consequentialism," *Ethics* 100:3 (1990): 586–615.

5. A. Phillips Griffiths, "Kant's Psychological Hedonism," *Philosophy* 66 (1991): 207–216.

6. Peter Atterton, "A Duty to Be Charitable? A Rigoristic Reading of Kant," *Kant-Studien* 98:2 (2007): 135–155.

7. Daniel Guevara, "The Impossibility of Supererogation in Kant's Moral Theory," *Philosophy and Phenomenological Research* 59:3 (1999): 593–624.

8. Richard L. Bowes, "Sacrifice and the Categorical Imperative of Human Security," *International Journal* 56:4 (2001): 649–664.

9. Dennis King Keenan, *The Question of Sacrifice* (Bloomington and Indianapolis: Indiana University Press, 2005).

10. Sydney Axinn, *Sacrifice and Value. A Kantian Interpretation* (Lenham: Lexington Books, 2010).

11. Axinn, *Sacrifice and Value*, 1.

12. Ibid., 110.

13. Immanuel Kant, *Critique of Pure Reason*, trans. and ed. by P. Guyer and A. W. Wood (Cambridge: Cambridge University Press, 1998), Bxvi/110. For this and for other of Kant's works, the first number refers to the pagination of the standard German edition of Kant's works, *Kants Gesammelte Schriften*, edited by the Royal Prussian—later German—Academy of Sciences (Berlin: Georg Reimer, later Walter de Gruyter & Co., 1900–). The second number refers to the page numbering in the English translation.

14. Cf. Peter Kreeft, *Summa of the Summa. Essential Passages of Aquinas* (San Francisco: Ignatius Press, 1990), 74–112.

15. Cf. Lanzetta, "Three Categories of Nothingness in Eckhart," 260.

16. Kenotic thinking featured in the thought of radical Pietists such as Zinzendorf and Wesley. Cf. Donald G. Dawe, *The Form of a Servant: A Historical Analysis of the Kenotic Motif* (Philadelphia: Westminster, 1963), 18; David T. Williams, *The Kenosis of God: The self-limitation of God-Father, Son, and Holy Spirit* (New York and Bloomington: iUniverse, 2009), 21.

17. This is not undisputed. As is known, Kant's parents were Pietists and his early education took place in the Collegium Fridericianum, a school established by the Pietist pastor F. A. Schultz. Although "attempts are frequently made to identify Pietist influences in Kant's moral and religious thought," it is a fact that "virtually all explicit references to Pietism in his writings or lectures are openly hostile." Allen W. Wood, "Kant's Life and Works," in Graham Bird (ed.), *A Companion to Kant*, (London: Blackwell, 2006), 11. Mature Kant was definitely not a Pietist; and yet, this does not mean that some elements in the Pietist thought have not played

any role in his education and in the establishment of a personal attitude toward knowledge and life.

18. Jacob Böhme, *Aurora*. In *Sämtliche Schriften*, ed. Will-Erich Peuckert (Stuttgart: Fr. Frommanns 1955–61). Trans. by William Law, *The Works of Jacob Behman* (London: Richardson, 1764), ch. 23, #17.
19. Cf. Redding, *Continental Idealism*, 58.
20. Ibid.
21. Kant, *Critique of Pure Reason*, A51–B75/50.
22. See, for example, the *Preface* to the first edition of the *Critique of Pure Reason* (Axx). As mentioned in the Introduction, the possibility of reading Kant's account of metaphysics in two different ways has been suggested by Gardner (*Kant and the 'Critique of Pure Reason,'* 30–33) and Redding (*Continental Idealism*, 2, 47, 62).
23. Immanuel Kant, *Jäsche Logik*, trans. and ed. by P. Guyer and A. W. Wood, *Lectures on Logic* (Cambridge: Cambridge University Press, 1992), 9:92/590.
24. Redding, *Continental Idealism*, 72.
25. Cf. Pinkard, *German Philosophy*, 227.
26. For a discussion of this passage, see Keenan, *The Question of Sacrifice*, 68.
27. Cf. Hegel, *Philosophy of Right*, §135A. Regarding Hegel's critique of Kant's categorical imperative, see Stephen Houlgate, *Freedom, Truth and History* (London and New York: Routledge, 1991).
28. Friedrich Nietzsche, *The Antichrist*, trans. H. L. Mencken (New York: Alfred A. Knopf, 1918), aphorism 11.
29. To this brief list might be added the standing attack against Kant's "ethics of self-sacrifice" conducted by Ayn Rand. Rand violently opposes Kant's idea of an autonomous moral law, countering it with her idea that the only moral purpose of one's life is the pursuit of one's own happiness or rational self-interest. Cf. Ayn Rand, *Philosophy: Who Needs It* (London: Penguins Book, 1982). I am not considering Rand's objections, since I think that her arguments are not particularly significant for our purposes. For a critique of Kant's notion of sacrifice based on Rand's thought, see Leonard Peikoff, "Kant and Self-Sacrifice," *Objectivist* 10 (1971): 1092–1104.
30. Milbank, *Being Reconciled*, 14.
31. Immanuel Kant, *Grundlegung zur Metaphysik der Sitten*, trans. M. Gregor, *Groundwork of the Metaphysic of Morals* (Cambridge: Cambridge University Press, 1997), 4:407/19.
32. Milbank, *Being Reconciled*, 14.
33. Ibid., 14–15.
34. Axinn, *Sacrifice and Value*, 1.
35. Pinkard, *German Philosophy*, 227.
36. Cf. Axinn, *Sacrifice and Value*, 110.
37. As we will see in Chapter 3, the section of the *Phenomenology of Spirit* focusing on the *cult* is very clear on this point. Cf. PG, 718/435.
38. See Redding, *Continental Idealism*, 2.

39. Immanuel Kant, *Kritik der Urteilskraft*, trans. W. S. Pluhar, *Critique of Judgment* (Indianapolis: Hackett, 1987), 5:434/301.

40. Redding, *Continental Idealism*, 72.

41. As noted in the Introduction, the German verb "*Verlassen*" is often used in kenotic literature to describe Christ's act of relinquishing his own divinity in the incarnation.

42. Cf. Atterton, "A Duty to Be Charitable?," 147ff.

43. It would be a mistake to assume Kant's reduction of religion to ethics. Conversely, Kant claims that "morality leads inevitably to religion" (RGV, 6:6/60), and argues that it makes a morally meaningful difference whether an agent believes or disbelieves. Cf. Matthew Caswell, "Kant's Conception of the Highest Good, the Gesinnung, and the Theory of Radical Evil," *Kant-Studien* 97:2 (2006): 184–209. See also Philip J. Rossi and Michael J. Wreen (eds.), *Kant's Philosophy of Religion Reconsidered* (Bloomington: Indiana University Press, 1991) and Stephen Palmquist, "Does Kant Reduce Religion to Morality?," *Kant-Studien* 83:2 (1992): 129–148.

44. Redding, *Continental Idealism*, 96ff.

45. "While an empirical concept can be *exemplified* (one can give a phenomenal presentation of the concept 'dog,' for example, by pointing to *this actual dog*) and a pure concept *schematised* (one can give a phenomenal presentation to the concept 'cause' by pointing to *this actual event of a ball smashing a window*) an idea can only be *symbolized*" (Redding, *Continental Idealism*, 96).

46. Another important *Darstellung* is beauty as a symbol of morality. Cf. Kant, *Critique of Judgment*, 5:351/225, and the entire §59.

47. "Since, after all, *revelation* can at least comprise also the pure *religion of reason*, whereas, conversely, the latter cannot do the same for what is historical in revelation, I shall be able to consider the first as a *wider* sphere of faith that includes the other, a *narrower* one, within itself (not as two circles external to one another but as concentric circles); the philosopher, *as purely a teacher of reason* (from mere principles *a priori*), must keep within the inner circle and, thereby, also abstract from all experience" (RGV, 6:12/64; emphasis added).

48. A more detailed analysis of the regulative role of religious notions for Kant is beyond the scope of this book. Good accounts of the notion of regulativity applied to religion in Kant include: Donald M. MacKinnon, "Kant's Philosophy of Religion," *Philosophy* 50, no. 192 (1975): 131–144.; Cathy Caruth, "The Force of Example: Kant's Symbols," *Yale French Studies* 74 (1988): 17–37; and Thomas Teufel, "Kant's Non-Teleological Conception of Purposiveness," *Kant-Studien* 102:2 (2011): 232–252.

49. Sylviane Agacinski, "We Are Not Sublime: Love and Sacrifice, Abraham and Ourselves," in *Kierkegaard: A Critical Reader*, in Jonathan Ree and Jane Chamberlain (eds.), 141.

50. Immanuel Kant, *Der Streit der Fakultäten*, trans. and ed. by A. W. Wood and G. Di Giovanni, *The Conflict of the Faculties*, in *Religion and Natural Theology* (Cambridge: Cambridge University Press, 1996), 7:63/283.

51. Of course, as Kierkegaard's *Fear and Trembling* (together with a large number of other philosophical and nonphilosophical reflections on this biblical episode) shows, several alternative interpretations of the *Akedah* can be offered. See Chapter 4.

52. Cf. MacKinnon, "Kant's Philosophy of Religion": 141.

53. For an account of this debate, see Chris L. Firestone and Nathan Jacobs, *In Defense of Kant's Religion* (Bloomington: Indiana University Press, 2008).

54. See, for instance, Vincent McCarthy, *Quest for a Philosophical Jesus* (Macon, Georgia: Mercer University Press, 1986).

55. See Allen W. Wood, 'Kant's Life and Works,' in Graham Bird (ed.), *A Companion to Kant* (Oxford: Blackwell Publishing, 1977).

56. This is also the direction pursued by Stephen Palmquist, *Kant's Critical Religion* (Aldershot: Ashgate, 2000) (17ff), with the idea of Kant's "Critical mysticism."

57. Robert B. Pippin, "Idealism and Agency in Kant and Hegel," *The Journal of Philosophy* 88 (1991), 540.

Chapter 2

1. Hegel's review of *Solgers Nachgelassene Schriften und Briefwechsel* (edited by Ludwig Tieck and Friedrich von Raumer) originally appeared in the *Jahrbücher für wissenschaftliche Kritik* 1828, no. 51/52, 53/54, 105/106, 107/108, 109/110.

2. See Jeffrey Reid, "Hegel, Critique de Solger. Le Problème de la Communication Scientifique," *Archives de philosophie* 60:2 (1997): 256.

3. Søren Kierkegaard, *The Concept of Irony with continual reference to Socrates*, edited by Howard V. Hong and Edna H. Hong (Princeton, NJ: Princeton University Press, 1989), 308.

4. The first edition was published in 1826. All the translations from this text are mine, unless otherwise noted.

5. When Solger speaks of the *finite* (*Endlich*), he refers to the world (*Welt*) and, and the same time, to the human being (*Mensch*).

6. Cf. Claudio Ciancio, *Il paradosso della verità* (Turin: Rosenberg & Seller, 1999), 102.

7. Plotinus, Third Ennead, Eight Tractate, Section 10, trans. Stephen MacKenna and B.S. Page. Another metaphor quite common in Neoplatonic philosophy is that of light: the light spreads out from its source, but does not diminish its source.

8. The kenotic dimension of Solger's thought has been noted by Marco Ravera, "Solger e la salvezza come non conciliazione" in Piero Coda and Graziano Lingua (eds.), *Esperienza e libertà* (Rome: Città Nuova, 2000), 35.

9. "The nothing of God" (*Das Nichts Gottes*) sounds odd in English, but not so odd in German. Theologically, the use of this notion dates back to Scotus Eriugena: the Logos, created and creating, is the first manifestation of the Nothing of God. Subsequently, this notion played an important role in the German mystical tradition

of Meister Eckhart and Jacob Böhme. Cf. Alois M. Haas, "Das Nichts Gottes und seine Sprengmetaphorik" in H. Herwig, I. Wirtz and Stefan Bodo Würffel (eds.), *Semiotik und Hermeneutik in Raum und Zeit* (Tübingen: Basel, 1999), 53–70.

10. The German text can help us to understand what Solger means: "*Folglich offenbart sich das Wesen als solches, oder wird wirkliches wesen nur dadurch, daß es dieses nichts aufhebt oder vernichtet*" (NS, 172).

11. In the *Phenomenology of Spirit* the object is always the experience of the consciousness, but it assumes different features depending on whether it is considered from the point of view of the consciousness or from the point of view of the spirit. More on this in the next chapter.

12. "*Und wenn wir uns des Ewigen und Wahren in uns bewusst werden, so thun wir weiter nichts als dass wir jenen Schein in sein nichts auflösen*" (NS, 31).

13. Even Kierkegaard seems to make this mistake. *The concept of Irony*, 318.

14. "When the soul enters the light that is pure, she falls so far from her own created somethingness into her nothingness that in this nothingness she can no longer return to that created somethingness by her own power." Meister Eckhart, Sermon DW1, in *Selected Writings*, ed. and trans. Oliver Davies (London: Penguin Books, 1994), 192.

15. Meister Eckhart uses the German term "*Seelenfunklein*."

16. This dynamic has been stressed very sharply by Valeria Pinto, *Filosofia e religione in K. W. F. Solger* (Naples: Morano Editore, 1995), 49–50.

17. "*Folglich offenbart sich das Wesen als solches, oder wird wirkliches wesen nur dadurch, daß es dieses nichts aufhebt oder vernichtet*" (NS, 172).

18. The absence of a Hegelian *Aufhebung* in Solger's thought has been stressed by Giovanna Pinna, *L'ironia Metafisica. Filosofia e teoria estetica in K.W.F. Solger* (Genova: Pantograf, 1994), 233.

19. Cfr. Solger's letter to Kessler, 16.5.1818, in NS, 631–633.

20. "Since the absolute being is not real at all and therefore unknowable, knowledge is made possible only by the moment of limitation or negation." Pinna, *L'ironia Metafisica*, 45.

21. Karl Wilhelm Ferdinand Solger, *Vorlesungen über Ästhetik*, hrsg. von K. W. L.Heyse (Darmstadt: Wissenschaftliche Buchgesellschaft, 1962). The original edition appeared in Leipzig in 1829.

22. Ibid., 125.

23. For discussions of Solger's statements about irony, see Gustav E. Mueller, "Solger's Aesthetics—A Key to Hegel (Irony and Dialectic)," in A. Schirokauer and W. Paulsen (eds.), *Corona*, (Durham, NC: Duke University Press, 1941), 212–227 (here 225–226); Garnett G. Sedgewick, *Of Irony Especially in Drama* (Toronto: University of Toronto Press, 1948), 17.

24. Solger, *Vorlesungen über Ästhetik*, 112–125. Josef Heller described Solger's philosophy as "an ironic dialectic." See Josef Heller, *Solgers Philosophie der ironischen Dialektik* (Berlin: Von Reuther & Reichard, 1928). See also Ulrich Dannenhauer, *Heilsgewissheit und Resignation: Solgers Theorie der absoluten Ironie* (Frankfurt am Main:

Peter Lang, 1988); Valerio Verra, "Tragische und künstlerische Ironie bei Solger" in A. Gethmann-Siefert (ed.), *Philosophie und Poesie. O. Poeggeler zum 60 Geburtstag* (Stuttgardt-Bad Cannstatt, 1988), 235–254.

25. Solger, *Vorlesungen über Ästhetik*, 311.
26. Mueller, "Solger's Aesthetics," 225.
27. Friedrich Schlegel, *Lyceumfragment* 37. On Schlegel's irony, see Peter Szondi, "Friedrich Schlegel and Romantic Irony, with Some Remarks on Tieck's Comedies" in Peter Szondi (ed.), *On Textual Understanding and Other Essays*, (Minneapolis: University of Minnesota Press, 1986).
28. Reid, "Hegel, Critique de Solger," 256.
29. Solger, *Beurtheilung der Vorlesungen über Dramatische Kunst und Literatur*, in *Nachgelassene Schriften*, 493–628.
30. Ibid., 513.
31. Kierkegaard, *The Concept of Irony*, 317–318.
32. Solger, *Vorlesungen über Ästhetik*, 96–97.
33. Marco Ravera ("Solger e la salvezza come non conciliazione," 54) writes that the repetition of the original act of God's self-alienation can be regarded as *sacrifice*. However, the question is not analyzed either in his paper or in other scholarship exploring Solger's thought.
34. Solger, *Vorlesungen über Ästhetik*, 97–98 (my italics).
35. This and the following passages are quoted in Hegel's review of *Solgers Nachgelassene Schriften und Briefwechsel*. I therefore use the translation of Hegel's *Solger's Posthumous Writings and Correspondence*, provided by I. Diana in *Encyclopedia of the Philosophical Sciences in Outline and Critical Writings*, ed. by E. Behler (New York: Continuum, 1990), 265–319.
36. Solger, *Vorlesungen über Ästhetik*, 136–156.
37. Ibid., 312.
38. One could argue that Solger's theological categories have to be conceived *à la Kant*, as concerned not with "theological objects," but with our mode of knowing these "objects," so that, for instance, "God" should be thought of not as a "metaphysical object" but as a regulative idea. Others could argue that Solger's theological categories have to be conceived *à la Hegel*, that is, as representations of ontological categories, so that, for instance, God should be thought of as the principle that brings about the totality of conceptual determinations that underlie both human knowledge and reality. Although both these interpretations are in principle legitimate, I believe that neither of them is sufficiently grounded in Solger's work to be pursued.
39. John N. Martin, *Themes in Neoplatonic and Aristotelian Logic: Order, Negation and Abstraction* (London: Ashgate Publishers, 2004).
40. Solger, *Vorlesungen über Ästhetik*, 97–98.
41. Ivi, 603.
42. Georg Wilhelm Friedrich Hegel, *Solgers Nachgelassene Schriften und Briefwechsel*, in *Berliner Schriften*, ed. by J. Hoffmeister (Hamburg: Meiner Verlag, 1956); trans. I. Diana, *Solger's Posthumous Writings and Correspondence*, in *Encyclopedia*

of the Philosophical Sciences in Outline and Critical Writings, ed. by Ernst Behler (New York: Continuum, 1990), 265–319 (here 293).

43. For an overview of Hegel's critique of Solger, see Jeffrey Reid, *Real Words. Language and System in Hegel* (Toronto: University of Toronto Press, 2007), 96–103.

44. Hegel, *Solger's Posthumous Writings*, 287.

45. Ibid, 295.

46. Ibid, 291.

47. Ibid.

48. Ibid., 292.

49. For a deeper analysis of Hegel's review, see Reid, "Hegel, Critique de Solger": 255–264. See also Mueller, "Solger's Aesthetics—A Key to Hegel," 212–27; and Remo Bodei, "Il primo romanticismo come fenomeno storico e la filosofia di Solger nell'analisi di Hegel," *Aut Aut* 101 (1967): 68–80.

50. For a detailed account of different definitions of privation and negation see Laurence R. Horn, *A Natural History of Negation* (Chicago and London: The University of Chicago Press, 1989).

51. "With Aristotle [. . .] logic, epistemology and ontology all interpenetrate each other, and these neat divisions between negation, abstraction and privation simply will not work." Raoul Mortley, *From Word to Silence, 2. The Way of Negation, Christian and Greek* (Bonn: Peter Hanstein, 1986), 259.

52. Paul Redding, *Analytic Philosophy and the Return of Hegelian Thought*, (Cambridge: Cambridge University Press, 2007), 82. Regarding Aristotle's two negations, see also Laurence R. Horn, *A Natural History of Negation*, ch. 1.1.

53. Aristotle, *Metaphysics*, Book V, 22. See also Book 10, 5.

54. Aristotle, *Metaphysics*, Book IV, 6, 1011^b. Cf. R. Mortley, *From Word to Silence*, 259.

55. Cf. Martin, *Themes in Neoplatonic and Aristotelian Logic*.

56. To be more precise, "Hegel regarded term negation as appropriate in particular contexts and inappropriate in others." This is what Paul Redding calls "Hegel's cognitive contextualism." Paul Redding, *Analytic Philosophy and the Return of Hegelian Thought*, 208 ff.

57. Cyril O'Regan, in his *The Heterodox Hegel* (Albany, NY: SUNY Press, 1994), writes that "Hegel makes a distinction between two kind of negative, a negative that is nonpositive, that is, a *privative* negative, and a *positive* negative" (179). Hegel's *Science of Logic* leads to identify the "positive negative" with the "determinate negative" and to consider the "privative negative" as secondary to the determinate negative. O'Regan also writes that "Hegel shows himself capable of designating the finite as nonbeing and evil, without raising the issue of the relation between these two categories or exploring their possible differences" (Ibid.). The question is problematic and would need more development.

58. PG 188/114–115.

59. Kierkegaard, *The Concept of Irony*, 317–318.

60. Georg Wilhlem Friedrich Hegel, *Science of Logic*, trans. A. V. Miller (Atlantic Highlands, NJ: Humanities Press International, 1989), 5:38/45–46.
61. Kierkegaard, *The Concept of Irony*, 309. This claim is repeated in the final line of the chapter dedicated to Solger: "[. . .] the thought that appeals to me most is that Solger was a sacrifice to Hegel's positive system" (323).
62. See, for example, the judgment passed by V. Descombes, *Le Même et l'Autre. Quarante-cinq ans de philosophie française (1933–1978)* (Paris: Minuit, 1979).
63. Reid's conclusion is that Solger and Hegel represent two opposite notions of *logos*: according to Hegel, the possibility of a language that is truth opposes a language that consists in representing the truth that is elsewhere—and this is the case of Solger. See Reid, "Hegel, Critique de Solger," 262.
64. "Spirit is this power only by looking the negative in the face, and tarrying with it. This tarrying with the negative is the magical power that converts it into being" (PG 32/19).

Chapter 3

1. The first number refers to the standard numbering of the paragraphs in the *Phenomenology*. The second number refers to the page numbering in the Miller edition. All the quotations are from the Miller edition, except when noted.
2. Consider what Hegel writes in the Preface: "The bud disappears in the bursting-forth of the blossom, and one might say that the former is refuted by the latter: similarly, when the fruit appears, the blossom is shown up in its turn as a false manifestation of the plant, and the fruit now emerges as the truth of it instead" (PG, 2/2).
3. "Entäußert." In his new translation of the *Phenomenology* available on the web <http://terrypinkard.weebly.com/phenomenology-of-spirit-page.html>, Terry Pinkard translates it as "emptied."
4. Terry Pinkard, *Hegel's Phenomenology: The Sociality of Reason* (Cambridge: Cambridge University Press, 1994), 71.
5. Pinkard, *Hegel's Phenomenology*, 77.
6. "All the moments which in virtue itself were supposed to be risked and sacrificed, are just such existences of the good, and hence are inviolable relationships. Consequently, the conflict can only be an oscillation between preserving and sacrificing; or rather there can be neither a sacrifice of what is one's own, nor a violation of what is alien" (PG, 386/232). See Pinkard, *Hegel's Phenomenology*, 109.
7. "The side of reality is itself nothing else but the side of individuality" (289/233). See Pinkard, *Hegel's Phenomenology*, 110.
8. Ibid., 135.
9. Ibid., 156.
10. PG, 505–509/308–309; cf. Pinkard, *Hegel's Phenomenology*, 158.

11. Pinkard, *Hegel's Phenomenology*, 159.

12. To regard sacrifice as deceptive if what is sacrificed is itself not really given up (as Hegel seems to suggest) does not necessarily implies that there cannot be any gain resulting from that sacrifice—but this gain appears in all its clarity only *retrospectively*. I will return to this point shortly.

13. According to Pinkard, this "faith" can be regarded as mainly represented by emotionalist religious movements such as Pietism or Jansenism. However, some objections can be raised against this identification. I will not analyze the question in more details, as it is not relevant to my argument. Cf. Pinkard, *Hegel's Phenomenology*, 166. For a detailed analysis of this episode, cf. Maurizio Pagano, "Alle radici della modernità: la lotta dell'illuminismo contro la fede," in Francesca Michelini and Roberto Morani (eds.), *Hegel e il Nichilismo*" (Milan: Franco Angeli, 2003), 57–84.

14. Miller translates *Zeichen* as "symbol." I prefer Pinkard's translation ("sign"), as "symbol" after Kant is usually associated with *Darstellung* and refers to a type of analogical presentation. Also "Representational thought of sacrifice" is Pinkard's translation, and better captures the German verbal form *vorstellt*. Miller translates it as "sacrifice in imagination."

15. Cf. Henry S. Harris, *Hegel's Ladder* (Indianapolis: Hackett Publishing, 1997), II, 190.

16. Miller has "surrender."

17. "In itself" is Pinkard's translation of "*an sich*." Miller translates it as "in principle."

18. Pinkard translates *Einzelnheit* as "individuality," whereas Miller translates it as "singleness."

19. Pinkard, *Hegel's Phenomenology*, 329.

20. Ibid., 329.

21. Ibid.

22. On Hegel's reading of Christianity as the "consummate" religion, see Giacomo Rinaldi, *Ragione e Verità* (Rome: Aracne, 2010), 80–85.

23. Redding, *Analytic Philosophy and the Return of Hegelian Thought*, 228.

24. Cf. Raymond Geuss, *Outside Ethics* (Princeton: Princeton University Press, 2005), 48.

25. Here I use the term "non-traditionalists" to refer not only to the so-called "revisionist" reading pioneered by Pinkard and Pippin, but more broadly to all those scholars who reject the traditional view that regarded Hegel's spirit as a metaphysical super-entity.

26. Redding, *Continental Idealism*, 149.

27. Pinkard, *Hegel's Phenomenology*, 135.

28. Clearly, when one speaks of "the legislator," one does not refer to a specific individual in flesh and blood, let alone the empirical existence of an all-knowing lawgiver; and nonetheless, the existence of a "point of view of the legislator" is usually not questioned.

29. Miller usually translates the Hegelian term *Aufhebung* as "supersession."

30. "What Hegel means by spirit does indeed only come into being through the readiness to let go of oneself and die." Stephen Houlgate, "Hegel, Derrida, and Restricted Economy: The Case of Mechanical Memory," *Journal of the History of Philosophy* 34:1 (1996): 82. This is argued at length in Stephen Houlgate, *Freedom, Truth and History: An Introduction to Hegel's Philosophy* (London & New York: Routledge, 1991), 206–221.

31. Some scholars disagree with this translation: for instance, Raymond Geuss prefers to use "representation" as a translation of *Darstellung*. Cf. Geuss, *Outside Ethics*, 48, note 18.

32. Williams, *Recognition*, 257.

33. This is the expression used by Miller to translate *Vorstellung*.

34. Martin Wendte argued that representation (*Vorstellung*) is characterized by the represented appearing as other to the representer. As a consequence, the otherness of God gets lost in the transition to thought. See Martin Wendte, *Gottmenschliche Einheit bei Hegel* (Berlin: de Gruyter, 2007), 165ff. My position on this matter will be clear in the second half of this chapter. For an excellent discussion of this problem, see Thomas A. Lewis, *Religion, Modernity, and Politics in Hegel* (Oxford: Oxford University Press, 2011), 162.

35. J. Murray Murdoch, Jr., "Deconstruction as Darstellung: Derrida's Subtle Hegelianism," *Idealistic Studies* 37:1 (2007): 38.

36. Robert B. Brandom, "The Structure of Desire and Recognition: Self-Consciousness and Self-Constitution," *Philosophy & Social Criticism* 33:1 (2007): 131.

37. Miller and Pinkard translate *darstellt* here as "exhibit."

38. Pinkard, *Hegel's Phenomenology*, 218. For a detailed analysis of this episode, see also Paul Redding, "Hegel, Fichte and the Pragmatic Context of Moral Judgement," in Espen Hammer (ed.), *German Idealism: Contemporary Perspectives* (London & New York: Routledge, 2007), 231–234.

39. Note that, interestingly, what has to be sacrificed by the "hard-hearted judge" is similar to what is sacrificed in Stoicism (the claim of independence from the world): in both cases there is a transition from a type of formal philosophical outlook to a distinctly religious stance.

40. John O'Donoghue (*Person als Vermittlung: Die Dialektik von Individualität und Allgemeinheit in Hegels "Phänomenologie des Geistes,"* Mainz: Grünewald, 1993) argues that incarnation represents the "objective and personal unity of man and God" (435), and builds on this claim the main thesis of his work, namely, that to understand personality means to understand incarnation. While I agree that there is a connection for Hegel between the development of personal identity and the representation of Christ's incarnation, and that the logic of mediation is integral to the concept of recognition, I think that O'Donoghue neglects to consider that the individual point of view (or personal identity) is overcome by Hegel in favor of an

intersubjective dynamic—that dynamic which is precisely depicted in the "forgiveness and reconciliation" episode.

41. Georges Bataille, "Hegel, la Mort et le Sacrifice," *Deucalion* 5: 21–43. Trans. J. Strauss, "Hegel, Death and Sacrifice," *Yale French Studies* 78 (1990): 9–28.

42. Williams, *Hegel's Ethics of Recognition*, 69.

43. Ibid.

44. Ibid.

45. About the practical relations of recognition, especially with reference to the notion of *Freilassen*, in tension with processes of unification, see Ludwig Siep, "Recht und Anerkennung," in Helmut Girndt (ed.), *Selbstbehauptung und Anerkennung* (Sankt Augustin: Academia Verlag, 1990), 61–76, and the contrasting account in Klaus Roth, "Selbstbehauptung und Anerkennung bei G.W.F. Hegel," in Girndt (ed.), *Selbstbehauptung*, 177–206.

46. Cf. Peter C. Hodgson, *Hegel and Christian Theology: A Reading of the Lectures on the Philosophy of Religion* (Oxford, New York: Oxford University Press, 2005), 39.

47. In *The Accursed Share*, Bataille refers to the rite of *potlatch*, practiced among indigenous peoples of the Pacific Northwest Coast, in which the participants destroy or burn goods as an example of pure sacrificial expenditure. However, Bataille himself recognizes that the overall goal of the ritual is a manifestation of power by a family or a tribe, so that he eventually admits that "the ideal would be that a potlatch could not be repaid." Georges Bataille, *The Accursed Share*, trans. R. Hurley (New York: Zone Books, 1993), 70.

48. Georg Wilhelm Friedrich Hegel, *Philosophy of Right*, trans. S. W. Dyde (Kitchener, Ontario: Batoche Books, 2001), 7:§25/44.

49. For Hegel "subjectivity" and "objectivity" are relative rather than absolute terms: "It is ordinarily supposed that subjective and objective are blank opposites; but this is not the case. Rather they pass into one another, for they are not abstract aspects like positive and negative, but have already a concrete significance." Hegel, *Philosophy of Right*, 7:§25/45.

50. In the *Philosophy of Right*, Hegel refers to this notion, or phase, of subjectivity as "particularity of will, as caprice with its accidental content of pleasurable ends." Hegel, *Philosophy of Right*, 7:§25/44.

51. Georg Wilhelm Friedrich Hegel, *Lectures on the History of Philosophy 1825–1826*, Vol. III, 20:80/120. ("For this and other of Hegel's work, I give the volume and page number from the German *Werke in zwanzig Bänden*, followed by the page or paragraph number to the mentioned English translation).

52. O'Reagan, *The Heterodox Hegel*, 216–231. For a theological account of Hegel's reception of Böhme's notion of kenosis, see Thomas J. J. Altizer, *The Gospel of Christian Atheism* (London: Collins, 1967). Introducing the section on kenosis, Altizer writes: "While this radical expression of Christian mysticism was driven underground by the ecclesiastical authorities of the Church, it continued to exist in a subterranean form, finally surfacing in Jakob Böhme and his circle, who provided the germinal source for the one thinker who created a conceptual portrait of the incarnate or kenotic movement of God: Hegel" (62–63).

53. "Self-consciousness exists in and for itself when, and by the fact that, it so exists for another; that is, exists only in being acknowledged" (PG, 178/111).

54. "This does not make selves unreal or fictional, it simply makes their reality, unlike that of nature, conditional upon their recognition by others." Cf. Paul Redding, "Hegel, Idealism and God: Philosophy as the Self-Correcting Appropriation of the Norms of Life and Thought," *Cosmos and History: The Journal of Natural and Social Philosophy* 3:2–3 (2007): 27.

55. "For Hegel, 'concrete' means 'many-sided, adequately related, complexly mediated' (we may call this 'concrete [H]') while 'abstract' means 'one-sided, inadequately related, relatively unmediated' (abstract [H]). A concept or universal can quite sensibly be characterized as concrete [H], and at the same time, without paradox, as abstract [E] [the empiricist sense]. Sense particulars, or 'sensuous immediacy,' will necessarily be abstract [H] and at the same time, unparadoxically, concrete [E]." George L. Kline, "Some Recent Reinterpretations of Hegel's Philosophy," *The Monist* 4, 8 (1964): 41.

56. "The Greek gods must not be regarded as more human than the Christian God. Christ is much more a Man: he lives, dies—suffers death on the cross—which is infinitely more human than the humanity of the Greek Idea of the Beautiful." Georg Wilhelm Friedrich Hegel, *Philosophy of History*, trans. J. Sibree (Kitchener: Batoche Books, 2001), 12:304/267

57. Analogously, "Hegel's philosophy of nature is just that, a *philosophy* of nature, not a competing scientific account of natural phenomena or a philosophy of science." See Robert B. Pippin, *Hegel's Practical Philosophy: Rational Agency and Ethical Life* (Cambridge: Cambridge University Press, 2008), 49.

58. Eberhard Jüngel credits Hegel with a deeply profound (but, according to Jüngel, misguided) understanding of the Trinity, which Jüngel uses to develop his own assertion that "God's being is in becoming" (Cf. Eberhard Jüngel, *God as the Mystery of the World: On the Foundation of the Theology of the Crucified One in the Dispute between Theism and Atheism*, trans. D. L. Guder (Grand Rapids, MI: Eerdmans, 1983). However, Jüngel understands Hegel in a traditionally metaphysical way. Conversely, once Hegel is approached from the point of view of the "post-Kantian" reading, the idea of God as a "being in becoming" can be regarded as Hegel's "original account."

59. Hegel, *Lectures on the History of Philosophy*, 15:89. Cf. also James Yerkes, *The Christology of Hegel* (Missoula, MT: Scholars Press, 1978), 136–137. Yerkes has the merit of having called attention to the mentioned Hegelian passages. He does not, however, make the connection between kenosis and the tradition of *Imitatio Christi*.

60. Hodgson, *Hegel and Christian Theology*, 281. Some lines below, Hodgson adds that for Hegel "religion, like art, is mostly a thing of the past." This comment does not do justice to the complexity of the relation between philosophy and religion in Hegel's thought.

61. "It was through Christianity that this Idea came into the world. According to Christianity, the individual as such has an infinite value as the object and aim of divine love, destined as mind to live in absolute relationship with God himself, and have God's mind dwelling in him: i.e. man is implicitly destined to supreme

freedom." Georg Wilhelm Friedrich Hegel, *Philosophy of Mind*, trans. W. Wallace & A. V. Miller, revisions M. J. Inwood (Oxford: Clarendon Press, 2007), 10:§428/101. Cf. Pippin, *Hegel's Practical Philosophy. Rational Agency and Ethical Life*, 134–135.

62. Georg Wilhelm Friedrich Hegel, *Lectures on the Philosophy of Religion*, vol. 3, ed. P. C. Hodgson, trans. R. F. Brown et al. (Berkeley: University of California Press, 1984), 60/125.

63. This dynamic has been beautifully illustrated by Stephen Houlgate: "[. . .] divinity consists not in superhuman majesty and power, but in living a finite human life of love. In Christ, therefore, we see that human 'frailty' (*Gebrechlichkeit*) does not cut us from God [. . .] but is precisely what enables us to manifest divine love must fully." Stephen Houlgate, "Religion, Morality and Forgiveness in Hegel's Philosophy," in W. Desmond, E.-O. Onnasch and P. Cruysberghs (eds.), *Philosophy and Religion in German Idealism*. (Dordrecht: Springer, 2004), 93.

64. Cf. Redding, *Analytic Philosophy and the Return of Hegelian Thought*, 228.

65. Hegel, *Philosophy of Right*, 7:§25/44.

66. Cf. Pinkard, *German Philosophy 1760–1860*, 227.

67. Brandom seems to suggest such an instrumentalist view when he insists that "For Hegel all transcendental constitution is social institution." Robert B. Brandom, *Tales of the Mighty Dead* (Cambridge, MA: Harvard University Press, 2002), 216.

68. Redding, "Hegel, Idealism and God": 29.

69. I believe Angelica Nuzzo provides an account along these lines when she contrasts the language of the ancient gods (the language of "concept") with the language of speculative philosophy (the language of "dialectic"). She writes: "Truth is not gained by an improbably flight in the abstractness of thinking (where the 'immortal gods' whose language we may imagine to speak are not the gods of truth but of mere fantasy). Truth is reached instead by recognizing and consequently rectifying (not revoking) its 'incarnation' in ordinary language. To put it in Hegel's figurative way, in speculative philosophy truth speaks the language of an incarnated god. The language of dialectic is not the incomprehensible language of fantastic gods (or of past metaphysics) but the language of 'actual spirit' (*wirklicher Geist*)." Angelica Nuzzo, "Vagueness and Meaning Variance in Hegel's Logic," in A. Nuzzo (ed.), *Hegel and the Analytic Tradition* (London and New York: Continuum, 2009), 65–66.

70. Hegel, *Lectures on the History of Philosophy*, 15:89. Yerkes underlines the importance of this passage, but seems to interpret it in a realist rather than idealist way. Cf. Yerkes, *The Christology of Hegel*, 274.

Chapter 4

1. Ronald M. Green, *Kierkegaard and Kant: The Hidden Debt* (Albany, NY: State University of New York Press, 1992), 183. This understanding is precisely the traditional picture that Green has challenged. The relation of Kierkegaard to Kant has been addressed by a significant number of scholars in the last century: Emil

Brunner, "Das Grundproblem der Philosophic bei Kant und Kierkegaard," *Zwischen den Zeiten* 2, 6 (1924): 31–47; Alfred Baeumler, "Kierkegaard und Kant über die Reinheit des Herzens," *Zwischen den Zeiten* 3, 2 (1925): 182–187; Helmut Fahrenbach, "Kierkegaards ethische Existenzanalyse (als Korrektiv der Kantisch-idealistischen Moralphilosophie)," in M. Theunissen and W. Greve (eds), *Materialien zur Philosophie Søren Kierkegaards* (Frankfurt am Main: Suhrkamp, 1979) (just to mention a few).

2. There is now an extensive literature on the comparison of Kant's and Kierkegaard's views on morality, especially in relation to: moral rigorism (Roe Fremstedal, "Kierkegaard's Double Movement of Faith and Kant's Moral Faith," *Religious Studies* 48:2 (2012): 199–220), radical evil (David A. Robert, *Kierkegaard's Analysis of Radical Evil*, New York: Continuum, 2006), hypothetical and categorical imperatives (Ulrich Knappe, *Theory and Practice in Kant and Kierkegaard*, in N. Cappelørn (ed.), *Kierkegaard Studies Monograph Series* 9, New York: Walter de Gruyter, 2004), and the highest good (Roe Fremstedal, "The concept of the highest good in Kierkegaard and Kant," *International Journal for Philosophy of Religion* 69:3 (2004): 155–171).

3. Karl Verstrynge, in his article "The Perfection of the Kierkegaardian Self in Regulative Perspective" (*Kierkegaard Studies Yearbook* 2004: 473–495) offers a valuable contribution to this line of thought. Verstrynge convincingly argues that if Kierkegaard's idea of God is interpreted within a regulative perspective, then the emphasis on the subject's pole of the God-relation does not turn Kierkegaard into a subjectivist.

4. Robert L. Perkins, 'For Sanity's Sake: Kant, Kierkegaard and Father Abraham," in R. L. Perkins (ed.), *Kierkegaard's Fear and Trembling: Critical Appraisals* (Tuscaloosa, AL: University of Alabama Press), 43.

5. Perkins writes that both Kant and Kierkegaard "are skeptical regarding the possibility of rational knowledge of God" (Ibid., 48). However, Kant is not just "skeptical." He is really "negative" regarding the possibility of a rational knowledge of God. A reading of *Philosophical Fragments* reveals that the same can be said of Kierkegaard.

6. A sketch of Kierkegaard expanding Kant's "cognitive humility" and "giving it an existential twist" is found in Edward F. Mooney, *On Søren Kierkegaard: Dialogue, Polemics, Lost Intimacy, and Time* (London: Ashgate), 224. As presented in the book, this sketch is extremely intriguing and promising, but it remains partially undeveloped.

7. Perkins, "For Sanity's Sake: Kant, Kierkegaard and Father Abraham," 46.

8. Cf. Green, *Kierkegaard and Kant*, 223.

9. Cf. John Lippitt, "What Neither Abraham nor Johannes de Silentio Could Say," *Proceedings of the Aristotelian Society*, Supplementary Volume 82 (2008), 80.

10. Philip L. Quinn, "Kierkegaard's Christian Ethics," in A. Hannay and G. D. Marino (eds.), *The Cambridge Companion to Kierkegaard* (Cambridge: Cambridge University Press, 1998), 349.

11. Ibid.

12. It might be objected that *Fear and Trembling* identifies the ethical with the divine: "The ethical is the universal and as such in turn the Divine. It is therefore

right to say that every duty, after all, is duty to God" (FT, 59). However, I agree with Lippitt (*Routledge Philosophy Guidebook to Kierkegaard and Fear and Trembling*, London: Routledge, 2003, 81–82) that it is misleading to regard this claim as a definition of "the ethical": Johannes here is *questioning* the very assumption that the ethical is the universal. As it is argued by Lippitt, "If *all* duties are duties to God, what room does this leave for specific, particular duties to God of the kind faced by Abraham? Is 'duty to God' in fact merely shorthand for ethical duty, duty to 'the universal'?" (102). I will return to this point shortly.

13. C. Stephen Evans, and Sylvia Walsh, "Introduction," in Søren Kierkegaard, *Fear and Trembling* (Cambridge: Cambridge University Press, 2006), xxi–xxii.

14. For a general overview on the topic, see Dewi Zephaniah Phillips and Timothy Tessin (eds.), *Kant and Kierkegaard on Religion* (London and New York: Macmillan and St. Martin's Press, 2000).

15. Of course the fact that *Johannes de Silentio* is critical of the Kantian reduction of (natural) religion to moral philosophy does not mean that *Kierkegaard* is equally critical—and even if *Kierkegaard* was effectively critical of such a reduction (something that should be demonstrated), this does not mean that his criticism was justified—in other words, the question whether Kant *actually* reduces religion to moral philosophy belongs to a different sphere of inquiry and cannot be addressed here.

16. Lippitt, *Routledge Philosophy Guidebook to Kierkegaard*, 102.

17. Cf. Palmquist, "Does Kant Reduce Religion to Morality?," 129–148.

18. Ronald M. Green, "Developing Fear and Trembling," in A. Hannay and G. D. Marino (eds.), *The Cambridge Companion to Kierkegaard* (Cambridge: Cambridge University Press, 1998), 271.

19. For the sake of completeness, it should be noted that Green's work has been criticized by some Kant scholars and Kierkegaard scholars. Cf. William C. Davis, "Review of *Kierkegaard and Kant: The Hidden Debt* by Ronald Green," *Religious Studies* 30:1 (1994): 119–121; Merold Westphal, "Review of *Kierkegaard and Kant: The Hidden Debt* by Ronald Green," *Theological Studies* 54:2 (1993): 389; Knappe, "Theory and Practice in Kant and Kierkegaard"; and Chris L. Firestone and Nathan Jacobs, *In Defense of Kant's Religion* (Bloomington: Indiana University Press, 2008). While I do not subscribe to the thesis (which sometimes surfaces in Green's work) that Kierkegaard "took steps to ensure that his debt to Kant would not be detected" (Davis, "Review," 119), I consider persuasive the case he builds concerning the influence of Kantian ideas on Kierkegaard.

20. Evans and Walsh, "Introduction," xxii.

21. Cf. Merold Westphal, "Kierkegaard and Hegel," in A. Hannay and G. D. Marino (eds.), *The Cambridge Companion to Kierkegaard* (Cambridge: Cambridge University Press, 1998), 110.

22. Of course this does not apply to *second* or *Christian* ethics, in the context of which the *social* dimension of *Sittlichkeit* plays a marginal role. Some critics, such as Mooney, have even suggested that the country parson's sermon at the end of volume two of *Either/Or* was perhaps directed at the Judge himself rather

than at the aesthete, and therefore might be regarded as a criticism of the "social ethics" advanced by Judge William. Cf. Edward F. Mooney, "Kierkegaard on Self-Choice and Self-Reception: Judge William's Admonition," in R. L. Perkins (ed.), *International Kierkegaard Commentary: Either/Or*, Part Two (Macon GA: Mercer University Press, 1995), 5–32.

23. Søren Kierkegaard, *Unscientific Postscript to Philosophical Fragments*, trans. Howard V. Hong and Edna H. Hong (Princeton, NJ: Princeton University Press, 1992), I, 50–51.

24. C. Stephen Evans, *Kierkegaard's Ethic of Love: Divine Commands and Moral Obligations* (Oxford: Oxford University Press, 2004), 76.

25. Curtis L. Thompson, "The end of religion in Hegel and Kierkegaard," *Sophia* 33, 2 (1994), 10–20, 14.

26. Cf. Paul Redding, "Hegel's Philosophy of Religion," in Graham Oppy and Nick Trakakis (eds.), *History of Western Philosophy of Religion*, Volume IV: Nineteenth-Century Philosophy & Religion (Chesam: Acumen, 2007).

27. As everything else regarding *Fear and Trembling*, this reading too is not uncontroversial. There has been a recent flurry of papers on the topic of what Abraham can and cannot say, and why—see, for instance, the exchange between John Lippitt ("What Neither Abraham nor Johannes de Silentio Could Say") and Michelle Kosch ("What Abraham Couldn't Say," *Proceedings of the Aristotelian Society*, Supplementary Volume 82 (2008), 59–77), or Daniel Conway ("Abraham's Final Word," in Edward F. Mooney (ed.), *Ethics, Love, and Faith in Kierkegaard*, (Bloomington: Indiana University Press, 2008), 175–195). An analysis of this debate is beyond the scope of this chapter; in my reading, I endorse the position expressed by Lippitt in the mentioned paper (as well as in Lippitt, *Routledge Philosophy Guidebook to Kierkegaard*, chapter 5 "The Sound of Silence: Problema III," 111–135).

28. Georg Wilhelm Friedrich Hegel, *Encyclopaedia Logic*, ed. and trans. Théodore F. Geraets, Wallis Arthur Suchting and H. S. Harris (Indianapolis: Hackett, 1991), 8:24/12.

29. Cf. Pippin, *Hegel's Idealism*, and Pinkard, *Hegel's Phenomenology*.

30. Redding, "Hegel, Idealism and God," 22; see also Heiner Bielefeldt, *Symbolic Representation in Kant's Practical Philosophy* (Cambridge: Cambridge University Press, 2003).

31. Cf. Merold Westphal, "Abraham and Hegel," in Robert L. Perkins (ed.), *Kierkegaard's Fear and Trembling: Critical Appraisals* (Tuscaloosa, AL: University of Alabama Press, 1983), 62–80, (here 71).

32. This expression is used, with reference to Kierkegaard's critique of Hegel, by Merold Westphal, *Kierkegaard's Critique of Reason and Society* (Macon, GA: Mercer University Press, 1987), 74.

33. "The state can afford to be liberal in this matter, and may overlook small details affecting itself. It may even give room within itself to congregations, whose creed prevents them from recognizing any direct duties to it" (Hegel, *Philosophy of Right*, 7:§270/209).

34. Jon Stewart, *Kierkegaard's Relations to Hegel Reconsidered* (Cambridge: Cambridge University Press, 2003), 315.

35. Ibid.

36. Agacinski, "We Are Not Sublime,'" 132.

37. The claim that the position presented in *Fear and Trembling* implies a rejection of the divine command theory is not undisputed. Traditional interpretations often endorse a reading of *Fear and Trembling* that suggests that first ethics should be suspended when contradicted by a direct command by God. A more sophisticated version of the interpretation that reads *Fear and Trembling* as supporting a divine command ethics is that which is offered by C. Stephen Evans ("Is the Concept of an Absolute Duty Toward God Morally Unintelligible?" in Robert L. Perkins (ed.), *Kierkegaard's Fear and Trembling: Critical Appraisals*, (Tuscaloosa: AL: University of Alabama Press, 1983), 141–151)). Evans substantially appeals to the peculiarity of Abraham's personal relationship with God, a relationship which is marked by trust and love. Other scholars, such as Green ("Developing Fear and Trembling," 266–267) and Lippitt (*Routledge Philosophy Guidebook to Kierkegaard*, 89ff; 145) have advanced the counter-argument that "*Fear and Trembling* hardly stresses the love of God."

38. Green, "Developing Fear and Trembling," 258.

39. Perkins, "For Sanity's Sake," 56.

40. Alestair Hannay, "Introduction," in Søren Kierkegaard, *Fear and Trembling* (Harmondsworth: Penguin Book, 7–40), 24.

41. Edward F. Mooney, *Knights of Faith and Resignation: Reading Kierkegaard's Fear and Trembling* (Albany, NY: State University of New York Press, 1991), 91.

42. Lippitt, *Routledge Philosophy Guidebook to Kierkegaard*, 152.

43. Ibid., 154. A similar claim is advanced by Mooney (*Knights of Faith and Resignation*, 81)—who, however, considers this position just an "intermediate" interpretation): "There are dilemmas and in such straits, ethics cannot guide, deliver us from wrong." Nevertheless, this aspect is emphasized less by Mooney than it is by Lippitt, who is skeptical about the "virtue ethics" to which Mooney's interpretation seems to lead.

44. Mooney, *Knights of Faith and Resignation*, 80.

45. An in-depth analysis of this claim is undertaken in Green, *Kierkegaard and Kant*, 190–97.

46. Søren Kierkegaard, *The Concept of Anxiety*, trans. and ed. Howard V. Hong and Reidar Thomte (Princeton, NJ: Princeton University Press, 1980), 20.

47. Michelle Kosch, *Freedom and Reason in Kant, Schelling, and Kierkegaard* (Oxford: Oxford University Press, 2006), 160. The same interpretative position is held by Philip L. Quinn ("Kierkegaard's Christian Ethics," 349), and Evans (*Kierkegaard's Ethic of Love*, 83).

48. John E. Hare, *The Moral Gap: Kantian Ethics, Human Limits, and God's Assistance* (Oxford: Clarendon Press, 1996), 1; the notion of "moral gap" is used by Quinn ("Kierkegaard's Christian Ethics," 349) and Evans (*Kierkegaard's Ethic of Love*, 82).

49. Kosch, *Freedom and Reason in Kant, Schelling, and Kierkegaard*, 160.

50. Søren Kierkegaard, *Either/Or*, Vol. II, trans. Howard V. Hong and Edna H. Hong (Princeton, NJ: Princeton University Press, 1987), 339–54.

51. Stephen Mulhall, *Inheritance and Originality: Wittgenstein, Heidegger, Kierkegaard* (Oxford: Oxford University Press, 2001), 386.

52. The legend of Agnete and the merman (FT, 82–87) supports, in my view, this specific reading of the double movement of faith. Other interpretations of the *Akedah* as a symbol of the double movement of faith have been suggested by Roe Fremstedal ("Kierkegaard's double movement of faith and Kant's moral faith"), Sharon Krishek (*Kierkegaard on Faith and Love*, Cambridge: Cambridge University Press, 2009), Edward Mooney (*Knights of Faith and Resignation*), and Johannes Sløk (*Da Kierkegaard tav*, Copenhagen: Reitzel, 1980).

53. In recent years, interpretative efforts have been made to substantiate a third option—namely, that "first ethics" should be revised and understood from a religious perspective (see, for example, John J. Davenport, "Faith as Eschatological Trust in Fear and Trembling: Against the Strong Divine Command Reading," in Edward F. Mooney (ed.), *Ethics, Love, and Faith in Kierkegaard*, 196–233). While I agree with Davenport's critique of a "strong divine command theory," my interpretation is different insofar as it regards Christian ethics (as interpreted by Kierkegaard) as grounded on regulativity.

54. According to Evans, religion is a "morality in a new key" insofar as one is guided not by "autonomous striving to realize one's own ideals, but grateful expression of a self that has been received as a gift." C. Stephen Evans, "Faith as the Telos of Morality: A Reading of Fear and Trembling," in Robert L. Perkins (ed.), *International Kierkegaard Commentary: Fear and Trembling and Repetition* (Macon, GA: Mercer University Press, 1993), 26.

55. Lippitt, *Routledge Philosophy Guidebook to Kierkegaard*, 157.

56. It has to be clarified that the divine command plays a role in the "second" Christian ethics, especially as it is presented in *Works of Love*. More on this shortly.

57. Mulhall, *Inheritance and Originality*, 386.

58. In this context, Kierkegaard's claim that the person who lacks an awareness of ethics lacks an awareness of God (cf. Søren Kierkegaard, *Concluding Unscientific Postscript to Philosophical Fragments*, trans Howard V. Hong and Edna H. Hong (Princeton, NJ: Princeton University Press, 1992), 244) becomes understandable, and not in contradiction with the position presented in *Fear and Trembling*, which is expressed from a different existential standpoint.

59. I model this term on Paul Redding's "cognitive contextualism." This term is used by Redding to describe the Hegelian idea that different forms of logic and corresponding forms of negation are appropriate in different contexts or in different cognitive orientations. Cf. Redding, *Analytic Philosophy and the Return of Hegelian Thought*, 208ff.

60. An excellent account of Kierkegaard's relations to Kant and Schelling on religion, with a particular focus on the notion of freedom, can be found in

Kosch (*Freedom and Reason in Kant, Schelling, and Kierkegaard*, especially 123–138). Kierkegaard's exposure to Schelling's thought might have played a role in the development of his own use of regulative notions; however, the problem to which regulative notions are meant to respond (that is, the application of moral ideas to the world) is, as mentioned, a peculiarly Kantian problem to which all the post-Kantians (including Kierkegaard, in my view) tried to respond in different way. Therefore, I don't regard the possible mediation of Schelling as particularly relevant here.

61. Allusions to Abraham as an exemplar for faith can be found in several commentators. Among them, it seems to me that the scholar whose interpretation is closer to mine is Lippitt. For Abraham as an exemplar for faith, see, for instance, Lippitt, *Routledge Philosophy Guidebook to Kierkegaard*, 157. However, as I am going to stress, I take Abraham as an exemplar for faith in what seems to me a *stronger* sense—that is, as a Kantian regulative notion.

62. In previous literature, a reading of Kierkegaard's idea of God in the spirit of Kant's notion of regulative concepts has been attempted by George Pattison ("'Before God' as a Regulative Concept," in N. J. Cappelørn and H. Deuser (eds.), *Kierkegaard Studies Yearbook* 1997, 70–84), and expanded by Karl Verstrynge ("The Perfection of the Kierkegaardian Self in Regulative Perspective"). However, Pattison focuses on the Kantian use of regulative concepts in the theoretical realm, whereas I suggest that it is their practical use that is particularly developed by Kierkegaard. Verstrynge's interpretation is more in line with my interpretation, which is particularly focused on the regulative use of the notion of sacrifice in *Fear and Trembling*.

63. "The use of Abraham also conveys a new emphasis on faith as way of life. This emphasis is meant to replace the centuries-old understanding of faith as merely an acceptance of dogmatic truths" (Green, "Developing Fear and Trembling," 259).

64. Mooney, *Knights of Faith and Resignation*, 84.

65. Ibid.

66. Johannes considers the case of a man who, having listened to the pastor preaching on the greatness of Abraham, goes home and plans to imitate Abraham by murdering his own son. Johannes concludes that the man "would probably be executed or sent to the madhouse" (FT, 24). I agree with Lippitt that Johannes here is "trying to make absolutely clear what is involved in praising Abraham for his action" (Lippitt, *Routledge Philosophy Guidebook to Kierkegaard*, 36); and in fact, a few lines below, he claims to have "the courage to think a thought whole." (FT, 25).

67. Cf. Lippitt, *Routledge Philosophy Guidebook to Kierkegaard*, 133.

68. Agacinski, "We Are Not Sublime," 141.

69. See Allen W. Wood, *Kant's Moral Religion* (Ithaca, NY: Cornell University Press, 1970), 160–174.

70. Westphal, "Abraham and Hegel," 64. See also Sylvia Fleming Crocker, "Sacrifice in Kierkegaard's Fear and Trembling," *Harvard Theological Review* 68:2 (1975), 125–139, here 135: "Faith, then, is a kind of openness, a passionate receptivity on the part of the historically existing individual to the revelation of God as a

Person [. . .]. This openness was the decisively significant feature of Abraham's relationship to God."

71. Redding, "Hegel, Idealism and God," 29.

72. As Roberts writes, the divine command (in Kierkegaard's "second" ethics) does not function "as the base of a moral theory." Robert C. Roberts, "Kierkegaard and Ethical Theory," in Edward F. Mooney (ed.), *Ethics, Love, and Faith in Kierkegaard* (Bloomington: Indiana University Press, 2008), 90.

73. Cf. Alastair Hannay, *Kierkegaard: The Arguments of the Philosophers* (London: Routledge and Kegan Paul, 1982), 242, 254.

74. Cf. Quinn, "Kierkegaard's Christian Ethics," 353ff.

75. Ibid., 362.

76. Søren Kierkegaard, *Practice in Christianity*, trans. Howard V. Hong and Edna H. Hong (Princeton, NJ: Princeton University Press, 1991), 107.

77. Ibid., 241–241.

78. Ibid., 34–35.

79. Quinn, "Kierkegaard's Christian Ethics," 370.

80. *Søren Kierkegaard's Journals and Papers*, ed. and trans. Howard V. Hong and Edna H. Hong, assisted by Gregor Malantschuk (Bloomington: Indiana University Press, Vol. 2, 1970), 2:1848 (1848), 319.

81. Put differently, "Christ's pattern for us is a down-to-earth one, full of concrete content to be imitated." See M. Jamie Ferreira, *Love's Grateful Striving: A Commentary on. Kierkegaard's 'Works of Love'* (Oxford: Oxford University Press, 2001), 82.

82. Coakley, "Kenosis: Theological Meanings and Gender Connotations," 192–210.

83. Groenhout, "Kenosis and Feminist Theory," 291–312.

84. John Lippitt, "True Self-Love and True Self-Sacrifice," *International Journal for Philosophy of Religion* 66, 3 (2009), 125–138.

85. Ibid., 131.

86. Cf. Quinn, "Kierkegaard's Christian Ethics," 362.

87. Lippitt, "True Self-Love and True Self-Sacrifice," 132.

88. Ferreira, *Love's Grateful Striving*, 129.

89. Gene Outka, *Agape: An Ethical Analysis* (New Haven, CT: Yale University Press, 1972), 21.

90. Ferreira, *Love's Grateful Striving*, 153.

91. Ibid., 258–259.

92. Kierkegaard, *Either/Or*, vol. II, 339–54.

93. "There is no longer anyone who does not need forgiveness because the loving one sees both self and other as equal in the light of the 'third' (God, or goodness)." Ferreira, *Love's Grateful Striving*, 204.

94. Cf. Terry Pinkard, "Objektivität und Wahrheit innerhalb einer subjektiven Logik," in Anton Friedrich Koch, Alexander Oberauer, and Konrad Utz (eds.), *Der*

Begriff als die Wahrheit: Zum Anspruch der Hegelschen "Subjektiven Logik," (Paderborn: Schönigh, 2003).

95. One might argue that Hegel is, after all, an anthropological *optimist*, whereas Kierkegaard is an anthropological *pessimist*.

96. Joakim Garff, *Søren Kierkegaard: A Biography*, trans. Bruce H. Kirmmse (Princeton, NJ: Princeton University Press, 2005), 491.

97. John Lippitt, "Review of *Either Kierkegaard/Or Nietzsche: Moral Philosophy in a New Key* by Tom P. S. Angier," *Ars Disputandi* 7 (2007). <http://www.arsdisputandi.org/publish/articles/000284/article.pdf>, accessed October 20, 2011.

98. Knud Ejler Løgstrup, "Settling Accounts with Kierkegaard's Works of Love," in Hans Fink and Alasdair MacIntyre (eds.), *The Ethical Demand* (Notre Dame, IN: Notre Dame University Press, 1997), 230. See also Ferreira, *Love's Grateful Striving*, 239.

99. Alexander Nehamas, *Nietzsche, Life as Literature* (Cambridge, MA: Harvard University Press, 1985), chapters 5–7.

Chapter 5

1. For this and other Nietzsche's works, Arabic numerals denote the section number rather than the page number (as it is customary in Nietzsche scholarship). Dennis K. Keenan ("Nietzsche and the Eternal Return of Sacrifice," *Research in Phenomenology* 33 (2003), 167–84) begins his inquiry by analyzing this paragraph. The consequences he draws belong to what I call "the postmodern approach" to Nietzsche (see below).

2. Diethe translates *Geschlecht* with *tribe* and *menschlichen Geschlechts* (in the previous sentence) as *human race*. I think that the word *tribe* can be misleading and I consider *species* a better translation in this context.

3. Again, I find the translation of *Geschlechter* as *tribes* quite reductive, so I translate it as *stocks*.

4. See the example of the opposition between the king Odysseus and the foot soldier Thersites in the *Ilias*, in Ken Gemes, "Postmodernism's Use and Abuse of Nietzsche," *Philosophy and Phenomenological Research*, 62:2 (2001), 337–360 (here 358).

5. "And if the lambs say to each other, 'These birds of prey are evil; and whoever is least like a bird of prey and most like its opposite, a lamb,—is good, isn't he?,' then there is no reason to raise objections to this setting-up of an idea of beyond the fact that the birds of prey will view somewhat derisively" (GM, I 13).

6. The Kaufmann edition of *Will to Power* (=WM) is sometimes unreliable, so I also provide references to the corresponding texts in the *Kritische Studienausgabe* (Berlin: de Gruyter, 1980).

7. This notion of sacrifice as "overflowing and bestowing" originating from "abundance in oneself" was later elaborated by Bataille to form his notion of sacrifice as *dépense* (expenditure). Cf. Georges Bataille, *Inner experience* (Albany, NY: State University of New York Press, 1998). More on Bataille in the next chapter.

8. "Never and nowhere has there hitherto been a comparable boldness in inversion [*Umkehren*], anything so fearsome, questioning and questionable, as this formula [god on the cross]: it promised a revaluation of all antique values" (JGB, 46.)

9. "The lie of the ideal has so far been the curse on reality; on account of it, mankind itself has become mendacious and false down to its most fundamental instincts—to the point of worshiping the opposite values of those which alone would guarantee its health, its future, its lofty right to its future." Friedrich Nietzsche, *Ecce Homo*, trans. W. Kaufmann, in *On the Geneaology of Morals and Ecce Homo* (New York: Vintage Books, 1989), *Preface*, section 2.

10. Gemes, "Postmodernism's Use and Abuse of Nietzsche." Cf. John Richardson, *Nietzsche's System* (New York: Oxford University Press, 1996).

11. Cf. Alan White, "Nietzschean Nihilism: A Typology," *International Studies in Philosophy*, 14:2 (1987).

12. Cf. WM, 866 (10[17] 12.462f), where the distance between the "average man" and the overman appears clearly, thus suggesting a link with the noble type. There is a quite general consent about this identification among Nietzsche commentators. Cf. Reginald John Hollingdale, *Commentary* to Friedrich Nietzsche (Harmondsworth: Penguin Books, 1973).

13. Gemes, "Postmodernism's Use and Abuse of Nietzsche," 358.

14. Kaufmann–Hollingdale translate "Whatever the cost in men," which I think is a bad translation. The original text is "*Arbeiten an ihrem Marmor, mag dabei von Menschen geopfert werden, was nur möglich.*" In this case, Ludovici's translation done under Oscar Levy's editorship is more faithful to the original.

15. See also WM, 975 (1[56] 12.24).

16. Friedrich Nietzsche, *The Greek State*, in *On the Genealogy of Morality*, trans. C. Diethe (Cambridge: Cambridge University Press, 2007).

17. Ibid.

18. Nietzsche, *The Greek State*.

19. "He finds the return to such simple, uncomplicated natures both impossible and undesirable." Gemes "Postmodernism's Use and Abuse of Nietzsche," 357.

20. Benedict R. Anderson (*Imagined Communities: Reflections on the Origin and Spread of Nationalism*, London: Verso, 1983) showed the connection between nationalism and self-sacrifice (7ff.).

21. "The great popular movements of modern times represent the herd-men's attempt to bring the unlovely and impossible Christian heaven down to earth." Crane Brinton, *Nietzsche* (Cambridge, MA: Harvard University Press, 1948), 107.

22. Kauffman translates "patriotism" instead of "nationalism."

23. Friedrich Nietzsche, *The Gay Science*, trans. W. Kaufmann (New York: Random House, 1974), 347.

24. Friedrich Nietzsche, *Sämtliche Werke. Kritische Studienausgabe*, 2nd edn., ed. Giorgio Colli and Mazzino Montinari, 15 vols. (Berlin and New York: de Gruyter, 1988). "Nationalism has become a religion—a secular religion where god is the nation." Josep R. Llobera, *The God of Modernity: The Development of Nationalism in Western Europe* (Oxford, UK and Providence, USA: Berg, 1994), 143, quoted

in Stefan Elbe, "'Labyrinths of the Future': Nietzsche's Geneaology of European Nationalism," *Journal of Political Ideologies*, 7:1 (2002): 77–96, 81.

25. Friedrich Nietzsche, *Human, All Too Human*, trans. M. Faber (Lincoln: University of Nebraska Press, 1984), 472.

26. Friedrich Nietzsche, *Assorted Opinions and Maxims*, trans. R. J. Hollingdale (Cambridge: Cambridge University Press, 1986), 293.

27. Nietzsche writes: "The mediocre nature at last grows so conscious of itself (—acquires courage for itself—) that it arrogates even political power to itself" (WM, 215; cf. 10[77] 12.500).

28. Cf. Henri Lichtenberger, *The Gospel of Superman* (New York: The MacMillan Company, 1912), 143.

29. "A symptom of the herd's domination of politics is the almost complete ignorance of the art of commanding." Ruth Abbey and Friedrick Appel, "Nietzsche and the Will to Politics," *The Review of Politics* 60:1 (1998), 83–114, here 101.

30. Nietzsche, *Assorted Opinions and Maxims*, 292.

31. "The politics of herd society has a corrosive effect on human excellence" (Abbey and Appel, "Nietzsche and the Will to Politics," 103).

32. This distinction was originally introduced by Ashley Woodward ("Nihilism and the Postmodern in Vattimo's Nietzsche," *Minerva—An Internet Journal of Philosophy* 6. <http://www.ul.ie/~philos/vol6/nihilism.html>) to distinguish two different approaches to the question of nihilism. I am extending this distinction to the notion of the will to power.

33. Pierre Klossowski, *Nietzsche and the Vicious Circle* (Chicago: University of Chicago Press, 1997). Other postmodern interpretations of Nietzsche are those of Georges Bataille and Gilles Deleuze.

34. Will Dudley, *Hegel, Nietzsche, and Philosophy: Thinking Freedom* (Cambridge: Cambridge University Press, 2002).

35. Klossowski, *Nietzsche and the Vicious Circle*, 46.

36. Daniel Warren Smith, "Klossowski's Reading of Nietzsche: Impulses, Phantasms, Simulacra, Stereotypes," *Diacritics* 35:1 (2005), 8–21, 10.

37. Klossowski, *Nietzsche and the Vicious Circle*, 70.

38. "Sacrifice can only sacrifice itself over and over (in an eternal return of the same) because what it seeks to overcome (the nihilistic revelation of truth that sublates sacrifice's negation) makes this sacrifice of itself both *necessary* and *useless*." Keenan, "Nietzsche and the Eternal Return of Sacrifice," 183.

39. Roger Caillois, *The Edge of Surrealism: A Roger Caillois Reader*, trans. Claudine Frank and Camille Naish (Durham: Duke University Press, 2003), 30: "Bataille believed that accomplishing a human sacrifice would be an irreversible point, preventing any possible turning back. It came close to happening. The victim had been found, it was the sacrificer who was missing. Bataille offered me the role. [. . .] Things didn't get beyond that."

40. Woodward, "Nihilism and the Postmodern in Vattimo's Nietzsche." Woodward continues: "In the historical sense, this constitutes a new era of valuation

and human flourishing after nihilism has been overcome [. . .] Nihilism will be overcome and human culture will be reinvigorated by new categories of valuation, a 'revaluation of all values.'

41. Wilfried Van der Will, 'Nietzsche and Postmodernism,' in Keith Ansell-Pearson and Howard Caygill (eds.), *The Fate of the New Nietzsche* (Aldershot: Avebury, 1993), 43–54, here 50. As Woodward ("Nihilism and the Postmodern in Vattimo's Nietzsche") stresses: "Van der Will asserts that Nietzsche's vision of postmodernity has little to do with the postmodernity celebrated by some French poststructuralist philosophers who cite Nietzsche as a prime influence in their thought."

42. Cf. Nicola Massimo De Feo, *Ragione e Rivolta. Saggi e Interventi 1962–2002* (Milan: Mimesis, 2005).

43. For an exploration of some of the qualities Nietzsche believes future rulers would need and the mechanisms they could use to exercise and legitimate their power (but without emphasis on the notion of sacrifice), cf. Abbey and Appel, "Nietzsche and the Will to Politics," 83–114.

44. "Shortly: Nietzsche's few are in every regard the contrast to the too-many, to the 'Heerdenmenschen'." Otto Kaiser, "Democracy and Aristocracy in Nietzsche's Late Writings," in Jürgen G. Backhaus and Wolfgang Drechsler (eds.), *Friedrich Nietzsche (1844–1900). Economy and Society* (New York: Springer, 2006), 238.

45. Dudley, *Hegel, Nietzsche, and Philosophy*.

46. Robert Williams, Review of *Hegel, Nietzsche, and Philosophy: Thinking Freedom* by Will Dudley, *Notre Dame Philosophical Reviews* (2003), <http://ndpr.nd.edu/review.cfm?id=1182>.

47. Ibid.

48. Dudley, *Hegel, Nietzsche, and Philosophy*, 183.

49. Cf. Nietzsche, *Assorted Opinions and Maxims*, II, 2: 333. Quoted in Dudley, *Hegel, Nietzsche, and Philosophy*, 185.

50. Dudley, *Hegel, Nietzsche, and Philosophy*, 185.

51. See, for instance, *Kritische Studienausgabe* 7[60] 12.315.

52. Nietzsche's critique hides an analysis that could be highly valuable in today's world. In fact, this risk is probably much higher nowadays than at the time of Nietzsche, because of the great impact of the media. It is almost superfluous, I think, to recall that the use of the media, marshaled to consolidate and enlarge the consent of the electorate, inevitably determines a still wider consent. It is the risk of what I call "mediatical dictatorship," namely, a dictatorship produced or induced by the media.

53. *Kreuzigen* literally means "crucify." Kauffman translates "sacrifice" and I think the translation is correct, although it loses the religious-metaphysical nuance of the expression.

54. Cf. Friedrich Nietzsche, *Thus Spoke Zarathustra*, trans. Walter Kaufmann (New York: Penguin Books, 1981), 3 "The Three Evil Things"; *Ecce Homo*, Destiny 4. Gemes ("Postmodernism's Use and Abuse of Nietzsche," 343) comments: "Consider his account of herd man: he is a mere collection of ever fluctuating, competing

drives, with different drives dominating at different times. Such an animal cannot take on genuine commitments to the future, for such a being has no genuine continuity over time."

55. Alexander Nehamas, *Nietzsche, Life as Literature* (Cambridge, MA: Harvard University Press, 1985), chapters 5–7.

56. Janko Lavrin, *Nietzsche: An Approach* (London: Methuen & Co., 1948), 118.

57. This ambiguity has been very well stressed by Herman Siemens, "Yes, No, Maybe So . . . Nietzsche's Equivocations on the Relation between Democracy and 'Grosse Politik,'" in Herman Siemens and Vasti Roodt, *Nietzsche, Power and Politics. Rethinking Nietzsche's Legacy for Political Thought* (Berlin and New York: de Gruyter, 2008), 231–268.

58. Cf. Horst Hutter (*Shaping the Future: Nietzsche's New Regime of the Soul and Its Ascetic Practices*, Lanham, MD: Lexington Books, 2006), who criticizes Nehamas by claiming that his Nietzsche has "no political dimension," "no wish to revolutionize society and culture" (xiii).

59. Frederick Appel, *Nietzsche Contra Democracy* (Ithaca: Cornell University Press, 1998), 168.

60. Robert B. Pippin, "Nietzsche's Alleged Farewell: The Premodern, Modern and Postmodern Nietzsche," in Robert B. Pippin (ed.), *Idealism as Modernism: Hegelian Variations* (Cambridge and New York: Cambridge University Press, 1997), 330–350, here 350.

Chapter 6

1. Coakley, "Kenosis: Theological meanings and gender connotations."
2. Groenhout, "Kenosis and Feminist Theory."
3. Kierkegaard, *Concluding Unscientific Postscript to Philosophical Fragments*, 171.
4. Redding, *Continental Idealism*, 172–173.
5. Nietzsche, *Thus Spoke Zarathustra*, "The Vision and the Enigma," 2.
6. Cf. Redding, *Continental Idealism*, 167.
7. This survey cannot be in any way exhaustive, and I am aware that I am neglecting many twentieth-century philosophical accounts of sacrifice that might provide an interesting contribution to the discussion. The philosophers I deal with here have been selected as meaningful in their relationship to the post-Kantian tradition.
8. Emmanuel Levinas, "Existence and Ethics," in J. Ree and J. Chamberlain (eds.), *Kierkegaard: A Critical Reader* (Oxford: Blackwell, 1998), 31.
9. Albert Camus, *Le mythe de Sisyphe*, in *Essais* (Paris: Gallimard, 1965), 117–118.
10. Bataille, "Hegel, la Mort et le Sacrifice," 9–28.
11. Alexandre Kojève, *Introduction to the Reading of Hegel* (New York: Basic Books, 1969).

12. Bataille's essay, for instance, provoked Derrida's piece "From Restricted to General Economy: A Hegelianism Without Reserve," in Jacques Derrida, *Writing and Difference* (London: Routledge & Kegan Paul, 1978), 25–77.

13. At best, Bataille's account of sacrifice can fit with Hegel's conception of sacrifice in Hinduism, where sacrifice expresses the "negative relationship" of the subjects with transcendence through the "negation of consciousness." However, this negative relationship is already overcome with the Greek cultus. Cf. Hegel, *Lectures on the Philosophy of Religion*, vol. II, 555/663.

14. Jacques Derrida, *The Gift of Death* (Chicago, IL: University of Chicago Press, 1995), 68.

15. John Lippitt provides good arguments for claiming that, as an interpretation of the message of *Fear and Trembling*, Derrida's reading is quite unconvincing, and I tend to agree. Cf. Lippitt, *Routledge Philosophy Guidebook to Kierkegaard and Fear and Trembling*, 159ff.

16. Jacques Derrida, *Of Grammatology*, trans. G. C. Spivak (Baltimore and London: The Johns Hopkins University Press, 1976), 44–45.

17. Cf. Peter E. Langford, *Modern Philosophies of Human Nature: Their Emergence from Christian Thought* (Dordrecht: Martinus Nijhoff Publisher, 1986), 230.

18. René Girard, *Things Hidden Since the Foundation of the World* (Stanford, CA: Stanford University Press, 1978), 64.

19. René Girard, *Deceit, Desire and the Novel* (Baltimore: Johns Hopkins University Press, 1965), 111. See also Girard, *Things Hidden*, 277: "the very detachment of the person who contemplates the warring brothers from the heights of his wisdom is an illusion." Cf. Eugene Webb, *The Self Between: From Freud to the New Social Psychology of France* (Seattle and London: University of Washington Press, 1993), 192.

20. René Girard, *Job: The Victim of His People* (Stanford, CA: Stanford University Press, 1987), 107.

21. Ibid.

22. The relevance of the Kantian distinction between truth and truthfulness in the context of Girard studies has been suggested by Michael Kirwan, "'Fuori dalle Città, tra le Città: René Girard e il Male Radicale," in Paolo Diego Bubbio and Silvio Morigi (eds.), *Male e Redenzione. Sofferenza e Trascendenza in René Girard* (Turin: Edizioni Camilliane, 2008), 133–150.

23. Immanuel Kant, "On the miscarriage of all philosophical trials in theodicy," in *Works of Emmanuel Kant: Religion and Rational Theology* (Cambridge: Cambridge University Press, 1992), 34.

24. Ibid.

25. Girard, *Things Hidden*, 203.

26. René Girard and Giann Vattimo, *Christianity, Truth, and Weakening Faith: A Dialogue*. Pierpaolo Antonello (ed.), trans. William McCuaig (New York: Columbia University Press, 2010), 39 and 46.

27. Cf. Luigi Pareyson, *Existence, Interpretation, Freedom. Selected Writings* (Aurora, CO: Davies Group Publisher, 2009).
28. See, for instance, Nietzsche, *Sämtliche Werke*, 7[60] 12.315.
29. Girard and Vattimo, *Christianity, Truth, and Weakining Faith*, 84.
30. Ibid.
31. Ibid., 94
32. Gianni Vattimo, *A Farewell to Truth* (New York: Columbia University Press, 2011), chap. 2, "The Future of Religion," section 3, "For a Nonreligious Christianity."
33. Redding, "Hegel, Idealism and God," 30.
34. This has been suggested, from different interpretative standpoints by Maurizio Pagano (*Hegel: La Religione e l'Ermeneutica del Concetto*, Naples: ESI, 1992) and Paul Redding (*Hegel's Hermeneutics*, Ithaca NY: Cornell University Press, 1996).
35. I am aware that a fully developed analysis of the legacy of nineteenth-century post-Kantian philosophy about the notion of sacrifice in twentieth century thought should take into consideration Žižek's account. Unfortunately, I do not have the space to explore the details of that reading here, especially because Žižek's account is strictly interdependent with Lacan's insight, which makes this question far too extended to be treated in these conclusive remarks. Cf. Slavoj Žižek, *Tarrying with the Negative: Kant, Hegel, and the Critique of Ideology* (Durham, NC: Duke University Press, 1993); *The Fragile Absolute—or, Why Is the Christian Legacy Worth Fighting For?* (London: Verso, 2000); *On Belief: Thinking in Action* (London and New York: Routledge, 2001, especially 70ff). On Žižek on sacrifice, see Keenan, *The Question of Sacrifice*, 105–133.

Bibliography

Abbey, Ruth, and Friedrick Appel. "Nietzsche and the Will to Politics." *The Review of Politics* 60, 1 (1998): 83–114.
Agacinski, Sylviane. "We Are Not Sublime: Love and Sacrifice, Abraham and Ourselves." In *Kierkegaard: A Critical Reader*, ed. Jonathan Ree and Jane Chamberlain (Oxford: Blackwell, 1998), 129–150.
Altizer, Thomas J. J. *The Gospel of Christian Atheism* (London: Collins, 1967).
Anderson, Benedict R. *Imagined Communities: Reflections on the Origin and Spread of Nationalism* (London: Verso, 1983).
Ansell-Pearson, Keith. *An Introduction to Nietzsche as a Political Thinker* (Cambridge: Cambridge University Press, 1994).
Appel, Frederick. *Nietzsche Contra Democracy* (Ithaca, NY: Cornell University Press, 1998).
Atterton, Peter. "A Duty to Be Charitable? A Rigoristic Reading of Kant." *Kant-Studien* 98:2 (2007): 135–155.
Axinn, Sydney. *Sacrifice and Value. A Kantian Interpretation* (Lanham, MD: Lexington Books, 2010).
Baeumler, Alfred. "Kierkegaard und Kant über die Reinheit des Herzens." *Zwischen den Zeiten* 3, 2 (1925): 182–187.
Bataille, Georges. "Hegel, la Mort et le Sacrifice." *Deucalion* 5 (1955): 21–43. Trans. J. Strauss, "Hegel, Death and Sacrifice." *Yale French Studies* 78 (1990): 9–28.
———. *The Accursed Share*, trans. R. Hurley (New York: Zone Books, 1993).
———. *Inner experience* (Albany. NY: State University of New York Press, 1998).
Bielefeldt, Heiner. *Symbolic Representation in Kant's Practical Philosophy* (Cambridge: Cambridge University Press, 2003).
Bodei, Remo. "Il primo romanticismo come fenomeno storico e la filosofia di Solger nell'analisi di Hegel." *Aut Aut* 101 (1967): 68–80.
Böhme, Jacob. *Aurora*. In *Sämtliche Schriften*, ed. by Will-Erich Peuckert. Stuttgart: Fr. Frommanns, 1955–61. Trans. by William Law, *The Works of Jacob Behman* (London: Richardson, 1764).
Bowes, Richard L. "Sacrifice and the Categorical Imperative of Human Security." *International Journal* 56, 4 (2001): 649–664.

Brandom, Robert B. *Tales of the Mighty Dead* (Cambridge, MA: Harvard University Press, 2002).
———. "The Structure of Desire and Recognition: Self-consciousness and Self-Constitution." *Philosophy & Social Criticism* 33:1 (2007): 127–150.
Brinton, Crane. *Nietzsche* (Cambridge, MA: Harvard University Press, 1998).
Brunner, Emil. "Das Grundproblem der Philosophic bei Kant und Kierkegaard." *Zwischen den Zeiten* 2:6 (1924): 31–47.
Caillois, Roger. *The Edge of Surrealism: A Roger Caillois Reader*, trans. Claudine Frank and Camille Naish (Durham. NC: Duke University Press, 2003).
Camus, Albert. *Le mythe de Sisyphe*, in *Essais* (Paris: Gallimard, 1965).
Caruth, Cathy. "The Force of Example: Kant's Symbols." *Yale French Studies* 74 (1988): 17–37.
Caswell, Matthew. "Kant's Conception of the Highest Good, the Gesinnung, and the Theory of Radical Evil." *Kant-Studien* 97:2 (2006): 184–209.
Ciancio, Claudio. *Il paradosso della verità* (Turin: Rosenberg&Seller, 1999).
Connolly, William. *Identity/Difference* (Ithaca, NY: Cornell University Press, 1991).
Conway, Daniel W. "Abraham's Final Word." In Edward F. Mooney (ed.), *Ethics, Love, and Faith in Kierkegaard*, (Bloomington: Indiana University Press, 2008), 175–195.
Crocker, Sylvia Fleming. "Sacrifice in Kierkegaard's *Fear and Trembling*." *The Harvard Theological Review* 68:2 (1975): 125–139.
Cummiskey, David. "Kantian Consequentialism." *Ethics* 100:3 (1990): 586–615.
Dannenhauer, Ulrich. *Heilsgewissheit und Resignation: Solgers Theorie der absoluten Ironie* (Frankfurt s. M.: Peter Lang, 1988).
Davenport, John J. "Faith as Eschatological Trust in Fear and Trembling: Against the Strong Divine Command Reading." In Edward F. Mooney (ed.), *Ethics, Love, and Faith in Kierkegaard* (Bloomington: Indiana University Press, 2007), 196–233.
Davis, William C. Review of *Kierkegaard and Kant: The Hidden Debt* by Ronald Green. *Religious Studies* 30:1 (1994): 119–121.
Dawe, Donald G. *The Form of a Servant: A Historical Analysis of the Kenotic Motif* (Philadelphia: Westminster, 1963).
De Feo, Nicola Massimo. *Ragione e Rivolta. Saggi e Interventi 1962–2002* (Milan: Mimesis, 2005).
Derrida, Jacques. *Of Grammatology*, trans. G. C. Spivak (Baltimore and London: The Johns Hopkins University Press, 1976).
———. "From Restricted to General Economy: A Hegelianism Without Reserve." In Jacques Derrida, *Writing and Difference* (London: Routledge & Kegan Paul, 1978), 25–77.
———. *The Gift of Death* (Chicago, IL: University of Chicago Press, 1995).
Descombes, Vincent. *Le Même et l'Autre. Quarante-cinq ans de philosophie française (1933–1978)* (Paris: Minuit, 1979).

Dudley, Will. *Hegel, Nietzsche, and Philosophy: Thinking Freedom* (Cambridge: Cambridge University Press, 2002).
Elbe, Stefan. "'Labyrinths of the Future': Nietzsche's Geneaology of European Nationalism." *Journal of Political Ideologies* 7:1 (2002): 77–96.
Evans, C. Stephen. "Is the Concept of an Absolute Duty Toward God Morally Unintelligible?." In Robert L. Perkins (ed.), *Kierkegaard's Fear and Trembling: Critical Appraisals* (Tuscaloosa, AL: University of Alabama Press, 1983), 141–151.
———. "Faith as the *Telos* of Morality: A Reading of *Fear and Trembling*." In Robert L. Perkins (ed.), *International Kierkegaard Commentary: Fear and Trembling and Repetition* (Macon, GA: Mercer University Press, 1993), 209–224.
———. *Kierkegaard's Ethic of Love: Divine Commands and Moral Obligations* (Oxford: Oxford University Press, 2004).
Evans, C. Stephen, and Sylvia Walsh. "Introduction." In Søren Kierkegaard, *Fear and Trembling* (Cambridge, MA: Cambridge University Press, 2006), vi–xxx.
Fahrenbach, Helmut. "Kierkegaards ethische Existenzanalyse (als Korrektiv der Kantisch-idealistischen Moralphilosophie)." In Michael Theunissen and Wilfried Greve (eds.), *Materialien zur Philosophie Søren Kierkegaards* (Frankfurt s. M.: Suhrkamp, 1979), 8–33.
Ferreira, M. Jamie. *Love's Grateful Striving: A Commentary on Kierkegaard's "Works of Love"* (Oxford: Oxford University Press, 2001).
Fichte, Johann Gottlieb. *The Science of Rights*, trans. A. E. Kroeger (London: Routledge & Kegan Paul, 1970).
Firestone, Chris L., and Nathan Jacobs. *In Defense of Kant's Religion* (Bloomington: Indiana University Press, 2008).
Fremstedal, Roe. "Kierkegaard's Double Movement of Faith and Kant's Moral Faith." *Religious Studies* 48:2 (2012): 199–220.
———. "The Concept of the Highest Good in Kierkegaard and Kant." *International Journal for Philosophy of Religion* 69:3 (2011): 155–171.
Gardner, Sebastian. *Kant and the "Critique of Pure Reason"* (London: Routledge, 1999).
Garff, Joakim. *Søren Kierkegaard: A Biography*, trans. Bruce H. Kirmmse (Princeton, NJ: Princeton University Press, 2005).
Gemes, Ken. "Postmodernism's Use and Abuse of Nietzsche." *Philosophy and Phenomenological Research* 62:2 (2001): 337–360.
Geuss, Raymond. *Outside Ethics* (Princeton. NJ: Princeton University Press, 2005).
Girard, René. *Deceit, Desire and the Novel* (Baltimore, MD: Johns Hopkins University Press, 1965).
———. *Things Hidden Since the Foundation of the World* (Stanford, CA: Stanford University Press, 1978).
———. *Job: The Victim of His People* (Stanford, CA: Stanford University Press, 1987).
Girard, René, and Giann Vattimo, *Christianity, Truth, and Weakening Faith: A Dialogue*, ed. Pierpaolo Antonello, trans. William McCuaig (New York: Columbia University Press, 2010).

Green, Ronald M. *Kierkegaard and Kant: The Hidden Debt* (Albany, NY: State University of New York Press, 1992).
———. "Developing Fear and Trembling." In A. Hannay and G. D. Marino (eds.), *The Cambridge Companion to Kierkegaard* (Cambridge, MA: Cambridge University Press, 1998), 257–281.
Griffiths, A. Phillips. "Kant's Psychological Hedonism." *Philosophy* 66, 256 (1991): 207–216.
Grøn, Arne. "Kærlighedens gerninger og anerkensdelsen dialektik." *Dansk Teologisk Tidsskrift* 54 (1991): 260–270.
Guevara, Daniel. "The Impossibility of Supererogation in Kant's Moral Theory." *Philosophy and Phenomenological Research* 59:3 (1999): 593–624.
Guibal, Francis. "Le signe hégélien. Economie sacrificielle et relevé dialectique." *Archives de philosophie* 60:2 (1997): 265–297.
Haas, Alois M. "Das Nichts Gottes und seine Sprengmetaphorik." In H. Herwig, I. Wirtz and Stefan Bodo Würffel (eds.), *Semiotik und Hermeneutik in Raum und Zeit* (Tübingen: Basel, 1999).
Habermas, Jürgen. *The Philosophical Discourse of Modernity* (Cambridge, MA: MIT Press, 1997).
Hannay, Alastair. *Kierkegaard: The Arguments of the Philosophers* (London: Routledge and Kegan Paul, 1982).
———. "Introduction." In Søren Kierkegaard, *Fear and Trembling* (Harmondsworth, UK: Penguin Book, 1985), 7–40.
Hansson, Mats G. *The Private Sphere: An Emotional Territory and Its Agent* (New York: Springer, 2008).
Hare, John E. *The Moral Gap: Kantian Ethics, Human Limits, and God's Assistance* (Oxford: Clarendon Press, 1996).
Harris, Henry S. *Hegel's Ladder* (Indianapolis. IN: Hackett Publishing, 1997).
Hartmann, Klaus. 'Hegel: A Non-Metaphysical View,' in Alasdair MacIntyre (ed.), *Hegel: A Collection of Critical Essays* (New York: Anchor Books, 1972).
Hatab, Lawrence J. *A Nietzschean Defense of Democracy: An Experiment in Postmodern Politics* (Chicago: Open Court Publishing Company, 1995).
Hedley, Douglas. *Sacrifice Imagined. Violence, Atonement, and the Sacred* (London: Continuum, 2011).
Hegel, Georg Wilhelm Friedrich. *Lectures on the Philosophy of Religion*, 3 vol. ed. P. C. Hodgson, trans. R. F. Brown et al. (Berkeley: University of California Press, 1984).
———. *Science of Logic*, trans. A.V. Miller (Atlantic Highlands, NJ: Humanities Press International, 1989), 45–46.
———. *Encyclopedia of the Philosophical Sciences in Outline and Critical Writings*, ed. E. Behler (New York: Continuum, 1990).
———. *Solgers Nachgelassene Schriften und Briefwechsel*. In *Berliner Schriften*, ed. J. Hoffmeister (Hamburg: Meiner Verlag, 1956); trans. I. Diana, *Solger's Posthumous Writings and Correspondence*, in *Encyclopedia of the Philosophical Sciences*

in Outline and Critical Writings, ed. Ernst Behler (New York: Continuum, 1990), 265–319.
———. *Encyclopaedia Logic*, trans. T. F. Geraets et al. (Indianapolis, IN: Hackett, 1991).
———. *Philosophy of History*, trans. J. Sibree (Kitchener, Ontario: Batoche Books, 2001).
———. *Philosophy of Right*, trans. S.W. Dyde (Kitchener, Ontario: Batoche Books, 2001).
———. *Philosophy of Mind*, trans. W. Wallace and A. V. Miller, revisions M. J. Inwood (Oxford: Clarendon Press, 2007).
———. *Lectures on the History of Philosophy 1825–1826*, Vol. III: Medieval and Modern Philosophy. Trans. Robert F. Brown (Oxford: Oxford University Press, 2009).
Heller, Josef. *Solgers Philosophie der ironischen Dialektik* (Berlin: Von Reuther & Reichard, 1928).
Hill, Thomas E. "Kantian Constructivism in Ethics." *Ethics* 99:4 (1989): 752–770.
Hodgson, Peter C. *Hegel and Christian Theology: A Reading of the Lectures on the Philosophy of Religion* (Oxford and New York: Oxford University Press, 2005).
Hollingdale, Reginald John. *Commentary to Friedrich Nietzsche* (Harmondsworth, UK: Penguin Books, 1973).
Honig, Bonnie. *Political Theory and the Displacement of Politics* (Ithaca, NY: Cornell University Press, 1993).
Horn, Laurence R. *A Natural History of Negation* (Chicago and London: The University of Chicago Press, 1989).
Houlgate, Stephen. *Freedom, Truth and History: An Introduction to Hegel's Philosophy* (London and New York: Routledge, 1991).
———. "Hegel, Derrida, and Restricted Economy: The Case of Mechanical Memory." *Journal of the History of Philosophy* 34:1 (1996): 79–93.
———. "Religion, Morality and Forgiveness in Hegel's Philosophy." In W. Desmond, E.-O. Onnasch and P. Cruysberghs (eds.), *Philosophy and Religion in German Idealism*. (Dordrecht: Springer, 2004).
Hutter, Horst. *Shaping the Future: Nietzsche's New Regime of the Soul and Its Ascetic Practices*, (Lanham, MD: Lexington Books, 2006).
Jaeschke, Walter. *Reason in Religion: The Foundations of Hegel's Philosophy of Religion*, trans. J. M. Stewart and P. C. Hodgson (Berkeley: University of California Press, 1990).
Jüngel, Eberhard. *God as the Mystery of the World: On the Foundation of the Theology of the Crucified One in the Dispute between Theism and Atheism*, trans. D. L. Guder (Grand Rapids, MI: Eerdmans, 1983).
Kaiser, Otto. "Democracy and Aristocracy in Nietzsche's Late Writings." In Jürgen G. Backhaus and Wolfgang Drechsler (eds.), *Friedrich Nietzsche (1844–1900). Economy and Society* (New York: Springer, 2006).
Kant, Immanuel. *Critique of Judgment*, trans. W. S. Pluhar (Indianapolis: Hackett, 1987).

———. "On the Miscarriage of All Philosophical Trials in Theodicy." In *Works of Emmanuel Kant: Religion and Rational Theology*, trans. and ed. Allen W. Wood and George di Giovanni (Cambridge: Cambridge University Press, 1992).

———. *Lectures on Logic* (Cambridge: Cambridge University Press, 1992).

———. *The Conflict of the Faculties*. In *Religion and Natural Theology*, trans. and ed. A. W. Wood and G. Di Giovanni (Cambridge: Cambridge University Press, 1996).

———. *Groundwork of the Metaphysic of Morals*, trans. M. Gregor (Cambridge: Cambridge University Press, 1997).

———. *Critique of Pure Reason*, trans. and ed. P. Guyer and A. W. Wood (Cambridge: Cambridge University Press, 1998).

Keenan, Dennis King. "Nietzsche and the Eternal Return of Sacrifice." *Research in Phenomenology* 33 (2003): 167–84.

———. *The Question of Sacrifice* (Bloomington and Indianapolis: Indiana University Press, 2005).

Kierkegaard, Søren. *Soren Kierkegaard's Journals and Papers*, ed. and trans. Howard V. Hong and Edna H. Hong, assisted by Gregor Malantschuk (Bloomington: Indiana University Press, 1970).

———. *The Concept of Anxiety*, ed. and trans. Howard V. Hong and Reidar Thomte (Princeton, NJ: Princeton University Press, 1980).

———. *Either/Or Vol. II*, ed. and trans. Howard V. Hong and Edna H. Hong (Princeton, NJ: Princeton University Press, 1987).

———. *The Concept of Irony with continual reference to Socrates*, ed. and trans. Howard V. Hong and Edna H. Hong (Princeton, NJ: Princeton University Press, 1989).

———. *Practice in Christianity*, ed. and trans. Howard V. Hong and Edna H. Hong. (Princeton, NJ: Princeton University Press, 1991).

———. *Concluding Unscientific Postscript to Philosophical Fragments*, ed. and trans. Howard V. Hong and Edna H. Hong (Princeton, NJ: Princeton University Press, 1992).

Kirwan, Michael. "Fuori dalle Città, tra le Città: René Girard e il Male Radicale." In Paolo Diego Bubbio and Silvio Morigi (eds.), *Male e Redenzione. Sofferenza e Trascendenza in René Girard* (Turin: Edizioni Camilliane, 2008), 133–150.

Kline, George L. "Some Recent Reinterpretations of Hegel's Philosophy." *The Monist*, 4, 8 (1984): 34–75.

Klossowski, Pierre. *Nietzsche and the Vicious Circle* (Chicago: University of Chicago Press, 1997).

Knappe, Ulrich. *Theory and Practice in Kant and Kierkegaard* (New York: Walter de Gruyter, 2004).

Kojève, Alexandre. *Introduction to the Reading of Hegel* (New York: Basic Books, 1969).

Kosch, Michelle. *Freedom and Reason in Kant, Schelling, and Kierkegaard* (Oxford: Oxford University Press, 2006).

———. "What Abraham Couldn't Say." *Proceedings of the Aristotelian Society Supplementary Volume* 82 (2008): 59–77.

Kreeft, Peter. *Summa of the Summa. Essential Passages of Aquinas* (San Francisco: Ignatius Press, 1990).
Krishek, Sharon. *Kierkegaard on Faith and Love* (Cambridge: Cambridge University Press, 2009).
Langford, Peter E. *Modern Philosophies of Human Nature: Their Emergence from Christian Thought* (Dordrecht: Martinus Nijhoff Publisher, 1986).
Lanzetta, Beverly J. "Three Categories of Nothingness in Eckhart." *The Journal of Religion* 72 (1992): 248–268.
Lavrin, Janko. *Nietzsche: An Approach* (London: Methuen & Co., 1948).
Levinas, Emmanuel. "Existence and Ethics." In Jonathan Ree and Jane Chamberlain (eds.) *Kierkegaard: A Critical Reader* (Oxford: Blackwell, 1998).
Lichtenberger, Henri. *The Gospel of Superman* (New York: The MacMillan Company, 1912).
Lippitt, John. *Routledge Philosophy Guidebook to Kierkegaard and* Fear and Trembling (London: Routledge, 2003).
———. "Review of *Either Kierkegaard/Or Nietzsche: Moral Philosophy in a New Key*, by Tom P.S. Angier." *Ars Disputandi* 7 (2007), <http://www. arsdisputandi.org/publish/articles/000284/article.pdf>. Accessed October 20, 2011.
———. "What Neither Abraham nor Johannes de Silentio Could Say." *Proceedings of the Aristotelian Society Supplementary Volume* 82 (2008): 79–99.
———. "True Self-Love and True Self-Sacrifice." *International Journal for Philosophy of Religion* 66:3 (2009): 125–138.
Llobera, Josep R. *The God of Modernity: The Development of Nationalism in Western Europe* (Oxford, UK and Providence, RI: Berg, 1994).
Løgstrup, Knud Ejler. "Settling Accounts with Kierkegaard's Works of Love." In Hans Fink and Alasdair MacIntyre (eds.), *The Ethical Demand* (Notre Dame, IN: Notre Dame University Press, 1997).
MacKinnon, Donald Mackenzie. "Kant's Philosophy of Religion." *Philosophy* 50, 192 (1975): 131–144.
Martin, John N. *Themes in Neoplatonic and Aristotelian Logic: Order, Negation and Abstraction* (London: Ashgate Publishers, 2004).
McCarthy, Vincent. *Quest for a Philosophical Jesus*. (Macon, GA: Mercer University Press, 1986).
Meister Eckhart. *Selected Writings*, ed. and trans. Oliver Davies (London: Penguin Books, 1994).
Millbank, John. *Being Reconciled. Ontology and Pardon.* (London and New York: Routledge, 2003).
Moltmann, Jürgen. *God in Creation: A New Theology of Creation and the Spirit of God*, trans. M. Kohl (San Francisco: Harper & Row, 1985).
Mooney, Edward F. *Knights of Faith and Resignation: Reading Kierkegaard's* Fear and Trembling (Albany: State University of New York Press, 1991).
———. "Kierkegaard on Self-Choice and Self-Reception: Judge William's Admonition." In Robert L. Perkins (ed.), *International Kierkegaard Commentary: Either/Or, Part Two* (Macon GA: Mercer University Press, 1995), 5–32.

———. *On Søren Kierkegaard: Dialogue, Polemics, Lost Intimacy, and Time* (London: Ashgate, 2007).
Mortley, Raoul. *From Word to Silence, 2. The Way of Negation, Christian and Greek* (Bonn: Peter Hanstein, 1986).
Mueller, Gustav E. "Solger's Aesthetics—A Key to Hegel (Irony and Dialectic)." In Arno Schirokauer and Wolfgang Paulsen (eds.), *Corona: Studies in Celebration of the Eightieth Birthday of Samuel Singer* (Durham, NC: Duke University Press, 1941).
Mulhall, Stephen. *Inheritance and Originality: Wittgenstein, Heidegger, Kierkegaard* (Oxford: Oxford University Press, 2001).
Murdoch, Jr., J. Murray. "Deconstruction as *Darstellung*: Derrida's Subtle Hegelianism." *Idealistic Studies* 37:1 (2007): 29–42.
Nehamas, Alexander. *Nietzsche, Life as Literature* (Cambridge, MA: Harvard University Press, 1985).
Nietzsche, Friedrich. *Sämtliche Werke. Kritische Studienausgabe*, 2nd edn., ed. Giorgio Colli and Mazzino Montinari, 15 vols. (Berlin and New York: de Gruyter, 1988).
———. *The Antichrist*, trans. H. L. Mencken (New York: Alfred A. Knopf, 1918).
———. *The Gay Science*, trans. W. Kaufmann (New York: Random House, 1974).
———. *Thus Spoke Zarathustra*, trans. Walter Kaufmann (New York: Penguin Books, 1981).
———. *Human, All Too Human*, trans. M. Faber (Lincoln: University of Nebraska Press, 1984).
———. *Assorted Opinions and Maxims*, trans. R. J. Hollingdale (Cambridge, MA: Cambridge University Press, 1986),
———. *Ecce Homo*, trans. W. Kaufmann, in *On the Geneaology of Morals and Ecce Homo* (New York: Vintage Books, 1989).
———. *The Greek State*, in *On the Genealogy of Morality*, trans. C. Diethe (Cambridge, MA: Cambridge University Press, 2007).
Nuzzo, Angelica. "Vagueness and Meaning Variance in Hegel's Logic." In A. Nuzzo (ed.), *Hegel and the Analytic Tradition* (London and New York: Continuum, 2009), 61–82.
O'Donoghue, John. *Person als Vermittlung: Die Dialektik von Individualität und Allgemeinheit in Hegels "Phänomenologie des Geistes"* (Mainz: Grünewald. 1993).
O'Regan, Cyril. *The Heterodox Hegel* (Albany: State University of New York Press, 1994).
Outka, Gene. *Agape: An Ethical Analysis* (New Haven, CT: Yale University Press, 1972).
Pagano, Maurizio. *Hegel: la Religione e l'Ermeneutica del Concetto* (Naples: ESI, 1992).
———. "Alle radici della modernità: la lotta dell'illuminismo contro la fede." In F. Michelini and R. Morani (eds.), *Hegel e il Nichilismo* (Milan: Franco Angeli, 2003), 57–84.
Palmquist, Stephen. "Does Kant Reduce Religion to Morality?." *Kant-Studien* 83:2 (1992): 129–148.
———. *Kant's Critical Religion* (Aldershot: Ashgate, 2000).

Pareyson, Luigi. *Existence, Interpretation, Freedom. Selected Writings*, ed. Paolo Diego Bubbio, trans. Anna Mattei (Aurora, CO: Davies Group Publisher, 2009).
Pattison, George. "'Before God' as a Regulative Concept." In N. J. Cappelørn and H. Deuser (eds.), *Kierkegaard Studies Yearbook 1997*, 70–84.
Peikoff, Leonard. "Kant and Self-Sacrifice." *Objectivist* 10, 9 (1971): 1092–1104.
Peperzak, Adriaan Theodoor. *System and History in Philosophy* (Albany: State of New York Press, 1986).
Perkins, Robert L. "For Sanity's Sake: Kant, Kierkegaard and Father Abraham." In Robert L. Perkins (ed.), *Kierkegaard's Fear and Trembling: Critical Appraisals* (Tuscaloosa, AL: University of Alabama Press, 1983), 46–61.
Phillips, Dewi Zephaniah, and Timothy Tessin (eds.), *Kant and Kierkegaard on Religion* (London and New York: Macmillan and St. Martin's Press, 2000).
Pinkard, Terry. *Hegel's Phenomenology: the Sociality of Reason* (Cambridge, MA: Cambridge University Press, 1994).
———. *German Philosophy 1760–1860: The Legacy of Idealism* (Cambridge, MA: Cambridge University Press, 2002).
———. "Objektivität und Wahrheit innerhalb einer subjektiven Logik." In Anton Friedrich Koch, Alexander Oberauer, and Konrad Utz (eds.), *Der Begriff als die Wahrheit: Zum Anspruch der Hegelschen "Subjektiven Logik"* (Paderborn: Schönigh, 2003).
Pinna, Giovanna. *L'ironia Metafisica. Filosofia e teoria estetica. in K. W. F. Solger* (Genoa: Pantograf, 1994).
Pinto, Valeria. *Filosofia e religione. in K. W. F. Solger* (Naples: Morano Editore, 1995).
Pippin, Robert B. *Hegel's Idealism: The Satisfactions of Self-Consciousness.* (Cambridge, MA: Cambridge University Press, 1989).
———. "Idealism and Agency in Kant and Hegel." *The Journal of Philosophy* 88:10 (1991): 532–541.
———. *Modernism as a Philosophical Problem* (Cambridge, MA: Cambridge University Press, 1991, 2nd ed. 1999).
———. "Nietzsche's Alleged Farewell: The Premodern, Modern and Postmodern Nietzsche." In Robert B, Pippin (ed.), *Idealism as Modernism: Hegelian Variations*, (Cambridge and New York: Cambridge University Press, 1997), 330–350.
———. "Hegel's Practical Philosophy: The Realization of Freedom." In K. Ameriks (ed.), *The Cambridge Companion to German Idealism* (Cambridge, MA: Cambridge University Press, 2000).
———. "What is the Question for which Hegel's Theory of Recognition is the Answer?." *European Journal of Philosophy* 8:2 (2002): 155–72.
———. *Hegel's Practical Philosophy: Rational Agency and Ethical Life* (Cambridge, MA: Cambridge University Press, 2008).
Polkinghorne, John (ed.), *The Work of Love: Creation as Kenosis* (Grand Rapids, MI: Eerdmans, 2001).
Quinn, Philip L."'Kierkegaard's Christian Ethics." In Alastair Hannay and Gordon Daniel Marino (eds.), *The Cambridge Companion to Kierkegaard* (Cambridge, MA: Cambridge University Press, 1998), 349–375.

Railton, Peter G., and Gideon Rosen. "Realism." In J. Kim and E. Sosa (eds.), *A Companion to Metaphysics* (Oxford: Blackwell, 1995).
Rand, Ayn. *Philosophy: Who Needs It* (London: Penguins Book, 1982).
Ravera, Marco. "Solger e la salvezza come non conciliazione." In Piero Coda and Graziano Lingua (eds.), *Esperienza e Libertà* (Rome: Città Nuova, 2000), 33–62.
Redding, Paul. *Hegel's Hermeneutics* (Ithaca, NY: Cornell University Press, 1996).
———. "Hegel, Fichte and the Pragmatic Context of Moral Judgement." In Espen Hammer (ed.) *German Idealism: Contemporary Perspectives* (London and New York: Routledge, 2007).
———. "Hegel, Idealism and God: Philosophy as the Self-Correcting Appropriation of the Norms of Life and Thought." *Cosmos and History: The Journal of Natural and Social Philosophy*, 3:2–3 (2007): 16–31.
———. "Hegel's Philosophy of Religion." In G. Oppy and N. Trakakis (eds.), *History of Western Philosophy of Religion*, Volume IV: Nineteenth-Century Philosophy & Religion (Chesam, UK: Acumen, 2007).
———. *Analytic Philosophy and the Return of Hegelian Thought* (Cambridge: Cambridge University Press, 2007).
———. *Continental Idealism: Leibniz to Nietzsche* (London and New York: Routledge, 2009).
Redhead, Mark. "Nietzsche and Liberal Democracy: A Relationship of Antagonistic Indebtedness?." *The Journal of Political Philosophy* 5:2 (1997): 183–193.
Reid, Jeffrey "Hegel, Critique de Solger. Le Problème de la Communication Scientifique." *Archives de philosophie* 60:2 (1997): 255–264.
———. *Real Words. Language and System in Hegel* (Toronto: University of Toronto Press, 2007).
Richardson, John. *Nietzsche's System* (New York: Oxford University Press, 1996).
Rinaldi, Giacomo. *Ragione e Verità* (Rome: Aracne, 2010).
Robert, David A. *Kierkegaard's Analysis of Radical Evil* (New York: Continuum, 2006).
Roberts, Robert C. "Kierkegaard and Ethical Theory." In Edward F. Mooney (ed.), *Ethics, Love, and Faith in Kierkegaard* (Bloomington: Indiana University Press, 2009).
Rossi, Philip J., and Michael J. Wreen. *Kant's Philosophy of Religion Reconsidered* (Bloomington: Indiana University Press, 1991).
Roth, Klaus. "Selbstbehauptung und Anerkennung bei G. W. F. Hegel." In Helmut Girndt (ed.), *Selbstbehauptung und Anerkennung* (Sankt Augustin: Academia Verlag, 1990), 177–206.
Sedgewick, Garnett G. *Of Irony Especially in Drama* (Toronto: University of Toronto Press, 1948).
Siemens, Herman. *Yes, No, Maybe So . . . Nietzsche's Equivocations on the Relation between Democracy and 'Grosse Politik.'* In H. W. Siemens and V. Roodt (eds.), *Nietzsche, Power and Politics: Rethinking Nietzsche's Legacy for Political Thought* (Berlin and New York: de Gruyter, 2008), 231–268.

Siep, Ludwig. *Anerkennung als Prinzip der praktischen Philosophie* (München: Alber, 1979).

———. "Recht und Anerkennung." In Helmut Girndt (ed.), *Selbstbehauptung und Anerkennung* (Sankt Augustin: Academia Verlag, 1990), 61–76.

Sløk, Johannes. *Da Kierkegaard tav* (Copenhagen: Reitzel, 1980).

Smith, Daniel Warren. "Klossowski's Reading of Nietzsche: Impulses, Phantasms, Simulacra, Stereotypes." *Diacritics* 35:1 (2005), 8–21.

Solger, Karl Wilhelm Ferdinand. *Vorlesungen über Ästhetik*, edited by K. W. L. Heyse (Darmstadt: Wissenschaftliche Buchgesellschaft, 1962).

Sorell, Tom, and G. A. J. Rogers, eds. *Analytic Philosophy and History of Philosophy* (Oxford: Oxford University Press, 2005).

Steward, Jon. *Kierkegaard's Relations to Hegel Reconsidered* (Cambridge, MA: Cambridge University Press, 2003).

Szondi, Peter. "Friedrich Schlegel and Romantic Irony, with Some Remarks on Tieck's Comedies." In Peter Szondi (ed.), *On Textual Understanding and Other Essays*, (Minneapolis: University of Minnesota Press, 1986).

Taureck, Bernard. *Nietzsche un der Faschismus: Eine Studie uber Nietzsches politisches Philosophie und ihre Folgen* (Hamburg: Junius Verlag, 1989).

Teufel, Thomas. "Kant's Non-Teleological Conception of Purposiveness." *Kant-Studien* 102:2 (2011): 232–252.

Thompson, Curtis L. "The end of religion in Hegel and Kierkegaard." *Sophia* 33:2 (1994): 10–20.

Van der Will, Wilfried. "Nietzsche and Postmodernism." In Keith Ansell-Pearson and Howard Caygill (eds.), *The Fate of the New Nietzsche* (Aldershot: Avebury, 1993), 43–54.

Vattimo, Gianni. *A Farewell to Truth* (New York: Columbia University Press, 2011).

Verra, Valerio. "Tragische und kunstlerische Ironie bei Solger." In D. Gethmann-Siefert (ed.), *Philosophie und Poesie. O. Poeggeler zum 60 Geburtstag* (Stuttgardt-Bad Cannstatt, 1988).

Verstrynge, Karl. "The Perfection of the Kierkegaardian Self in Regulative Perspective." *Kierkegaard Studies Yearbook* 2004: 473–495.

Ward, Keith. "Kant's Teleological Ethics." *The Philosophical Quarterly* 21, 85 (1971): 337–351.

Webb, Eugene. *The Self Between: From Freud to the New Social Psychology of France* (Seattle and London: University of Washington Press, 1993).

Weeks, Andrew. *Boehme: An Intellectual Biography of the Seventeenth-Century Philosopher and Mystic* (New York: State University of New York Press, 1991).

Wendte, Martin. *Gottmenschliche Einheit bei Hegel* (Berlin: de Gruyter, 2007).

Westphal, Merold. "Abraham and Hegel." In Robert L. Perkins (ed.), *Kierkegaard's Fear and Trembling: Critical Appraisals* (Tuscaloosa, AL: University of Alabama Press, 1983), 62–80.

———. *Kierkegaard's Critique of Reason and Society* (Macon, GA: Mercer University Press, 1987).
———. *Kierkegaard and Hegel*. In Alastair Hannay and Gordon Daniel Marino (eds.), *The Cambridge Companion to Kierkegaard* (Cambridge, MA: Cambridge University Press, 1988), 101–124.
———. Review of *Kierkegaard and Kant: The Hidden Debt* by Ronald Green. *Theological Studies* 54:2 (1993): 389.
White, Alan. "Nietzschean Nihilism: A Typology." *International Studies in Philosophy* 14:2 (1987), 29–44.
Wildt, Andreas. *Autonomie und Anerkennung. Hegels Moralitdtskritik im Lichte seiner Fichte-Rezeption* (Stuttgart: Klett-Cotta, 1982).
Williams, David T. *The Kenosis of God: The self-limitation of God-Father, Son, and Holy Spirit*. (New York and Bloomington: iUniverse, 2005).
Williams, Robert R. *Recognition: Fichte and Hegel on the Other* (Albany: State University of New York Press, 1992).
———. *Hegel's Ethics of Recognition* (Berkeley: University of California Press, 1997).
Williams, Robert. Review of *Hegel, Nietzsche, and Philosophy: Thinking Freedom*, by Will Dudley. *Notre Dame Philosophical Reviews* (2008), <http://ndpr.nd.edu/review.cfm?id=1182> (Last accessed: 16.05.2012).
Wood, Allen W. *Kant's Moral Religion* (Ithaca, NY: Cornell University Press, 1970).
———. "Kant's Life and Works." In Graham Bird (ed.), *A Companion to Kant* (Oxford: Blackwell Publishing, 2006).
Woodward, Ashley. "Nihilism and the Postmodern in Vattimo's Nietzsche." *Minerva— An Internet Journal of Philosophy*, 6 (2002), <http://www.ul.ie/~philos/vol6/nihilism.html> (Last accessed: 16.05.2012).
Yerkes, James. *The Christology of Hegel* (Missoula, MT: Scholars Press, 1978).
Žižek, Slavoj. *On Belief: Thinking in Action* (London and New York: Routledge, 2001).
———. *Tarrying with the Negative: Kant, Hegel, and the Critique of Ideology* (Durham, NC: Duke University Press, 1993)
———. *The Fragile Absolute—or, Why Is the Christian Legacy Worth Fighting For?* (London: Verso, 2000).

Index

absolute, the, 39–40, 43, 50, 79, 113
Agacinski, Sylviane, 94, 102
Altizer, Thomas J.J., 180n52
Anderson, Benedict, 191n20
Anti-Climacus. *See* Kierkegaard, Søren
Appel, Frederick, 137–38
Aquinas, Thomas, 2, 21
Aristotle, 7, 54–55
Augustine of Hippo, 169n32
Axinn, Sydney, 19, 28

Bacon, Francis, 78
Bataille, Georges, 1, 15, 16, 76, 114, 131, 149–52, 163, 180n47, 190n7, 192n39, 195n13
Böhme, Jacob, 2, 5, 22–23, 78, 171n18, 173n9
Bonaparte, Napoleon, 124–25

Caillois, Roger, 131
Camus, Albert, 147
Christ, 2, 4, 12, 13, 34, 35–36, 37, 48, 51, 53, 67, 69–70, 71–72, 73, 74, 79–82, 84–85, 100, 102, 105–106, 108, 109, 111, 112, 116, 126, 144, 155, 156, 157, 159, 179n40
Christianity, 12, 72, 79–80, 84, 101, 121, 127–28, 181n61
Coakley, Sarah, 4, 108, 141
Copernicus, Nicolaus, 20

Davenport, John J., 187n53

De Feo, Nicola M., 132
democracy, 127–32, 136–37
Derrida, Jacques, 1, 15, 16, 19, 149, 152–54, 163
Dudley, Will, 130, 133–35

Eckhart, Meister, 2, 21–22, 41, 42, 173n9
Evans, C. Stephen, 91, 98, 186n37

faith, 66–67, 72, 85, 87, 89, 91–95, 96, 98, 99–104, 112, 114, 115–16, 144, 172n47, 187n52, 188n61
Ferreira, M. Jamie, 110, 114
Feuerbach, Ludwig, 8, 83, 84, 104, 146
Fichte, Johann Gottlieb, 3, 8, 29, 45, 104

Gadamer, Hans-Georg, 158
Gardner, Sebastian, 6
Garff, Joakim, 115
Gemes, Ken, 122
Girard, René, 1, 15–16, 149, 154–58, 159
Green, Ronald M., 89, 96, 97, 99, 184n19
Groenhout, Ruth, 4, 108, 141

Hannay, Alastair, 96–97
Hare, John E., 98, 110
Hartmann, Klaus, 6
Haufniensis, Vigilius. *See* Kierkegaard, Søren

Index

Hedley, Douglas, 167n1
Hegel, Georg Wilhelm Friedrich, 2, 6, 7, 9, 11–13, 15, 26, 28, 29, 37, 38, 39, 41, 49, 52–57, 58–59, 61–85, 90–95, 98, 101, 102–103, 111–16, 133, 143–44, 146, 148, 149–51, 153, 160, 163, 164, 165, 168n6, 175n38, 180n49, 181n53, 195n13
   Phenomenology of Spirit, 26, 41, 55–56, 61–75, 76, 79, 111, 149–51, 174n11, 177n64, 177n2, 177n6
   Lectures on the Philosophy of Religion, 76–79, 82, 93
Heidegger, Martin, 158
Hodgson, Peter C., 81, 181n60
Hölderlin, Friedrich, 79

Idea, 44, 45
intersubjectivity, 7, 81, 85, 113, 179n40. *See also* recognition
irony, 43, 44–46, 56

Judge William. *See* Kierkegaard, Søren.
Jüngel, Eberhard, 181n58

Kant, Immanuel, 5, 6, 7–8, 10, 11, 14, 15, 19–38, 49, 69, 79, 82, 83–84, 87–90, 92, 93, 94–95, 96, 98, 99–100, 101, 102–103, 105, 110, 111, 113, 114–15, 116, 133, 139, 141, 142, 143, 147–48, 152, 153, 156, 160, 161–62, 164, 170n13, 170n17, 171n29, 172n43, 175n38, 184n15, 187n60
   The Conflict of the Faculties, 34
   Critique of Judgement, 29
   Critique of Practical Reason, 25–27, 32, 96
   Critique of Pure Reason, 20, 24, 29, 170n13
   The Metaphysics of Morals, 29–30, 36
   Religion within the Boundaries of Mere Reason, 19, 31–32, 33–35, 69, 88–90, 105, 172n47

Kantian paradox, 6–8, 9, 10, 11, 23–25, 28–29, 37, 83–84, 104–105, 111, 114–15, 138, 142–44, 169n19
Keenan, Dennis K., 19, 190n1
kenosis, 2–5, 8, 20–27, 29, 30, 35, 36–37, 40, 42, 70, 73, 76, 78–79, 80, 82–83, 85, 104–11, 112, 116, 125, 141, 144, 145, 151, 153, 157, 158–60, 161, 162, 163–65
kenotic sacrifice. See *kenosis*.
Kierkegaard, Søren, 9, 11, 13, 14, 15, 37, 39, 46, 56, 57, 70, 85, 87–116, 137, 144, 145, 147, 152–53, 157, 160, 162–63, 165, 184n15, 187n58, 187n60
   Fear and Trembling, 87–104, 144, 183n12, 185n27, 186n37, 187n52
   The Concept of Irony, 39, 57
   Works of Love, 88, 102, 104–11, 113–14, 115, 144, 152
Klossowski, Pierre, 130–31, 138
Kojève, Alexandre, 58, 147, 149

Leibniz, Gottfried Wilhelm, 21, 23
Levinas, Emmanuel, 147
Lippitt, John, 97, 98, 108, 109, 115, 183n12
Livy, 96
Løgstrup, Knud Ejler, 116
Louis XIV, 65
Luther, Martin, 2, 22

Merleau-Ponty, Maurice, 58
Millbank, John, 19, 26, 27–28
Mooney, Edward F., 41, 101, 184n22, 186n43
Moltmann, Jürgen, 4, 167n4
Mulhall, Stephen, 187
mysticism, 2, 22–23, 36, 41–42, 52, 58, 78, 173n9, 180n52

Nancy, Jean-Luc, 1
Newton, Isaac, 71

Index

Nietzsche, Friedrich, 5, 7, 8, 13–15, 20, 26, 37, 88, 103, 104, 115, 116, 117–39, 141, 142, 144–46, 147, 148, 151, 154, 158, 160, 163, 165, 193n52
  Beyond Good and Evil, 117–19, 122–23, 127–28, 191n8
  The Genealogy of Morality, 118–21, 122, 123, 126–27, 132
  The Greek State, 126–27
  Human, All Too Human, 129
  The Will to Power, 119, 121, 123, 129, 132–33, 191n12
Nuzzo, Angelica, 182n69

O'Donoghue, John, 179n40
Outka, Gene, 110
O'Regan, Cyril, 78, 176n57

Pareyson, Luigi, 158, 159
Pattison, George, 188n62
Perkins, Robert, 96, 183n5
perspectivism, 4, 7, 9, 22–27, 29, 37, 142–45, 155–57, 158, 159–60, 161–62
Plotinus, 40
Pinkard, Terry, 6, 8, 25, 28, 37, 63, 64, 68–69, 71, 74, 83, 104, 111, 142, 143, 178n13, 178n25
Pippin, Robert B., 6, 38, 138, 169n29, 178n25

Quinn, Philip L., 88, 98, 105, 106

Rand, Ayn, 171n29
recognition, 6–7, 9, 11, 12, 15, 28, 65, 73–75, 79, 90–95, 113, 115, 148, 153. *See also* intersubjectivity
Redding, Paul, 6, 7, 24, 29, 71, 84, 142, 144–45, 172n45, 187n59
regulative sacrifice. *See* regularity
regularity, 8, 9–11, 12, 13, 14–15, 16, 24, 30–37, 49, 51, 80, 84, 87, 89–90, 93, 95, 96–104, 105, 109, 110, 116, 133, 135–39, 142, 144, 145–46, 147–49, 153–54, 160, 162, 163–64, 165, 172n48, 175n38, 183n3, 187n53, 187n60, 188n62
Reid, Jeffrey, 177n63
Richardson, John, 122
Ricoeur, Paul, 148, 158, 163
Ravera, Marco, 175n33

Sartre, Jean-Paul, 58
Schelling, Friedrich Wilhelm Joseph, 11, 29, 49–50, 79, 99, 187n60
Schlegel, August Wilhelm, 45
Schlegel, Friedrich, 45
Siep, Ludwig, 7
Silentio, Johannes de. *See* Kierkegaard, Søren
Smith, Daniel W., 130–31
Solger, Karl Wilhelm Ferdinand, 9, 11, 38, 39–59, 61, 70, 113, 142–43, 147, 151–52, 173n5, 175n38
  Nachgelassene Schriften und Briefwechsel (Posthumous Writings), 39, 41, 47–48, 51
  Lectures on Aesthetics, 44, 48
Sophocles, 46
Spinoza, Baruch, 55
Stewart, Jon, 90, 94
Strauss David, 83
Suso, Henry, 2
symbol, 8–10, 11, 15, 16, 27–28, 31–35, 37, 49, 51, 59, 67, 80, 87, 88, 89–90, 92–96, 98, 99–100, 102, 103, 105, 116, 142, 143, 144, 147–49, 151, 153–54, 157, 160, 162–63, 187n52
symbolic sacrifice. *See* symbol

Tauler, John, 2

Van der Will, Wilfried, 132
Vattimo, Gianni, 157, 158–60
Verstrynge, Karl, 183n3

Wendte, Martin, 179n34
Westphal, Merold, 90
Wildt, Andreas, 7
Williams, Robert, 7, 76

Woodward, Ashley, 131–32, 192n32
Yerkes, James, 181n59
Žižek, Slavoj, 1, 16, 19, 163, 196n35

www.ingramcontent.com/pod-product-compliance
Lightning Source LLC
Chambersburg PA
CBHW020653230426
43665CB00008B/426